NAPOLEON

AND THE

REBEL

NAPOLEON

AND THE

REBEL

*A Story of Brotherhood,
Passion, and Power*

MARCELLO SIMONETTA AND NOGA ARIKHA

palgrave
macmillan

First published in 2011 by PALGRAVE MACMILLAN® in the United States—a division of St. Martin's Press LLC, 175 Fifth Avenue, New York, NY 10010.

Where this book is distributed in the United Kingdom, Europe, and the rest of the world, this is by Palgrave Macmillan, a division of Macmillan Publishers Limited, registered in England, company number 785998, of Houndmills, Basingstoke, Hampshire RG21 6XS.

Palgrave Macmillan is the global academic imprint of the above companies and has companies and representatives throughout the world.

Palgrave® and Macmillan® are registered trademarks in the United States, the United Kingdom, Europe and other countries.

ISBN: 978-0-230-11156-1

Library of Congress Cataloging-in-Publication Data

Simonetta, Marcello, 1968–
    Napoleon and the rebel : a story of brotherhood, passion, and power / Marcello Simonetta and Noga Arikha.
        p.   cm.
    Includes bibliographical references and index.
    ISBN 978-0-230-11156-1 (hardback)
    1. Bonaparte, Lucien, prince de Canino, 1775–1840.   2. Napoleon I, Emperor of the French, 1769–1821—Family.   3. Princes—France—Biography.   I. Arikha, Noga.   II. Title.
DC216.6.S56   2011
944.05092—dc22
[B]
                                                                    2011003100

A catalogue record of the book is available from the British Library.

Design by Letra Libre

First edition: June 2011

10 9 8 7 6 5 4 3 2 1

Printed in the United States of America.

CONTENTS

ILLUSTRATIONS

Chapter One, p. 1: Jean-Baptiste Wicar, portrait of Lucien Bonaparte dressed as president of the Council of the Five-Hundred, engraving, Museo Napoleonico, Rome, n. 522 (1800). This is one of the depictions of Lucien as the hero of the coup d'état of Brumaire (November 10–11, 1799).

Chapter Two, p. 55: Andrea Appiani, portrait of the Marquesa de Santa Cruz, oil on canvas, Accademia di San Luca, Rome. This portrait of Lucien's Spanish mistress was executed in 1805 by Appiani, who was selected by Napoleon as the "first Italian painter."

Chapter Three, p. 107: Guillaume Guillon Lethière, portrait of Lucien Bonaparte and Alexandrine de Bleschamp, oil on canvas, private collection, New York (1802). The title of this painting, inspired by Francisco Goya's *Maya Desnuda,* is *The Sleep of Venus.* Courtesy Alan Roche.

Chapter Four, p. 153: François-Xavier Fabre, portrait of Lucien Bonaparte at the Villa Rufinella, oil on canvas, Museo Napoleonico, Rome, n. 17 (1808). Lucien is posing with a book in his hands to show that he has chosen the contemplative life.

Chapter Five, p. 193: "Universal murderer of domestic happiness or the fraternal tyrant," engraving, Houghton Library, Harvard University, Call Number 007257673 (December 24, 1810). This caricature depicts Lucien and his family arriving in England after being expelled from Italy by Napoleon.

Epilogue, p. 241: Jean-Auguste Dominique Ingres, portrait of the family of Lucien Bonaparte, drawing (Photoreproduction, Museo Napoleonico, Rome; original preserved at the Fogg Art Museum, Cambridge MA) (1815). From left to right, with their poses and birthdates: Anna Jouberthon (standing, 1799), Jeanne (sitting, 1807), Louis (standing, 1813), Paul (sitting, 1809), Charles (standing, 1803), Alexandrine (sitting, 1778), Christine (or Lili, standing, 1798), Letizia (standing, 1804), Charlotte (or Lolotte, sitting, 1795).

ACKNOWLEDGMENTS

First and foremost, we wish to thank Countess Albalisa Faina for having graciously given us access to the Archivio Faina in Perugia, a treasure trove of Bonaparte documents. We are also grateful to Father Abele Calufetti, at the Archivio dei Frati Minori di Lombardia in Milan, and to Roberto Lanzi for having shared his digital pictures of both archives.

Particular thanks go to Massimo Colesanti, president of the Fondazione Primoli, and to the valiant archivist Valeria Petitto, for their steadfast support; as well as to their next-door neighbor, Giulia Gorgone, director of the Museo Napoleonico, who has shared her vast knowledge about the Bonaparte family.

Pierre Rosenberg and Marc Fumaroli both wrote warm letters of recommendation for us to access respectively the Archives Diplomatiques at the Ministère des Affaires Etrangères and the Bibliothèque de l'Institut de France in Paris. Sylvie Biet was very helpful when we consulted the Fonds Masson at the Bibliothèque Thiers in Paris. Inge Dupont and Maria Molestina assisted us in consulting Bonaparte autographs at the Morgan Library and Museum in New York. Patricia Tyson Stroud kindly suggested the importance of the Mailliard Papers in the Manuscripts and Archives at Yale University Library. The late Geneviève Madec-Capy conveyed to us her enthusiasm for the life and works of Lethière.

Maria Teresa Caracciolo and Isabelle Mayer-Michalon in Paris were wonderful partners in the researching and writing of the catalogue *Un homme libre* for the 2010 exhibition about Lucien at the Musée Fesch in Ajaccio. Ludovica Cirrincione D'Amelio and Angelica Zucconi gave us good advice in Rome over Memmo's excellent *amatriciana*. Olivier Bernier in New York, Peter Hicks at the Fondation Napoléon in Paris, and Louis-Napoléon Bonaparte Wyse in Brussels provided us with useful tips during the course of the research. Christophe Leonzi provided us with the current name and recipe for a Corsican pastry that Lucien loved.

We are grateful to our agent, Elizabeth Sheinkman of Curtis Brown, for believing in this book and for the enthusiasm with which she set out to find it a home. Our editors at Palgrave Macmillan, Alessandra Bastagli, who acquired the manuscript and edited its beginning, and Luba Ostashevsky, who finished the job steadfastly, helped us improve the first draft. We also wish to thank Debby Manette for her precise copyediting.

We began writing in the summer of 2008, at the Sicilian house of Gea Schirò and Alessio Planeta, whom we thank for their wonderful hospitality. The text benefited in its initial stages from the generous and sharp-eyed editorial input of Joan Juliet Buck and Marie d'Origny, marvelous friends and readers both.

We would not have set out on writing this book at all if Jonathan Kagan had not purchased the Lethière picture representing Lucien and Alexandrine. His passion for and knowledge of artistic, literary, and political matters have been a constant inspiration to us, as has been Ute Wartenberg Kagan's affectionate encouragement.

This book is dedicated to a late father and a new child: Avigdor Arikha, and our son, Vigo Luciano. The one left us just before being able to meet the other, who was born just as the book was completed, in a time of great sadness and great joy.

PREFACE

This book started with a painting. In the summer of 2005, a collector in New York acquired an unusual, erotic portrait of a couple, set in an artificially ancient room. The painter, a half-black Frenchman called Guillaume Guillon Lethière from the Caribbean island of Guadeloupe, depicted a sensuous, curvaceous woman languidly lying on a chaise longue, her nakedness barely concealed by a thin gauze, her pubic hair visible beneath it—surprising for a neoclassical work such as this. The man, dark and handsome, chin resting on right hand, is gravely but covetously contemplating this resting beauty; his left hand rests on a partially unrolled writ. A wilted laurel wreath lies at his feet; a satyr's profile looms in the left corner. The names of the two lovers are inscribed in Greek under the chaise longue: Alexandra and Lukiano.

It emerged that the painting was a double portrait of Lucien Bonaparte, brother of Napoleon, and Alexandrine de Bleschamp, then his mistress; but the story behind this picture remained mysterious. As we began to investigate, we realized how much there was to uncover. Lucien was acknowledged by historians for his crucial role in the coup that brought Napoleon to power but little had been said about him beyond that, because he had not been a player in Napoleonic Europe. His story, which is also that of Alexandrine, who became his wife against the wishes of Napoleon, had not been properly told, because it was the story of a man who chose to lead a private life in part for the sake of love.

Lucien did tell his own story, however, in his lengthy, detailed *Mémoires*. A first volume was published during Lucien's lifetime, and an edition later appeared in three volumes, in 1883. But the editor, a retired colonel called

Theodore Iung, in his zeal to demonstrate that the author was an "enemy of the truth, like his brothers," had not published the work in its entirety.[1] We needed to consult the manuscript and see what had been left out. On a November morning in 2007, we went to the Archives of the Quai d'Orsay, the French Ministry of Foreign Affairs, where we found the three microfilmed reels containing Lucien Bonaparte's *Mémoires* (ironically numbered 1814, 1815, and 1816, the years of the Napoleonic decline and the beginning of the Restoration). We started looking at some passages of the text, and, realizing they were missing from Iung's edition, we ordered a digital copy of the microfilm. After perusing it at leisure, we ascertained that Iung had omitted about half the text.

This was shocking: The pages cut by Iung, and ignored by subsequent historians, contain arresting and fascinating details that re-create a whole world that, as a result, lay hidden from view for nearly 200 years. Large sections recounting episodes of Lucien's adolescence, youth, and maturity, and describing his loves and hatreds, had been erased. Most egregiously, the editor had ignored countless anecdotes about Lucien's relationship with his brother Napoleon as well as with his other siblings and in-laws, his mother, and his children. Throughout the unpublished *Mémoires* one sees Lucien thinking, worrying, loving, mocking, wondering, discovering, planning. He gives his views and judgments on everyone in his family, on counts and princes encountered in Spain and Italy, on France's savvy politicians Talleyrand and Fouché, on artists and writers.

However, one major disappointment for us was that the description of Lucien's first encounter with Alexandrine, which we had hoped to locate in these papers, was nowhere to be found. The key to the painting had still not emerged. For some weeks, we wondered how this could be. It did not seem possible that the passionate, Stendhalian soul that was Lucien would have never written about the moment that would change his life. Perhaps he had destroyed this intimate section, in a moment of rage or shame; perhaps she had. Then again, the papers could have been hidden elsewhere. We had known for a while that a branch of Lucien's Italian family, the Faina, had inherited some important artworks, as well as some letters, the originals of which had been seized by Napoleon III, who had them destroyed as soon as Alexandrine died in 1855. He might have had good reason to do so, since his claim to the throne rested on his being the son of Louis, one of the Bonaparte brothers, by Hortense, daughter of Joséphine Beauharnais by her first marriage—and it is likely that Louis was not in fact his father.

Eventually, we tracked down the Faina family heirs, who live in Milan. They kindly sent us two hefty typewritten volumes containing detailed summaries of the materials preserved in the archive: hundreds of letters exchanged between family members over more than a century, from the early 1800s until the early 1900s. Many were letters to and from Lucien, Alexandrine, their children, and their grandchildren, and all were unpublished. But more surprises lay ahead: At the very end of the second volume, there was a short section of "literary writings" by the prolific couple; it consisted in a list of works—and of items listed simply as fragments of the *Mémoires.*

We clearly had to take a look at these fragments, so we made an appointment to visit the archive, which was housed in the old Faina family property on the outskirts of Perugia. Countess Albalisa Faina née Roncalli, a distinguished lady in her seventies, welcomed us warmly and took us to a nearby building, unlocking the door to the dusty family archive. We took from the shelves some of the bulky folders and excitedly started browsing through them. One of the first ones we opened was the bound fragment from the *Mémoires,* in a hand that we had become familiar with from the Quai d'Orsay papers. And there it was, in a little notebook: Lucien's first-person account of his meeting with Alexandrine.

Before dying, Alexandrine had managed to stash the most private family papers in some hidden corner, probably anticipating the move by her imperial nephew, Napoleon III. Her caution paid off, since she managed to prevent the destruction of many documents that illuminate her own life and that of her beloved husband, Lucien.

The *Mémoires,* published and unpublished, are the main source for our book. Because Lucien's story has never been told in its entirety before, and because his humane voice has been drowned out by history, we have decided to take him at his word, trying to be as faithful to his lively recollections as possible. Memory can be self-serving, and Lucien's was no exception in this regard; but rather than judge him, as his detractors have often done, we chose to let the memoirist speak and be heard. We generally gave him the benefit of the doubt, unless we had positive proof that his memory or retelling were widely off the mark. As historians, we have revised his dating and corrected voluntary omissions and exaggerations. Throughout, we have inserted amendments that take into account the facts we have found out through historical scholarship, through other firsthand documents, and through the testimonies, memoirs, and letters of his contemporaries.

We have also decided to leave for the most part untouched his dialogues with Napoleon and others, which Lucien himself reported (he used a shorthand to transcribe them), because they are precious for their fly-on-the-wall quality, regardless of their veracity. Family life—Bonaparte family life in particular—is a complicated business, and Lucien had the talent of catching his relatives and even himself off guard, providing future generations with revelations about Napoleon and the circles of power around him.

It is thanks to Lucien's testimony that we were able to draw an intimate picture of the family that was the epicenter of European life in the first decades of the 1800s. The story of Lucien and Alexandrine offers us the opportunity to reflect upon the values adopted by those on the margins of power, often against the odds, and reveals how private passions can rule over politics. Lucien is an unusual figure: an ambitious politician who turned the notion of a private life into a political statement, a brilliant man who was inconstant in his passions but whose passions were absolute, a man of principle who could contradict himself, a stylish writer who remains unknown as a literary figure, a philanderer whose eventual devotion to one woman shoved him to the sidelines of history. For all his flaws, we find him the most humanly admirable of the Bonaparte siblings. We hope to have done him justice in these pages.

ONE

YOUTH
1775–1799

There is yet one country in Europe, capable of legislation; and that is the island of

Corsica. The valour and constancy with which that brave people hath recovered and

defended its liberty would well deserve that some wise man should teach them how to

preserve it. I have some presentiment that one day that little island will astonish Europe.

—Jean-Jacques Rousseau, *On the Social Contract*

THE ORANGERIE AT CHATEAU DE ST. CLOUD

A FEW MILES OUTSIDE OF PARIS

November 10, 1799 (19 Brumaire, year

VIII in the calendar of the Revolution)[1]

Dark and slender, Lucien Bonaparte, president of the Council of the Five-Hundred, sat in the crowded chamber at St. Cloud. He wore the attire of the office—a red toga over his suit and a revolutionary scarf wrapped and knotted around his waist. He was intently watching the heated debate among the Council's members. Earlier that afternoon, the twenty-five-year-old Lucien had provoked this debate when he announced the resignation of Paul Barras, the head of the Directory, which had been governing France with increasing ineptitude since 1795. Barras's official letter of resignation, so remarkably restrained for a man whose raw ambition was notorious, had been met with dismay and disbelief by the members of the Council.

Speakers were jostling to hold the floor, passions were strong and voices high-pitched. The many arguments Lucien heard were contradictory, and the session was stalling. He was hoping for a quick vote on the resolution that would hand governing powers to his older brother, Général Napoleon Bonaparte. After a decade of bloody coups and terrorizing bloodshed, despotic rule and internal instability, massive deprivation and brutal war, the brilliant military leader would take over and ensure that France was properly, justly governed at last. The plan had been long gestated and was unfolding now, albeit more slowly than predicted.

All of a sudden, the doors at the far end of the Council chamber were thrown open. Lucien was seriously myopic, and at this distance, in the dim

November light, he could just make out the silhouettes of four uniformed grenadiers escorting a short man toward the rostrum. He heard angry shouts and shrieks directed at the intruder: "Down with the tyrant! Down with the dictator!"

The short man was Général Bonaparte. The session had been dragging on for too long: He had felt the urge to cut short the useless debates and take over as planned. But the Council chamber was no battlefield, and armed soldiers were not allowed in the hall. Napoleon tried to make his way to the podium but encountered stubborn resistance. The Council members shouted at him with increasing intensity. Some men approached him with their knives drawn, one even ripping a grenadier's coat. The rabble threw punches at the general and pushed him. Napoleon opted for a slow retreat, walking backward toward the exit, apparently bruised, some blood running on his left cheek. His was an egregious tactical mistake, likely to break momentum and favor the Bonapartes' enemies. Moments before, victory had seemed within reach. Now a spectacular defeat loomed. As soon as the unwelcome intruder left the hall, the mood of the Council switched dramatically.

There were louder chants now: "Outlaw him! Motion to outlaw!" Lucien knew very well the meaning of such revolutionary language: It was a call for immediate imprisonment and capital punishment. In a matter of minutes, everything seemed to have collapsed. After weeks of painstaking preparations, Napoleon's untimely appearance was turning him into a dishonorable scapegoat. And by a tragic irony, Lucien found himself in the position of having to put to a vote the death sentence for his own brother, so clamorously demanded by the furious crowd.

Lucien reluctantly rose to his feet and slowly started walking toward the podium, where he was preceded by some verbose orators. He needed to delay the vote on his brother's capital sentence. The only way out was to exercise his right to speak as member of the Council, not as its president. Eventually, among jeers and threats, he took the stand and spoke thus: "I am going to oppose this motion. Suspicions raised so lightly lead to mad excesses. A small, even if formally faulty, irregularity cannot erase so many triumphs, so many services given to our homeland."

A rumbling of murmurs and protests interrupted him: "Time is running out! Let's vote the proposition!"

Lucien tried to continue his speech, but his famous eloquence was no match for the chaotic Council. Since his appeal to silence passions failed, he took off his toga and left it theatrically on the podium, saying: "There is no liberty left in here. Your President, in sign of public mourning, is abandoning the symbols of the popular magistracy."

This one gesture had an effect greater than any of his words. Many representatives invited him to take his seat back. Instead, fearing for his life in that mayhem, Lucien walked down the podium toward the middle of the room, where he spotted a group of friends and supporters. A dozen of soldiers headed by Général Frégeville surrounded and shielded Lucien. Some Council members cried: "Let's follow our president!" Others shouted back: "Liberty has been violated!"

While waiting to take the stand, Lucien had managed to tell the general that soon he no longer would be able to answer for the situation in the Council and that Napoleon should send someone to rescue him within the next ten minutes. Now Lucien was able to step out into the courtyard where troops were gathered, waiting for orders, and where his brother was saddling up. Lucien also mounted the horse of a dragoon and requested a drumroll. When the drums stopped, a deep silence fell and, in the looming dusk, in a strong, animated voice, Lucien addressed the soldiers:

CITIZENS! The majority of that Council is at this moment held in terror by a few representatives of the people, who are armed with knives, and are surrounding the tribune, threatening their colleagues with death and proposing the most awful deliberations.

I declare to you that these audacious brigands, who are doubtless inspired by the fatal genius of the English government, have risen in rebellion against the Council, demanding that the General charged with the execution of the Council's decree be outlawed, as if the word "outlaw" were still to be regarded as the death-warrant of persons most beloved by their country.

I declare to you that this small number of enraged people have outlawed themselves by their attacks upon the liberty of the Council. In the name of those who, for so many years, have been victims or the plaything of those miserable children of Terror, I consign to the soldiers the charge of rescuing the majority of their representatives; so that, protected against daggers by bayonets, we might be able to deliberate on the fate of the Republic.

Général, and you, soldiers, and you, citizens, you will acknowledge as deputies of France only those who come to join you with their President. As for those who remain in the Orangerie to vote for outlaws, let force expel them! They are no longer the representatives of the people, but the representatives of the dagger.

Vive la République![2]

After this harangue, the troops cried "Vive Bonaparte!" but hesitated to act. It was evident that they were not fully prepared to turn their bayonets against the national representatives.

Deathly pale and uncertain before the angry crowd, but astride his horse, Napoleon cried: "If anyone resists, kill, kill, kill! Yes, follow me, follow me, I am the god of battles!" It was an ineffective cry at best. From his own horse, Lucien promptly hissed: "Will you hold your tongue, for God's sake? You're not talking to your Mamelukes!" With that, Lucien bent over, grabbed his brother's sword, and drew it, exclaiming loudly: "I swear that I will stab my own brother to the heart if he ever attempts anything against the liberty of Frenchmen."[3]

Upon hearing this rousing promise from Lucien, the soldiers marched into the Orangerie and chased away all the protesters, some of whom escaped by jumping out of the windows. By nightfall, Lucien had passed all the necessary resolutions, and Napoleon Bonaparte became first consul of the French Republic.

LIBERTY, EQUALITY, FRATERNITY

The words Lucien uttered and the gesture he made were brilliantly timed; the rhetoric could not have been more effective. They also appear, in retrospect, to have been sincere: Lucien saw himself and his brother as the defenders of republican liberty, those who would stand as the bulwark both against the Revolution's bloody excesses and against the return to monarchy, so fresh still in the memory of the nation.

On that day in November, the first consul-to-be was battered, silent, as if paralyzed, his face slightly bloodied, his strategic genius on hold, while his fiery and fearless brother roused the revolutionary troops, swearing that his elder brother would pay with his life if ever he were to harm the freedom of France. If Napoleon was able to take power on that day, it was thanks to his brother Lucien.

But it was hard for Napoleon to feel gratitude. The competition between these two siblings started early. Lucien was nine years old when, in 1784, he entered the military school in Brienne. Upon his arrival, he was given a full physical examination, and Napoleon, who was six years older and had spent the last five years there, meticulously reported the information about his younger brother in a letter to one of their uncles: "He is three feet, eleven inches and six lines in stature." Such careful attention to a brother's height might seem excessive, and one cannot but wonder whether Napoleon had already become self-conscious about his short stature and afraid that even his younger brother would surpass him. The report went on: "He is in the sixth class in Latin, and is to learn the different branches of instruction. He shows much talent and good will, and we have reason to hope that something good can be made of him. He is healthy, strong, quick and rash, and he gives satisfaction in the beginning. He is very familiar with French, and has entirely forgotten Italian. He will write a postscript to my letter. I will not help him, that you may note his progress. I hope he will write to you more frequently than he did at Autun."[4]

The praise, though generous enough, was paternalistic, even professorial, and somewhat impersonal. According to Lucien, Napoleon did not welcome him at Brienne with much warmth. Napoleon inspired fear in Lucien as well as in his schoolmates. His presence was vaguely threatening, his manner serious and unappealing. He was decidedly unpopular at the school. In contrast, Lucien was a tender boy, capable of deep affection.[5] Later in life Lucien grew convinced that the lack of tenderness in his older brother must have contributed to his own reluctance as an adult to bend before him.

The brothers overlapped only for a few months at Brienne, and in October 1784, Napoleon left for the Royal Military School in Paris. Four months later, the boys' father, Charles Bonaparte—a well-respected, middle-class, Tuscanbred Corsican patriot—died in France (in Montpellier, where he had sought medical treatment). He left behind eight children (five boys and three girls) and their mother, the iron-willed, thirty-two-year-old Letizia. She could not continue to afford the best education Charles had always insisted their children receive—going almost bankrupt in the process—other than by sending Lucien to the seminary. Moreover, by becoming a priest, Lucien would eventually provide the stable income they all needed now; the plan was for him to succeed to the canonship of an uncle in San Miniato, in Tuscany. So it was that in 1786, Lucien entered the seminary in Aix-en-Provence.

Lucien had not been consulted on this decision and was deeply unhappy about it. But in Aix he was delighted to be reunited with his beloved uncle, the priest Joseph Fesch—his mother's half brother—with whom he was to study. In 1/81, Fesch had accompanied the then seven-year-old Lucien on the sea voyage from Ajaccio, Corsica's capital, to Marseille, on the way to his first college in the town of Autun. The boy had been constantly seasick, and arrived at destination pale and skinny, in sharp contrast to the rosy Fesch, a bon vivant who tried to initiate his young nephew into the pleasures of wine. It was perhaps a little too much too early: Lucien was so put off that he would never touch wine again.[6]

In 1786, eleven-year-old Lucien knew immediately that the seminary was no place for him. Soon after his nephew's arrival, Fesch left Aix for Lyon, in pursuit of more lucrative employment. Once he had worn out the uniform he had brought from Brienne, Lucien had no compunction displaying his unhappiness at having to wear a priest's clothing, swiftly turning it to rags. Teachers reprimanded him, calling him a "little devil, a real little devil who breaks everything."[7] Lucien would remain fundamentally bored and friendless for three years, until Joseph, the eldest of the Bonaparte siblings, came to see him.

The relationship between Lucien and Joseph was as warm as Lucien's relationship with Napoleon was cold. Joseph had been the only family member by their father's deathbed in Montpellier and had subsequently cut short his military studies, which had become unaffordable, and returned home to Ajaccio. As the firstborn, Joseph had promised Charles that he would assume the role of pater familias after his father's death. He excelled in this paternal role, lavishing affection and attention on Lucien. Quickly realizing that the priesthood was not the boy's calling, Joseph took him back home.

Their mother welcomed them, as did their two younger brothers, Louis and Jérôme, and two younger sisters: Pauline, a charming, dark-haired eight-year-old, and little Caroline. Napoleon was there too, on a short leave from the military. Their sister Elisa, eldest of the girls, was at the Royal College of Saint-Cyr on the continent. Eight children, no father: It was a heavy burden for Letizia. Her elderly brother-in-law, the archdeacon Lucien, after whom the third son had been named, helped with the administration of their finances. He was bedridden but nevertheless wielded extraordinary authority. He had always been highly respected by Corsicans, especially since he was close to their exiled leader, Pasquale Paoli, author of the 1755 constitution that freed Corsica from Genoese rule and turned it into a representative republic. Paoli was living in England, having fled there in 1769 after the French crown had secretly bought the rights to the mostly Italian-speaking Corsica from the Genoese. Joseph himself soon left for Tuscany to attend university at Pisa, where he studied law. There he also befriended Pasquale's brother Clemente Paoli and became deeply involved in the Corsican independence movement.

The day soon arrived for Napoleon to leave and return to his regiment. He embraced a tearful Lucien, but when he advised him to study his Latin well since he was to be a priest, the boy's tears quickly dried up. Napoleon knew perfectly well that Lucien had no interest whatsoever for the priesthood. There was nothing to say. The affectionate moment had not lasted long.

In the absence of his older brothers, fourteen-year-old Lucien suddenly found himself the eldest child, and by right the head of the family. This is not a role one takes on lightly in a Corsican clan. He was old enough now, he thought, to choose a career for himself. The canonship his mother was relying on for future income, which would make him the richest man in the family, could very well be passed on to Louis or to Jérôme if Louis didn't care for it either. But since Letizia was not happy with Lucien's dislike of the priestly state, the boy wanted to hide his feelings from her. Instead, he hatched a plan that settled the question once and for all.

Using the scissors of his faithful nanny Saveria, he cut up his priest's robe and chopped up his round priest's hat, which he threw out of a window. Saveria was horrified; Letizia was outraged. As punishment for this doubly sacrilegious act, she ordered her son to stay in his room, putting him on a diet of bread and water, while measurements were taken for a new, secular outfit. Clearly his punishment was to last only for as long as it took to make the clothing. His nanny and nine-year-old sister Pauline did not have the heart to have the boy stick to the harsh regime. Pauline snuck him sweets, especially a Corsican pastry called palcotelle (today called falculelle) that Lucien would crave for the rest of his life.[8]

Regardless of the punishment, this act of rebellion was Lucien's first taste of liberty from oppressive rules. And its upshot was a beautiful, brand-new green suit, a source of joy and a cause for gratitude toward his forgiving mother. His will to study followed—including Latin, as he promised Letizia—and from then on he spent hours in the well-stocked family library, reading the Roman historians, the Italian epic poets, and the Enlightenment philosophers with increasing pleasure and excitement.

Napoleon was still a young sublieutenant, based mostly in Auxonne, near Dijon. But he already burned with revolutionary zeal and was imbued with dreams of glory. He wrote in his diary a "draft for a memorial concerning monarchical authority" against Europe's twelve monarchies, describing in detail how each of those crowns had been usurped, arguing that the monarchs merited dethronement.[9] Meanwhile, the movement of antimonarchists was growing increasingly angry and vociferous throughout France. On July 14, 1789 the people of Paris marched to the Bastille, unlocked its gates, and freed the prisoners held captive there. The Revolution had begun rocking the world.

Exactly two months later, Napoleon, by then a full lieutenant, hurried back to Corsica, which was quickly integrated into the revolutionary government. Lucien noted that his brother had much grown in the last few years but that he was "small and ugly," especially in comparison with Joseph.[10]

Napoleon was also warmer than he had been in Brienne, or even on his last visit home. Both brothers had matured, and this time they were on better terms—Napoleon was not particularly friendly, but he was cordial enough on the long walks or rides they took together in the Corsican mountains, encountering their countrymen, the peasants and shepherds. The proud lieutenant showed Lucien drafts of his philosophical and political writings, fascinating texts, though filled with spelling mistakes that the younger brother did not dare point out, praising instead Napoleon's otherwise striking *History of Corsica*.[11]

The brothers' interest in the island was genuine but also opportunistic. They felt that the patriotic legacy of their father would open doors for them. Lucien enthusiastically embraced the principles of liberty, equality, fraternity, a triad that had become the slogan of the Revolution. The recent Declaration of the Rights of Man had enshrined these principles as the core of a new, morally sound political order, one in which justice would reign and limited and democratic power would represent the people. Lucien was eager to play a part in the realization of these noble goals.

Corsicans tended to take the principles of the Revolution as a given, since they conceived themselves as equal, free, and united, and class differences were minimal on the island. For a young boy who identified with France, was schooled in the classics and steeped in the history of republican Rome, the slogan, and the events under way in its name on the continent, rang like a loud call to action. Lucien was eager to follow in the footsteps of his elder brothers, both enviably engaged in public activities, and he began with political activism at home.

Lucien thus joined the local Jacobin Club, where Joseph was a departmental official. There the bookish teenager was surrounded by simple country people. Although still a mere fourteen-year-old, he had no difficulty finding words when he took the podium for the first time, making an elaborate, eloquent speech about the rights of man, proudly and brilliantly armed with his classical training in rhetoric. He talked of Paoli as of a giant taller than all Greek and Roman heroes, who had defended his country like Epaminondas, the general who liberated Thebes from Spartan rule. The speech was met with a loud ovation, clapping, shouting, and much boot-stomping—the audience's enthusiastic reaction was overwhelming. Inspired by the collective adoration, Lucien's words escalated into a torrential flow. He found himself predicting the return of Paoli—even though it was highly unlikely at this point—electrifying the room with love, admiration, and gratitude for the man. Suddenly he was a prophet in the eyes of these passionate people, who embraced him as he descended the podium, showering him with praise. The crowd brought him back in triumph to his house, where his surprised and slightly frightened mother welcomed him. As he repeated the story of his oracular feats day after day, exhausting himself in the process, she also became concerned about where his newfound talent and the inevitable intoxication of success might take such a young man. But she held off from voicing her concern.

Lucien was now established as a young leader in Ajaccio. He had discovered that he could hold an audience captive, and suddenly he was more beloved by the people than were his elder brothers. They too attended the Club, but quietly, and never from the podium. While Napoleon merely kept on writing his thoughts, Lucien was speaking well and loud. He had found a voice, heard applause, felt approval.

IN THE NAME OF THE FATHER

On the first anniversary of Bastille Day, July 14, 1790, Pasquale Paoli came home. The islanders were deliriously happy to see their *Babo*, as they called him—Corsican Italian for "father"—back after twenty long years of exile.

The sixty-five-year-old but still combative leader had stopped in Paris to receive the title of lieutenant of Corsica, although his most inspiring meeting was not with the Jacobins, who were de facto ruling France, but with his former opponent, King Louis XVI. Paoli's years in England had turned him into a convinced advocate of constitutional monarchy. His political activity had been curtailed in exile, but he had hardly been idle and had been embraced by England's intellectual, artistic, and political elite. Most notably, he had frequented the Literary Club founded by Samuel Johnson and Joshua Reynolds, which—besides including Johnson's and Paoli's own biographer James Boswell (for whom Paoli was "one of those men who are no longer to be found but in the lives of Plutarch"[12]) and the playwright Oliver Goldsmith, included the likes of Edmund Burke, Adam Smith, and Edward Gib-bon—had a decisive influence on his views.

Corsica had been incorporated into France by the French National As-sembly in 1790, which meant that Corsican exiles were allowed to return to the island. One such exile was Paoli. He wanted to celebrate this union of forces for liberty, and he returned to his native island in the belief that France might foster the form of government he had lived under happily in England. His first action upon returning was to send a letter of congratulations to the National Assembly, stating that he had decided to leave England to come live and die among his compatriots, to enjoy his rights as a free citizen of Corsica.

Charles Bonaparte had sided with Paoli during the war of independence, and Letizia, in Lucien's glorious recollection, was among the many women who, accompanied by their children, set out to welcome him when he ar-rived in Ajaccio, in June 1791. It was a joyous, celebratory occasion, and in town all ordinary business stopped, to await the hero's arrival. Joseph was the head of the delegation sent from the Jacobin clubs of Ajaccio and Bastia to welcome Paoli at the port.

The return of the revolutionary hero was Lucien's political rite of passage. Eager to impress him, Lucien searched the home library for good sources. He ransacked and memorized especially two political thinkers, the French Jean Bodin and the English Joseph Needham, trusting that their sentences would be unfamiliar enough that no one would recognize them. And he also chose for his speech a dramatic subject from popular Corsican history, the heroic death by starvation of the Corsican patriot Guagno.

Lucien ran along with a throng of people to meet the beloved leader. Paoli went up to the podium of the Jacobin Club, reluctantly taking his seat in an imposing armchair that seemed too regal for his natural modesty. And when the moment came, Lucien, overcoming his initial stage fright, declaimed the words that were his as well as those of the great thinkers, emphasizing in particular "the preference that the people should give to a re-publican government."[13] Hoping all along that neither Joseph nor Napoleon would identify his scholarly source, he spoke with passion and conviction. He saw Paoli smile and address a few words to his brothers—compliments, as it would turn out. By the end of the speech, the audience cheered and

raved. But the best was still to come: The other members of the Club announced Lucien's second speech, the one he had composed about Guagno.
The young orator finally could show his mettle to the man who mattered,
without hiding behind the words of others. He put all his ardor into his
retelling of the dramatic story of the Corsican martyr, who exhaled his last
breath uttering the name of Paoli as "the avenger of liberty."[14] The speech
was a triumph; Paoli was moved to tears.

This was a turning point for Lucien. He had a strong need to be recognized by an elder, especially since his father was no longer there to approve or
disapprove. He could only mature by speaking up and by being heard. And
his desire to be adopted by a paternal figure was amply fulfilled when, at the
end of his speech, Paoli embraced him, exclaiming, "I see that you would like
to be my little Tacitus," and compared him to Charles Bonaparte, who also
had been unusually erudite as a young man.[15] When he authoritatively but
gently admonished Lucien for conflating liberty with the republican form of
government, rather than with constitutional monarchy, the teenager became
flustered and felt as if his world were suddenly collapsing. But Paoli, seeing
the boy's strong response to the criticism, went on: "I see that you are as good
as your father was, and if this suits you, and the Signora Letizia, we will no
longer part."[16] Paoli thereupon invited Lucien to spend a few months with
him in his house in Rostino, up in the mountains, during the summer and
fall of 1791.[17]

The brothers—Joseph especially—approved of the plan, and Lucien, at sixteen, thus became Paoli's informal secretary—a role his own father had held
two decades earlier. "Your father," Paoli would muse, "was my best friend.
Younger than me, he studied many books, while I learned to know men.
Had he lived longer, he would have been my natural heir."[18] Paoli became
the paternal figurehead Lucien missed—not to mention a political mentor.

The house in Rostino was a peaceful former convent, surrounded by
chestnut forests and herds of sheep whose bleating reverberated through the
mountains together with the echoes of stanzas of the Italian poet Tasso, sung

by Paoli in his booming voice, and by the shepherds. Those were a happy few months for Lucien: His sense of the world expanded as the old leader debated history with him, talking at length about the past and future of Corsica and France. Paoli thought of England not as a monarchy but as "a wise, powerful republic" whose model France should emulate.[19]

Paoli had much to say about America: He was convinced that the founding fathers, especially Benjamin Franklin (whom he had met) and George Washington himself, would have preferred a constitutional monarchy to a republic but that the Americans' decision to adopt the latter had been dictated by their hatred of England rather than by their love of republican ideals. He also believed that, given the continuous expansion of U.S. territory, a republican government would have much less homogeneous control over the country than a constitutional monarchy. As for slavery, it was the "American leprosy"[20] that had corrupted a nation with great potential, whose inhabitants were dangerously inclined to replace the aristocracy of blood with the "aristocracy of the dollar."[21]

Lucien was deeply struck by many of Paoli's ideas. The young man's sharp and curious mind took it all in, processed the new thoughts and the unexpected provocations. But he was not completely convinced. Paoli's Anglophilia seemed to connote a firm dislike of France, which Lucien found unacceptable. He could not help remaining skeptical about his mentor's tendency to idealize the moral superiority of his islanders and the pride they took in their freedom—celebrated once by Jean-Jacques Rousseau. But he was too respectful of the old man to express his misgivings.

Napoleon, however, openly clashed with Paoli and grew suspicious of his younger brother's allegiance to a man he saw as anachronistic. A political divide was opening between the Bonaparte clan and the Paoli faction—between those who stood for France and political renewal and those who wanted to advance the cause of Corsican nationhood. Deep down, Paoli was a true Corsican, who could not forgive a perceived betrayal or disobedience without resorting to a fierce vengeance. One day Lieutenant Napoleon Bonaparte provocatively declared to him that the Corsicans, no matter how pure their customs were, still practiced the ancient system of family vendettas—hardly an indication of advanced civility. He was justifying his position against that of Paoli.

Lucien found himself caught between the restless ambitions of his generation and the allegiance to the ideals of his newfound father figure. In May 1792, fourteen-year-old Louis, the younger brother of Lucien and Napoleon, always ready to spy on the latter's behalf, found on Lucien's desk a pamphlet by him attacking a member of the local Jacobin Club. Napoleon was furious. He sought to undermine seventeen-year-old Lucien by criticizing the pamphlet's form, saying: "I have seen your pamphlet: it is worthless. There are too many words and too few ideas. You go after pathos. This is not the way to address the people. They are more sensible and sensitive than you think. Your prose will do more harm than good."[22]

Lucien—who was in Ucciani, in the mountains, with the rest of his family—responded with equally harsh words; he was suspicious of his brother's political motives, and on June 24, 1792, he wrote to Joseph, who had remained in Ajaccio: "In Napoleon I have always detected an ambition which is not wholly selfish, but is greater than his love for the public welfare. I believe that in a free state he would certainly be a dangerous man. . . . He seems to me inclined to become a despot, and I think he would become one, were he a king, and that his name would be a terror to posterity and to sensitive patriots."[23]

Young Lucien's evident insight into Napoleon's character should give one pause, for his diffidence was very probably justified, even in 1792. "I believe him capable of being a turncoat," Lucien said of his brother, perhaps on the basis of daily observations, of family life, or of his premonition that Napoleon would be a "terror to posterity." And this was no ordinary time. Being on the right side in those frantic days was a matter of life and death. The Terror had started in earnest that year, and the shiny blade of the guillotine had been bloodied incessantly in the last few months. In August Napoleon became a captain.

On January 21, 1793, Louis XVI was executed. The news quickly reached Corsica. France was plunged from weak monarchy into wild anarchy. Paoli, already horrified by the bloody turn the Revolution had taken, was devastated. "Unhappy nation!" he told Lucien. "Our Corsica cannot be ruled by these monsters!"[24] Paoli had met Louis XVI in Paris in 1790, when the meek king had engaged the island leader in an open-hearted conversation about the virtues of republics and had declared himself ready to give up his crown were he persuaded that doing so would bring happiness to the people. The execution of the sincere, naive monarch provoked enormous emotional and political distress in those who had felt loyal to him and, less evidently, in the liberals, regardless of their views about monarchism. The man who had fought for Corsican independence now justified his love for England by saying that since Corsica would never actually be independent, he would "rather have it led by thinking heads than by rolling heads."[25]

Paoli had tried to persuade the sons of Charles Bonaparte of his views, but in spite of the horrors taking place in France, he had failed to turn them to his side. They felt French, after all, and had faith in their country. Now that the king had been killed, Paoli incited the Corsicans to revolt against the French republic, organizing the local leaders and assembling the mountain dwellers into troops. "Woe to whomever sides with that horde of brigands!" he exclaimed. "I will not spare anyone, not even Charles' sons!"[26] This burst of rage, so uncharacteristic of the old chief, frightened Lucien, who, though no longer his secretary, was still in his thrall. It was a barely veiled threat, a warning of what was in store for the family if they did not follow Paoli's directives.

FIGHT OR FLIGHT

Lucien was perplexed at the choice that presented itself now between a Corsica that had turned against France and a France that no longer was the country Corsicans wanted to be associated with. In his memoirs he recalls being sent back by Paoli from the mountains to Ajaccio and his family. He found the city barricaded, and heard shots—the National Guard was patrolling. He was stopped at the gates: To be allowed entry, Napoleon and Joseph had to be alerted of his arrival, and the latter had to come fetch him. After arriving, Joseph grabbed Lucien's arm and told him to be very quiet. The anti-French movement had been quickly repressed, by Joseph himself, in alliance with the departmental administration and Napoleon, who had been named commander of the Corsican National Guard while on leave from the army. Whatever remained of Lucien's hope for reconciliation between Paoli and his brothers began to fade.

Lucien recorded in his memoirs the striking scene that awaited him at home, and though he probably embellished it in his retelling, it captures poignantly the family dynamic.[27] His mother was surrounded by all of his siblings. Napoleon was seated on a window recess, wearing the handsome uniform of the National Guard and holding little Caroline, who was playing with his watch chain. Louis sat alone in a corner painting puppets, Pauline and Jérôme played together, and, embroidering next to Letizia, acting grown up, sat fourteen-year-old Elisa—brought home by Napoleon when the revolutionary edict to abolish monasteries had shut down her exclusive school for girls at Saint Cyr, a venerable institution founded by Louis XIV.

"Finally," his mother said as Lucien entered, "here he is: I was afraid that Paoli the magician would not let him come back." Lucien replied, "On the contrary, Mother. It is the general himself who sends me." Napoleon chuckled and scoffed. Joseph suggested it might be best to send the little ones out of the room. "Do I also need to go?" asked Elisa, whose curiosity was aroused. "Yes, little girl," said Joseph, "even though you are a *grande demoiselle de Saint Cyr.*" Her mother concurred, asking her to take the others with her. Elisa curtseyed to Letizia, Joseph, and Napoleon. To the younger Lucien she gave an affectionate little slap on the hand, whispering to him "You will tell me everything, right?" The two had become the best of friends since she had returned to Corsica, and Lucien fully intended to keep her informed of what was going on.

Lucien recounted to his mother and elder brothers that Paoli was plotting an insurgency. They listened, dumbstruck. Letizia occasionally voiced her surprise and then her conviction that Paoli would fail because the Corsican cities no longer cared about national sovereignty—his was clearly a lost cause.

But when Lucien finally—painfully—reported the threatening phrase that Paoli had let escape against the Bonaparte brothers, all hell broke loose. The three men got up at once, angrily strode around the room, exclaiming, "What? He said what? He said that? That's too much!" Napoleon exploded.

"We will see about that! *Compère* Pascal! He hasn't gotten me yet! He declares war on us! For me, I don't hate the idea of war. I haven't waged it yet, but will happily start with him."

Joseph was enraged as well, but his bouts of anger tended not to last long in the presence of those angrier than he. Quite calmly, shrugging his shoulders, he replied to the irate Napoleon: "War! It's easier said than done! I understand that you might love war, but with what, and whom, are you going to wage it?"

Letizia, irritated but quiet until now, seconded Joseph. "Yes, with what will we wage war on him, Napolione? You know that each mountain fighter is worth four times as much as one of us. Oh, if they were all on our side, I wouldn't hesitate to fight myself, just like Napolione. But this is different."

Meanwhile Napoleon kept on muttering "He said that, he really said that. Fine. Fine, we'll wage war." When Letizia asked Napoleon what should be done now, he replied: "I have to admit that I don't like wars without artillery. That devil of Paoli has prevented the building of roads, so there is no use for cannons on the island. We have to stand ready for an attack."

The conversation turned to strategy. It was a proper family council—transcribed word for word, or reinvented, by Lucien—by the end of which it had become clear that urgent measures would have to be taken immediately to ensure the Bonapartes' safety and a possible escape to France.

They conferred late into the evening, but as Lucien prepared to take his leave, Joseph reminded him that there were to be two sessions at the Jacobin Club the next day which he should attend, since he could not go that evening. Lucien was surprised, saying "Tomorrow? But what do you mean? My dear brother, tomorrow I have to go back to Paoli!"

Letizia, hearing this, burst out: "Are you mad? This time he won't let you come back here! Now that he needs to know everything that happened here, he'll keep you hostage! Have you promised to return?"

Joseph reassured his mother. "Well, he would hardly be able to keep him hostage if Lucien were returning in good faith, upon his word that he would be back. In any case I hope he hasn't given his word." But Lucien stood by his mentor, saying "Good God! I did not need to promise I'd return. Neither I nor he ever doubted it for a moment."

Joseph and Letizia expressed relief, and Lucien went on to explain his special relationship with Paoli. "My dear Mother, my dear Joseph, it is exactly for the good reason that I did not need to promise that it is as if I did. It's as if—" He was interrupted as his mother and brother debated whether Lucien was bound to go back. Letizia said, "Come on! If he had promised . . . promised. . . . He does not have the right to. I say he could not have, he should not have promised, because . . . because he is a minor and cannot make any commitments without my permission."

Joseph confirmed, "This is legally true, but we do not need to go there. Luckily he has not promised anything. So you can, you must stay with us, my dear Lucien." At which point Lucien protested, "But this is awful! They will say that I have betrayed Paoli." His mother reassured him. "They'll say that of us all, my dear, and in neither case will it be true. It's of Paoli that one will say he betrayed France. In Ajaccio that's all they've been talking about." Still, Lucien insisted, "But they're wrong. Paoli could not have betrayed the France to which he swore his allegiance; and besides, I heard him say that there is never any treason in the means one uses for the love of one's country."

Letizia confessed that she did not think of Paoli as a traitor—that simply was not his nature—but she had noticed his increasing detachment from Jacobin France, and, given the pain and indignation he must have felt upon the execution of Louis XVI, whom he venerated as a saint, she had predicted what fateful steps he would take. Joseph had had the same foreboding. And he could not trust a republican Corsica led by Paoli; he would much rather see the alliance with France preserved and remain a French citizen—the madness there would not last, because bloodshed never lasted. Paoli had designated Charles his potential successor—the whole family was aware of Paoli's faith in the patriarch—but there were no guarantees now. Joseph tried to explain to Lucien why Paoli was at once wrong and still a great man: He was remaining heroically faithful to his ideal of an independent Corsica, but this was not realistic or possible, and hence bad politics. A revolt against France would entail the island's alliance with England, France's great enemy, especially since France had supported the American independence from Britain; and England would have used such an alliance for its own strategic interest against France. This was why, even if Paoli could not forgive Charles's children for abandoning him, Lucien had to realize that his mentor was the one who was forcing them to abandon him.

Lucien was not convinced. Joseph tried another tack, arguing this time that Paoli was right to admire the English model—but that if everyone had abandoned it when King Charles I had been decapitated, then the perfect English state that existed now would never have come into being.

Letizia and Joseph, during Napoleon's absence from the room, were finding all sorts of arguments to build a strong case against Paoli, like lawyers trying to win over a judge. By the end, Lucien was nearly in tears. "So it's decided! Your duty is to abandon the dear friend our father admired so much! And me? Yes, everyone will say I betrayed him! And he, he will accuse me of having betrayed him! Oh God!"

Joseph attempted to calm him: "No, Lucien, no, do not fear being accused of treason: It is only normal for someone your age to submit to the will of your mother and to your older brothers, who are men as capable as Paoli to judge what behooves their honor and interests, as well as yours."

Those simple, much more emotionally sensitive words had their intended effect. Lucien finally realized what was at stake. He relented, and all at once he felt at peace. He accepted that it would be possible for him always to admire Paoli while promising never to seek him out again. Joseph was relieved. "We'll talk more tomorrow," he said, "once you've rested, and we'll find a way to reconcile your duty to your family with the consideration that you owe your host—and that we owe, in form, to our great compatriot."

After Lucien had awoken from a long sleep, the conversation resumed over a large family meal. By dessert, talk had turned to the growth of English power in India—a country, Napoleon mused, where one could find fortune. He declared that if he failed to be promoted he would join the British forces there and return a rich nabob, wealthy enough to pay for the three sisters' dowries. While Joseph gallantly assured the captain that his merit would take him far even without protection from his superiors, Lucien was quietly struck by his brother's shameless display of greed.

But the main point of the discussion was to find a decent way for Lucien to end his relationship with Paoli. Clearly the young man would have to write him a letter. Together the family crafted a brief, rather cold missive that glossed over Lucien's reasons for not returning while making the point that this decision was now a family matter.

⁂

Lucien's political apprenticeship was over. He was awakening to the urgent realities of a world in disarray, where debates were all but theoretical. When, the next morning, he went to the Jacobin Club—by now renamed Société Populaire (Popular Society)—he embraced his new political position, buoyed by the fervent atmosphere and the participants' moving speeches. As he climbed the podium, the words came easily to him; he was already detached enough to be able to express warmly his respect, admiration, and love for the *père de la patrie* (father of the country) while describing the tense situation as a matter of security, a preventive measure the citizens of Ajaccio had rightly taken against unforeseen dangers, given that the leader no longer wanted to be French. Taking rhetorically astute byways and without belaboring the point, in effect Lucien announced his rupture with Paoli.

⁂

On the continent, the Revolution was increasingly bloody. On the island, exchanges at the Popular Society were not nearly as dramatic as those at the National Assembly in Paris, and politics remained orderly thanks in part to Joseph—but civil war was raging. Napoleon had entirely reorganized the National Guard, which regained the efficiency it had lost under Paoli. And Lucien was becoming an ardent anti-Paolist because, in 1793, the leader had Corsica renounce France, and strive once again to become independent.

In late February 1793, a French fleet stopped at Ajaccio on its way to what would be an ill-fated mission against Sardinia. Its commander was Admiral Laurent de Truguet, whose right-hand man Napoleon had become. The presence of this fleet in the port ensured that Corsican patriots stayed away from the city, and the Bonaparte family came to rely on it for its safety. But once it was gone—and Napoleon along with it, charged with the conquest of the small island of Maddalena, off the coast of Sardinia—the *montagnards,* or mountain people, gathered their forces and, under Paoli's leadership, took control of several towns around Ajaccio.

By this point, the tricolored flag of revolutionary France flew only over a few coastal cities. Life was getting riskier by the day for anti-Paolists, and it was increasingly pressing for the Bonapartes to organize their departure. Joseph no longer played a role in the island's administration; Napoleon, back half victorious from Maddalena, was in Bastia, a city in northern Corsica, with the people's representatives, trying to boost the defense against the Paolists. Lucien left the island without his family at the head of a deputation of Corsican Jacobins, to seek help against the Paolist insurgents. He followed one Huguet de Sémonville, ambassador to Constantinople for the French Republic.[28] While briefly in Corsica, the ambassador had given a speech in French at the Popular Society: No one had understood it, so Lucien immediately translated it into Italian (Corsicans were Italian speakers). Lucien's fiery eloquence had impressed the ambassador, a shrewd man who perceived the ardor of this young Bonaparte. Determined to take him under his wing, he immediately asked Lucien to be his private secretary, and Lucien accepted, in the vague hope of following him to the East. Lucien sailed with him to Marseille in the spring of 1793, unable to shake off an uncanny premonition of what was to come. Here their paths separated.

JACOBINS, "THE DEVILS OF THE CONTINENT"

Lucien had last been in the South of France as a seminary student, four years earlier. Now, age eighteen and in charge of a political mission, he felt he was returning an important man. As soon as he landed in Marseille, he was brought to the local Popular Society, to deliver his urgent message about the situation in Corsica. The meeting was held in a deconsecrated church, dark and dank, filled with men wearing revolutionary red caps and noisy women in the galleries. The arrival of the Corsicans was announced by the president, and a hearing was granted immediately.

Once again, Lucien's words flowed. He started by demanding help for the Corsican patriots, and, as he later recalled, for the very first time he "experienced how much the passions of those who listen have power over those who speak."[29] He preached strongly against Paoli, the traitor who had "abused the national confidence" and was about to deliver Corsica up to the English—the *perfide Albion* that would be plundering its rich forests to build its navy.[30] He was carried away by the gallery's response to his words, enjoying their effect, increasingly seeking to provoke and excite. The mere mention of England roused the crowds, and for hours Lucien heaped insult upon insult on his former mentor.

When he finally stepped down from the podium, he was enveloped by the warm embrace of the crowd and assaulted by the garlic breath of his revolutionary brothers, an unpleasant surprise that reminded him of where and who he was: a Corsican in France. Motions were swiftly passed—to send troops to Ajaccio and a deputation of three members to accompany Lucien and his delegation to Paris, where they would denounce Paoli's treason. It was midnight by the time Lucien could leave.

Despite his exhaustion, Lucien had trouble finding sleep that night. Once he did, he fell into agitated dreams. Paoli kept appearing in his mountain chief garb, fully armed. Instead of being irritated with Lucien, he was full of love, staring at him calmly and with tender benevolence, ignorant of his protégé's betrayal. Lucien knew in his dream that he had willingly betrayed his mentor and felt shame—but not repentance. Paoli then wanted to push Lucien away, but Lucien could not move. He got up from the armchair he had been sitting in and extended his hand, but Lucien hesitated to touch it. By the time Lucien made up his mind, the venerable old man, piercing him with an indignant gaze, disappeared like a shadow. Lucien tried to call after him, but the words remained stuck in his throat. The nightmare kept recurring throughout the night.

Lucien was woken up next morning by the bustling noises of the city's market and immediately realized what he had done. He had been a rabble-rouser. He had spoken against the man who had been his teacher and idol, he had uttered words in direct contradiction to everything he had learned from him, he had even voted for his arrest warrant—and the men with whom he was to go to Paris were revolting, filthy, smelly, brutish, and wild.

He went to the window and saw a sea of colorful caps—a throng of behatted people milling about the streets. The local deputies came to take him to breakfast, and he stepped out into the crowds, on to the Cannebière, the famous commercial stretch of Marseille. He was surprised by the jovial atmosphere, the commotion so early in the day, the men in hats, the well-dressed women and pretty children. Lucien and the deputies managed to elbow their way to the Cannebière Café and to find a seat. People came and went, though a group of a dozen individuals stood in the room, chatting. He followed their conversation distractedly. "When did they start?" "At nine." "Did they play well their roles?" "Yes, as far as I know. But the crowd was too thick and it was hard to get close." "Too bad. It is a beautiful day," said the plump lady at the counter. "And a good one too," added an ugly hunch-backed man with a bloodshot, malicious eye—his unforgettable face recalled that of Marat, the radical revolutionary journalist who would be stabbed to death in his bath the following July. Another rather sickly man jumped in: "That's very interesting. Do you think we'll still find a good seat? I need to sit to watch this." "Oh no," replied yet another, "that's impossible, your legs tremble with pleasure at the sight, don't they, you sensitive patriot!"

Lucien asked his new colleagues what spectacle these people were talking about and whether this was a festival day. The most zealous of them exclaimed, "It's better than that!" and led him to a window: It looked onto a side street at whose end was a square that seemed the focal point of all the to-do. "Here, you see!" chuckled the colleague, pointing at the square. "It is only about twenty aristocrats who are making a tumble!"

And there it was: the guillotine, its blade red with blood. The condemned were the city's richest merchants. Yet the shops were open, selling the goods of those very people whose heads were being chopped off; passersby were eating, drinking, laughing, celebrating the bloodshed and enjoying the show. One of Lucien's travel companions grinned. "These twenty market-grabbers want to spit and sneeze in the Revolution's basket!"[31]

Lucien was nauseated, horrified, and terrified. He would certainly not go to Paris, the capital of Terror. This time he used his persuasive powers to get himself off the hook and stay in Marseille. The argument he resorted to was not so far-fetched: He should be in charge of the rescue efforts for Corsica. He also tried flattery, persuading the least brutish of his three garlic-eating colleagues that they would be quite capable of fulfilling the Paris mission on their own.

Lucien tried to go back to the island. The news from there was not at all reassuring, and he had no idea what had happened to his family. The French representatives, including Napoleon, had apparently been kicked out of Bastia, and Paoli's insurrection was gaining ground. Lucien made his way to Toulon, from where the crossing to Ajaccio was shorter than it was from Marseille. When he arrived, he learned that a French frigate had just entered port. Curious to see who or what she carried, he followed the crowd and saw fugitives and refugees descending the ship's gangway. And there, suddenly, were his mother and siblings, walking down to the pier! There was a tumult. Lucien felt anxious and uneasy as he tried to reach them through a noisy mob—these were surely the same people who watched the daily beheadings of their compatriots, though here their shouts were not unfriendly.

The family was safe, and unharmed. They all waved at Lucien, who made his way to the dock, overjoyed. He embraced Elisa and the children, and the fat, pink-cheeked uncle Fesch, who had joined the rest of the family in Ajaccio. Trailed by the oddly well-intentioned crowd, they made their way to a modest hotel. They badly needed rest: The crossing, which normally was not very long, had lasted a good sixty hours. Finally closing the door on the chaos outside, and after putting the children to bed, Letizia turned to Lucien and told him what had happened.

After Lucien's departure, she said, the situation had become desperate. The Jacobins' revolutionary zeal had thrown a majority of Corsicans into the Paolist camp, and Letizia was alone with the three girls and the two little boys, deprived of the protection usually afforded by the three elder sons. Knowing full well that if Ajaccio fell to Paoli's men the family would be endangered, she sent the youngest children, Jérôme and Caroline, to stay nearby with her mother, Madame Fesch.

One night Letizia awoke to see her bedroom invaded by *montagnards*. She sat up, terrified, convinced they had come for her and the children. But torchlight illuminated the face of one of the men: It was Costa, who had long been devoted to the family. He was the chief of Bastelica, a nearby town in the middle of the island, deep in the forest at the foot of the mountains. Costa had called the Jacobins "the devils of the continent" but soon saw that his fellow Corsicans were turning into devilish creatures as well.[32] A nephew of his had encountered Paolist troops in the mountains, heading for Ajaccio, where, he was told, they were to "take all the children of Charles alive or dead." When Costa learned this, he immediately assembled his men and ran to Ajaccio to save the family, preceding their enemies only by a few miles.

Letizia and the children had little time to get ready. They could pack only their clothes, and, surrounded by their escort, they escaped the city in the middle of the night. The men who had opened the gates to Costa must have believed they were doing Paoli a favor—little did they know they had ensured the Bonapartes' flight. Whether Paoli really meant what he had said, the *montagnards* took their stated mission seriously, and Paoli must have been aware that they would do so.

It was a night of high anxiety for them all. Letizia, surrounded by three of her children, accompanied by Fesch, who was no fighter, marched in the dark, across the mountains, marshes, and forests, aware that a deadly encounter with the enemy could occur at any point. The day broke. They rested in a forest for a little while, from where they had a view of the coast. They saw flames rising up into the sky: "Madame, that is your house which is burning," one of Costa's men told Letizia. She replied: "Ah, never mind! We will build it up again much better—vive la France!"[33]

They marched on for another night, keeping their eye on the coast, until, arriving at the tower of Capitello, they finally caught sight of a French flotilla, which quickly intercepted the distress signals they sent from the beach. A small boat approached and brought the Bonaparte family back to the frigate, safe, and bound for Bastia; from there, they went to Calvi, where they stayed with friends. Joseph rejoined them, as did Jérôme and Caroline, who had been escorted there, and Napoleon, after another, vain attempt at retaking Ajaccio. It was clearly unsafe to remain in Corsica, and so they sailed for Toulon, where they arrived on June 13, 1793.[34]

Despite Letizia's assurances, Lucien could not bring himself to believe that *Babo* had given the order to catch his mother and younger siblings "alive or dead." But his rage was now boundless. His remorse vanished: He would have rejoined the deputation to Paris, had it not already left; he wanted Paoli to know that he had signed his arrest warrant. The family was destitute, their house burned down, the precious library reduced to ashes—along with his and Napoleon's writings. The Bonapartes had never been very rich; but now they were refugees whose sole possessions were the clothes on their backs. Letizia had managed to salvage a tiny stash of gold and a small jewelry case but nothing more. And all this was Paoli's doing.

FUNERALS AND WEDDINGS

It was August 1793 and the refugees' lives were fraught with uncertainty and danger. Everyone had to make ends meet, improvising and inventing opportunities. Joseph was unemployed, in Paris with Napoleon, who was trying to obtain the promotion that was due to him after his partially successful mission in La Maddalena. Lucien was in Marseille. As it happened, a Corsican friend of Letizia's had a relation named Jacques Pierre Orillard de Villemanzi, who held the lucrative post of commissary of wars in Marseille. He was a kind and elegant man, with whom Lucien quickly became friends. Villemanzi was eager to help out the young Bonaparte, offering to lend Lucien some money and then naming him keeper of supplies to the army in the small town of Saint-Maximin, near Marseille—a job that an underage Lucien secured by using Joseph's birth certificate. Villemanzi also generously gave him the use of a pied-à-terre in his house.

For Lucien, the post at Saint-Maximin did not sound like a dream job, but the salary was decent and would be essential, especially for Letizia, who was struggling to support the five younger children. The state provided an allowance to Corsican exiles, but it was a minimal amount, consisting for the most part of bread, basic goods, and ammunition.

Villemanzi owed his post to his protector, Général Jean-Francois Carteaux, who would have to approve Lucien for the job; and he soon obtained for Lucien an audience with the general. As the young Bonaparte was soon to learn, the revolutionaries did not make much use of intellectually refined generals such as Paoli: Carteaux had been a bad painter who became a bad military leader in spite of himself. He was a soldier's son, a coarse, haughty, pathetic character, at once sentimental and cruel, who shed tears for future widows and orphans before any battle he ordered. During the four-month siege of Lyon, in the summer of 1793, he unleashed a frightening group of roughs called the Revolutionary Army and authorized a fearsome plundering of the rebelling city. Next he moved to quash the beginnings of a revolt in Marseille, where his very presence was enough to settle the unrest.

Lucien was not eager to make the general's acquaintance, but it had to be done—he was in the hands of Villemanzi, who insisted there was no other way. As the two friends walked through the noisy halls of Carteaux's headquarters in an old administration building, they saw half-drunk soldiers who sang, chatted and cursed, played cards and dominoes, and drank. When they saluted the bemedaled general, he promptly exclaimed, turning to Villemanzi: "So this is your young friend, the Corsican patriot in exile? Boy, he is freakishly skinny! Can you vouch for his honesty? You need incorruptibility, the first virtue of the immortal Maximilien Robespierre! What a man! What a saint." Lucien then had to endure an endless rant filled with nonsensical curses, lachrymose descriptions of military prowess, and panegyrics to the republic and to liberty. The audience ended with "You will take your post, won't you? Service to the Republic first. Farewell, young man: I am in a rush."[35]

So it was that Lucien had a job, with six months' pay in advance, which he gave to Letizia, and an allowance to move, which he immediately put to use. He left Marseille for Saint-Maximin the next day. It was a short trip inland, and Letizia promised Lucien that if his brothers' situation in Paris did not soon improve, she would come live with him. But a few days after his arrival, he received a letter announcing that Napoleon had been appointed a major in the artillery division of the troops destined to besiege Toulon. Like Corsica, the fortified Toulon, fearing the approaching Terror, had suddenly surrendered to the English fleet (strengthened by help from the Spaniards), and the revolutionaries were urgently organizing its recapture. As for Joseph, he would soon be named commissioner of wars.

At the time, it was deemed patriotic for cities to adopt classical names, and in a fashionable show of republicanism, the revolutionaries renamed Saint-Maximin "Marathon." Lucien was welcomed in the town with all the honors; his reputation had preceded him. He quickly discovered that the locals were devotees of the flourishing cults of "Reason" and the "Supreme Being" instigated under the rule of Robespierre. He also saw that they were harmless and for the most part uneducated.

Soon upon his arrival, the mayor informed him that a good twentieth of the population was in jail—in an ex-monastery—as "suspects," under orders from the district of Brignoles, of which the town was part. Selecting whom exactly to arrest had been a strange exercise for the mayor and local police. One criterion was clothes: Anyone who wore garments luxurious enough to offend those who lived in misery was locked away. Aristocrats, intellectuals, and those who did not wear the Jacobin red cap were added to the list. Thankfully no one had been executed yet. But anyone risked being sent to the dank, dark prison in the town of Orange, where the revolutionary Tribunal operated nonstop to send people to the scaffold—doing so no less efficiently than the infamous Tribunal in Paris under the auspices of its ruthless public prosecutor, Fouquier de Tinville, who merrily boasted that "heads were falling like tiles." So far, the incarcerated citizens of Saint-Maximin were safe, yet their days were numbered, and something needed to be done.

Lucien learned the details of this situation from a pleasant-looking, pink-hued, white-toothed, fat middle-age man who had quietly attended his meeting with the mayor. He turned out to be a defrocked monk who had taken the classical name of Epaminondas—his religious name was Father Bruno. Shrewd and quick, he would soon become a useful ally for Lucien.

He was the president of the local revolutionary committee, to which he introduced the Corsican. Lucien's status of patriotic refugee, together with his oratorical skills, personal charm, and youth, endeared him to the local population, especially to the women in red caps, rich and poor alike, who turned up each evening with their embroidery work and cheered loudly whenever Lucien appeared at the podium. In short order he succeeded Epaminondas as president of the committee: The ex-monk was happy to leave the seat to him, and there was not much competition, given that all the educated citizens were in jail.

From this position, Lucien established a "little dictatorship."[36] He gloried in self-satisfaction, but, aware of his hubris—"the main engine of all the good and evil one does"—he forced himself to control it. Though dealing with simple people, most of them illiterate, he avoided the temptation of abusing his easily earned power, setting out instead to help them, in alliance with Epaminondas, who keenly felt the duty to care for the prisoners. The classical name Lucien adopted was that of Brutus, Caesar's killer—a historically loaded name, to be sure, but also an acutely theatrical one. And it was theater that Lucien resorted to in his mission to improve the lot of these hapless villagers. He managed to free a few of the detainees, bettered the conditions of those who had to stay in jail, passed a resolution guaranteeing that no one would be sent to the infamous prison in Orange, and initiated a series of performances where the prisoners played roles in republican, patriotic pieces. He even forced one well-born lady to act a part in Voltaire's play *Brutus*—and in so doing she obtained her release from jail.

Meanwhile, in Paris, Queen Marie-Antoinette did not have such luck: Dressed in a white dress and a white bonnet, her hands tied, she was carted to the guillotine on October 16, 1793. Lucien's intention was to distract everyone from the fear and horror of that year, and to a large extent he succeeded.

Carteaux was sent to Toulon in September 1793 to suppress a Royalist insurrection, but he could not dislodge the enemy. Challenged by Napoleon, then twenty-four years old and an artillery officer, to detail his war plan to the Convention—as the Assembly was then called—the rambling general showed once again his incompetence in military matters and was recalled from duty in November. Napoleon was appointed *chef de battallion* (major) after Général Dugommier had taken over the mission, and was nicknamed Captain Cannon. Once he was given a free hand in the siege operations, the English fleet finally fell under French fire. Lucien, perhaps sent to Toulon in his role as military store keeper, witnessed his brother's fearless exploits and was deeply impressed.

Captain Cannon indefatigably supervised the positioning of each of the batteries, which were dangerously exposed to enemy fire. One day Lucien followed him, but Napoleon, turning toward him, said: "Are you not going to leave? This is not your place." "But you are right here, my brother." "No doubt I am, and everyone here has to obey me. So leave at once. This is not your job: to each his own."[37] So Lucien moved a bit farther away. The moment he left his place, a cannoneer who had been standing next to him was killed by a bullet that just missed Napoleon's left leg. The battlefield was evidently not Lucien's territory. Napoleon thrived on it, and enjoyed an uncanny invulnerability. Toulon fell in December 1793. This was Napoleon's first triumph. From then on, as the writer and chronicler Alexandre Dumas put it, "History grabbed him and was never to leave him alone."[38]

In a letter signed Brutus Bonaparte, Lucien celebrated this victory against the Royalists: It announces "with joy" to the Convention deputies, "from the field of glory, walking through the blood of traitors, that your orders were executed and that France has been avenged; neither age nor sex have been spared. Those who were only wounded by the republican cannon were finished off by the sword of freedom and the bayonet of equality."[39] The battle had been ferocious, the carnage horrific. But though the bloodthirsty language was not unusual at the time, it seems decidedly out of character even for Lucien, prone as he was to oratorical excesses: Throughout his life he consistently avoided violence whenever he could and, seeing no thrill in battles, pursued peaceful solutions rather than wars. He would always deny being the author of this letter, which nevertheless stuck to his revolutionary name.

In 1794, the Terror was at its height. It reached an odious apogee that summer, under the rule of Robespierre: More heads rolled then than since the guillotine had begun its sinister work the year before. It was not only aristocrats and political "enemies" but also writers, scientists, and philosophers, who were being executed with their whole families.

Napoleon managed to avoid being dragged into the dark cesspool. Maximilien Robespierre had a younger brother named Augustin, who was superintendent of the army in the Alps. A member of the Convention, he was nicknamed "Bonbon" for his sweetness and many good deeds at the height of the Terror—in stark contrast with his brother. He fought for amnesties and against the persecution of Christians, and, horrified by the endless fratricide that raged in the country after the king's death, he tried to stop Maximilien. This man who saved lives was welcomed in the towns of southern France with cries of "vive Robespierre!" Napoleon got along with Augustin—the two met in Nice, where Bonaparte, a general of brigade now, was commanding the artillery. In the wake of the Toulon victory, Napoleon's name was beginning to mean something; and Augustin, who witnessed the victory, informed his brother of the young general's talents, convincing him to consider Bonaparte for nothing less than the post of commander of Paris.

The promotion of Napoleon to general in 1793 enabled the Bonaparte family to settle more comfortably in a château near Antibes. Lucien came from Saint-Maximin to visit for a few days. As he took a walk with Joseph and Napoleon, the latter announced what he had been offered and inquired of them what he should do. Lucien rejoiced at the notion of "reaching the capital" at last. But Napoleon had already made up his mind: He would turn down the offer. He observed, looking Lucien sharply in the eye: "This is not something to be enthusiastic about. It is not as easy to save one's head in Paris as it is in Saint-Maximin. Augustin is an honest fellow, but his brother does not kid around. He will have to be obeyed. To serve that man? No, never! I know how useful I would be to him by replacing that idiot of a commander of Paris; but *that is what I do not want to be.* It is not the right time. The army is the only honorable place for me today; be patient, *I will command Paris later on.*"[40]

Napoleon's sudden fame was nevertheless a boon for Lucien, who thought he might be able to use the influence of his brother's name to get the villagers out of jail. The feared agents of the Public Safety Committee, Paul Barras (the man who later would become leader of the Directory) and Stanislaus Fréron, were craving more capital executions. Just as towns all over France were imprisoning more "suspects," when the two men learned in Marseille that no one from Saint-Maximin had been delivered to the guillotine—that the villagers were actually *entertaining* themselves with theater and music—they decided to take action.

One day, an old woman ran up to Lucien and told him breathlessly: "In the name of Heaven, citizen president, come and defend us: they are carrying off our children to Orange. Remember what you promised us." Lucien immediately demanded that the alarm bell be sounded and ran along with a hundred or so members of the Popular Society to the prison. Half a dozen carts were already loaded with chained prisoners, bound for Orange. Barras's men, wearing tricolored scarves and plumed hats, stood at the gates with a few gendarmes, while a secretary wrote down the victims' names. Lucien did not waste a second. He ordered the men to leave "in the name of the law." He knew exactly what he was doing: "The Revolutionary Committee has not ordered any delivery of the prisoners," he declared. "The Popular Society is about to assemble; come there and present your authority. Gendarmes, release the suspects." At first the men branded him a "moderate," stated the names of those who had sent them, and ignored Lucien. But, alerted by the bell, a large number of villagers and relatives of the condemned arrived. Some were armed. Lucien ordered the release of the prisoners, and by the power of numbers he got his way. The thirty-odd prisoners were returned to the jail, its gates closely guarded by their fellow citizens. The delegate sent by Barras began to tremble when Lucien asked for his papers. Instantly changing his manner and complimenting the Popular Society of Saint-Maximin, he confessed that he had "nothing further to say, since the revolutionary committee is presided over by a Corsican patriot." Thereupon he abruptly departed, followed by his men.

Lucien described that day as "one of the happiest of my life."[41] He had actually saved lives. His way with words, presence of mind, determination, and self-confidence had served him in action. The "petty store-keeper"—as a resentful Barras would later label Lucien in his *Mémoires,* calling his oratorical style at the Popular Society "demagogic bawling"[42]—had become the town's heroic savior.

Lucien had been assiduously and successfully courting the attentions of his innkeeper's illiterate but charming daughter, Christine Boyer. Pierre-André Boyer, the girl's father, a conventional bourgeois who had not adopted a fancy classical name, was not going to allow his daughter's lover to get away with his courting. After a committee meeting at which Lucien had been spouting equality, Boyer, turning Lucien's words against him, said: "You who have so much to say about principles, why do you not start practicing your morality by marrying my daughter, since in not doing so you are injuring her reputation?"[43] The remonstrance was uttered in public, in the presence of a large gathering. There would not have been much of a choice for Lucien. And on May 4, 1794, while the Terror raged, Lucien married Christine. She was twenty-two and he was just nineteen—underage, in fact, since the legal age of marriage for males was twenty-one. So, just as Lucien had used his older brother Joseph's birth certificate to get the job in Saint-Maximin, he used it again to marry. The marriage certificate was in the name of Brutus Bonaparte—Lucien's revolutionary name.

Lucien's family was furious with him for rashly marrying beneath his station, and especially for not requesting Letizia's consent. But Christine was by every account a delightful young woman, endowed with a lovely smile and dark, southern looks whose charms were not diminished by the visible marks of smallpox; she was graceful, gentle, affectionate, and kind. And Lucien's love was amply reciprocated. Although malicious gossip would later claim that she was pregnant before they married, the records report the facts: She gave birth to their first daughter, Charlotte, no less than eleven months after the wedding day.

Lucien's marriage was shortly followed by that of Joseph, who wed Julie Clary, the daughter of a wealthy silk merchant from Marseille, on August 1, 1794. It was as good a choice as that of Lucien had seemed absurd. Meanwhile, Napoleon, whose irritation with Lucien was extreme, was engaged to Julie's sister Désirée, but he treated her with capricious indifference. Love was not foremost on his mind: The political scene was changing dramatically and, with it, the fortunes of the Bonapartes.

ALL ROADS LEAD TO PARIS

France bathed in its own blood, until the henchmen of the Terror became victims of their own deeds. The countdown to the end of that ghastly period began with Georges Jacques Danton's death, on April 5, 1794. The raucous orator literally spent the last of his powerful voice defending himself against fabricated charges in a revolutionary show trial whose deadly legal machinery he himself had created. His speechless head was severed and shown to the people of Paris, who had long idolized him. But the eloquent leader of the Revolution prophesized that his partners in crime would soon follow his fate.

With eerie punctuality, only two weeks after the fifth anniversary of Bastille Day, on July 28, Robespierre—"the most cruel hypocrite and the greatest coward of them all," in Lucien's words[44]—was guillotined. Those who ordered his execution were his erstwhile allies, including Barras, Fréron, and Fouché.

Young Augustin Robespierre, Napoleon's supporter, volunteered to follow his brother to death on the scaffold on the same day. The Thermidor purges—so-called because they began in the month of Thermidor, the revolutionary calendar's equivalent of mid-July to mid-August—lasted for a few months. It was a time of extreme tension and distress for the Bonaparte family. In the wake of the fall of the mighty Robespierre and of the Jacobin Convention, chaos and revenge raged, and many compromised officers and civil servants were removed from their posts. Because of his association with Augustin, on August 11, Napoleon was arrested in Nice, but he was detained only until the twentieth: his skills were needed, and the game of political expediency trumped the dictates of revenge.

For his part, Lucien eventually left Saint-Maximin, since the military store had been dismantled, and his job with it—by the time he married, in fact, he was already out of work. Moreover, he faced the double danger of being denounced to the military authorities for failing to have himself conscripted to the army as his age warranted and harmed for his Jacobin fervor, even though, in his view, he had performed "the parody of what the Convention wanted," refusing to be associated with the excesses of his fellow Jacobins.[45] And so Lucien went to the quiet, small town of St. Chamas as inspector in the military administration. The drawback was that his adored wife and baby had to stay behind for a while with Christine's father in Saint-Maximin.

At least the job did not require full-time commitment, and his days in St. Chamas were spent pleasantly, often in social engagements with local families. One day in August 1795, while in the company of his friends and as he was declaiming a poem to redeem a pledge, Lucien was called to the door: A military man wanted him. He was surprised to see Auguste Rey, the son of a couple in Saint-Maximin who had been among the prisoners he had saved. The sixteen-year-old wore the uniform of the Compagnons de Jésus (Companions of Jesus), a southern sect of brutally vengeful anti-Jacobins. "Well, Auguste, what do you want with me, and how are your parents?" Lucien asked. The response was unexpected: "March, brigand, and give me your hands!" Auguste arrested Lucien on behalf of the new administration of Saint-Maximin, handcuffing him and taking him away. Auguste brandished his sword to make Lucien walk faster, and the boys that accompanied Rey kept taunting him. Lucien asked: "Where are you going to take me? Are you going to cut my throat as a recompense for having saved your parents?" Auguste replied: "No, you have nothing to fear on that score. I shall take you to the prison of Aix." Lucien was startled: "To the prison of Aix! Why, it is only a few days since the prisoners were massacred there! It is as bad as the prison of Orange."[46]

In Aix, Lucien found himself in a big cell with a hundred other hapless inmates. The walls and mattress straw were stained with the blood of previous victims. The next day, he wrote to his mother and brothers to inform them of what had happened. And he composed a pleading letter to Auguste's father: He had, after all, saved their lives.[47] He also wrote to the Corsican Représentant du Peuple (Representative of the People), invoking his pitiful situation as compatriot, husband, and father, claiming he had left his office three months before 9 Thermidor (July 27, 1794, when Robespierre was arrested and condemned to death) and that no Jacobin "legal homicide" had taken place under his watch.[48]

After six weeks of agony in the crowded prison cell, an order of liberation came from Paris. It was signed by Napoleon. Struggling for his career, Napoleon had endured the humiliating demotion to the position of infantry brigade, and taken medical leave while trying to buy time. But on Barras's recommendation, he was nominated military advisor to the Committee of Public Safety for the Italian campaign whose preparation was under way. In that capacity Napoleon managed to get his brother out of jail.

Lucien went straight to Marseille, where the rest of the family, including Letizia, had found refuge under Joseph's wing. He found the city's mood much changed. Its inhabitants, once so eager to enjoy the gory death shows set up by the Jacobin Convention, were happily celebrating its defeat. Across the country, the counterrevolutionaries and monarchists were the new heroes. A new republican constitution was decreed in August, in the name of equality and the division of power: The government would consist of two legislative chambers—the Council of the Five-Hundred and the Council of the Elders—topped by the executive Directory made up of five Council members, whose unofficial leader was Barras. But to the outrage of those who celebrated the end of Jacobin tyranny, the deputies of the old Convention determined that they themselves should constitute two-thirds of the chambers, without any elections.

Seeing no reason to linger in Marseille, Lucien hastened to Paris, where he arrived on September 27, 1795, and met Napoleon. Jacobin uprisings in the months preceding Robespierre's death had led to a heavy military presence in the capital. New revolts now came from the right: Royalists clamored nationwide for the rejection of the "law of the two-thirds," without success in the provinces, where the assemblies accepted the constitution wholesale. But in Paris, the revolt came to a head on October 5, 1795, just a few days after Lucien's arrival: Royalists marched against the Directory, which had taken residence in the Tuileries, the royal palace. The scene might have looked frighteningly similar to the coup of August 10, 1792, when the king was captured, and which Napoleon had witnessed firsthand: That had been his first experience of the bloody consequences of battle, and indeed no other battlefield ever made a stronger impression on him. At the time, Napoleon had observed that if the king had mounted his horse, he would have won that fateful day. But today the rebels were the king's supporters; they were not a hungry, tired, desperate rabble but a well-organized, well-dressed, angry but disciplined crowd. The military was in place, facing it.

When Barras frantically called on generals to come rescue the Directory, only a handful responded, Bonaparte and Carteaux foremost among them. Ironically enough, before the Revolution, Carteaux had painted an equestrian portrait of Louis XVI and then had stormed the Tuileries. For the third and last time now, the long-winded and cowardly general was switching sides. Barras immediately made Napoleon commander of Paris. Lucien remembered the prophecy Napoleon had uttered less than two years earlier, that he would "command Paris later on." As determined to defend the Tuileries as he had been in attacking Toulon, Napoleon requisitioned the artillery and used lethal grapeshot against the rebels. Heavy rain discouraged them and washed away the blood of a few hundred casualties in the streets.

Impressed by Napoleon's zeal, Barras named him second in command of the Army of the Interior. Napoleon asked Fréron, who was about to take the post of proconsul of Marseille, to take Lucien with him as his personal secretary. Fréron had been close to Robespierre and an enemy of Lazare Carnot, now a minister in the Directory government, so his political career was on the wane. But he was a libertine, a lover of women and drink—an "excellent revolutionary" albeit "effeminately literary" according to his friend Barras, with whom he had overseen the Jacobin bloodshed in the South; and although Lucien had opposed the bloodshed, he did not demur from befriending Fréron.[49] Under the influence of Fréron's grand ways, Lucien took advantage of the trip to Marseille to perform his oratory at Aix, where he had been imprisoned, and in various southern towns. In Marseille, Fréron lived like a "Persian viceroy," illuminating his house day and night, staging bullfights and plays, impressing the city's high society with his ready wit and seductive air, with a sophistication borne of his upbringing with aunts of Louis XVI himself.[50]

Lucien's sister Pauline also was in Marseille and most probably met Fréron through her brother. She was fifteen and already a beauty—petite, fair-skinned, with dark hair and eyes and a sensuous mouth. Fréron was forty-two, the father of two children by his mistress, an ex-actress in Paris. He

set out to seduce the beautiful Pauline and succeeded immediately. Within a
few days there was talk of marriage. The brothers were puzzled by the match;
and Letizia firmly refused to consent to Pauline's nuptials with the former
terrorist (as the architects and abettors of Terror were now called), whom she
believed was incapable of sustaining his grandiose lifestyle for long. Lucien
ended his stint as Fréron's aide but on November 1, 1795, took the Directory
office in earnest. One week later, Napoleon had Lucien nominated commissioner of war with the Army of the North based in Antwerp, then part of the
Netherlands.

Before taking service, Lucien spent a month in Paris. It was by far the most
exciting time he had ever had in his life. After the Terror, Paris was a wild
and festive town. The signs of indigence were everywhere: The city was filthy
and fetid, babies lay abandoned on the streets next to feral dogs and dead
animals. But the streets were also the stage for celebration. After years of fear,
persecution, war, and death, the pursuit of pleasure was the order of the day.
Now that the forced, moralistic "celebrations" Robespierre had imposed in
true dictatorial style were over, the parks were full, music was performed in
the open air, a dozen theaters staged bawdy plays every evening, salons re-
opened, and surviving aristocrats began to return. People met again at balls,
gambling and dancing through the night, consuming ices and watching fireworks. There was even a subscription dance for victims of the Terror, whose
survivors wore red ribbons around their necks. Everyone read avidly, as new
novels were printed in a flurry of literary creation. Transparent gauze dresses
were all the rage, as were vaguely Oriental, sexy drapes and eccentric outfits;
love affairs blossomed. Conversation shone, gossip at last turned on matters
of Eros rather than Thanatos. The pagan gods and ancient heroes of neoclassical art populated houses and public squares.[51]

Lucien was enamored of politics. He spent his days at the Assembly
listening to the debates, buttonholing deputies to share his profuse thoughts
with them. At night, he frequented the famously elegant, sought-after salon
of Barras, who now revealed that he was in fact Vicomte Paul de Barras. No

less of a libertine than Fréron, Barras was creepily attractive and dissolute; and in his case as in Fréron's, his aristocratic pedigree had not gotten in the way of his revolutionary zeal. Unlike Fréron, though, he was an operator who, after overturning Robespierre, stayed on top and became rich by bribing the military to his advantage. As head of the Directory, he was even more powerful now.

Barras was also lucky in love: His mistress was Madame Tallien, née Thérésia Cabarrus, a half-Spanish, petite, dark beauty. She had met her husband Jean-Lambert Tallien—a moderate ally of Robespierre—during the Revolution, first as a married woman, in the studio of the renowned society painter Elizabeth Vigée-Lebrun, then as one of the first divorcées of the new republic, when Tallien had saved her from jail. (Her first husband had been an exiled aristocrat.) Now Tallien was a jealous man, and his wife was celebrated as the most voluptuous woman of the time; according to Britain's prime minister, William Pitt, she "would be capable of closing the gates of hell."[52] The hostess of the Barras salon, she had filled the walls with artworks that once belonged to Queen Marie-Antoinette. Her wild hairdos and transparent Greek-style tunics often dipped in scented oil set a new fashion trend and made the men dizzy, including Lucien, who called her "a true Calypso" and innocently flirted with her.[53] He was learning to thrive in Parisian salons. Hungry for life and culture, he was dazzled by the refinement and freedom of thought, by the intellectual energy and sensuality of this reborn world, so different from the rough environment in which he had lived. Now he was frequenting the best minds of the best society, exercising his artistic eye and literary mind.

Napoleon had also met the "female dictator of beauty"; he had tried his luck with her, but Mme Tallien rejected him with a much-remarked measure of disdain that made him look rather ridiculous. Barras was keen to push him instead into the arms of Madame Joséphine de Beauharnais, the widow of the Marquis de Beauharnais, a general who had been guillotined, and by whom she had two children. Rumor was that she had had an affair with Barras.

Given the many beauties in Paris, Lucien was unimpressed with this older woman, notably thin-waisted but with declining looks and rotten teeth, although Napoleon "noticed her, or rather was noticed by her."[54] Not brilliant in any way, but elegant, stylish, and worldly; this half Creole knew how to put to advantage her natural charms enough to be well known, and well received, in Parisian society.

After that month of blissful revelry, Lucien reluctantly left for the Netherlands without his wife and child. Soon after, on March 2, 1796, Napoleon married Joséphine. Her dowry was quite unusual: Barras made Napoleon commander of the army dedicated to fighting a campaign in Italy. As if following his younger brother's bad example, Napoleon had not asked for Letizia's consent.

An unapproved union to a wife regretfully left at home was the only thing the two brothers now had in common. While Napoleon, immediately after marrying, led thousands of troops in what turned out to be the first of his many triumphal campaigns, Lucien, alone in Antwerp, was scrambling to obtain one miserly horse for his own use. Unhappy with his petty role, devoured by boredom and dissatisfaction, he spent his time reading newspapers and pamphlets. After six weeks of this useless life, he left his post and returned to Paris. It was an act of insubordination that might cost him dearly, but he counted on his brother's protection not to be discharged.

VIVE LA RÉPUBLIQUE!

In mid-May 1796 the French army occupied Milan in the fight against the Austrians. Lucien quickly set out from Paris to join Napoleon there— it is unclear why, though it is likely that he planned to ask the general to give him another job, perhaps also to try to convince him to let Pauline marry Fréron, whom she still loved. On his way, he stopped in Genoa, where some volunteers had gathered to sail to Corsica in an attempt to deliver the island from the English occupation brought on by Paoli. The leader of those officers was Costa, the man who had saved his family from *Babo's* vendetta and whom Lucien embraced with affection and gratitude. Lucien was tempted to accompany them to Ajaccio, but he was more eager to find his heroic brother. During his brief stay in Genoa, the news arrived that Corsica had risen against Paoli, who had returned to London some months earlier.

Lucien hoped to partake of the celebratory mood that had crowned the victorious French entry into the northern Italian capital. But Napoleon and his army had left to suppress an uprising in Pavia, in the northern Italian plains. On his way there, Lucien passed through the burned ruins of a village plundered by the French and saw corpses of soldiers and civilians alike. And when he entered the beautiful city of Pavia, he was shocked to see how badly it had been pillaged; peasants who had refused to surrender lay dead on the ground, their bodies tended to just as Lucien arrived. There was blood everywhere, and hawkers were selling stolen goods in the streets. Even the most necessary of wars, he thought, brings a host of miseries to the people involved in it.

He hurried on. When he finally managed to catch up with the busy general, he found that his brother had no time for him; Napoleon's welcome was cold and unfriendly. Lucien spent half a day with him, feeling awkward at best. If at the siege of Toulon Lucien had been out of place, here he was out of order, as Napoleon made abundantly clear. The young man had extravagantly deserted his post, gone to Paris and come to Italy without seeking anyone's permission, and now was wandering around aimlessly.

Furious and impatient with his irresponsible brother, Napoleon nevertheless found him a commissary's post in Marseille. But Lucien was restless and lost, full of energy and desperate for a purpose. Accompanied by Christine and little Charlotte, he returned to Paris instead. Exasperated, Napoleon wrote to Minister Carnot, one of the five leaders of the Directory, a powerful man who had also been a key revolutionary:

> One of my brothers, a commissary of the War Department at Marseille, has gone to Paris without permission. This young man has a certain amount of talent, but at the same time a very ill-balanced mind. All his life he has had a mania for plunging into politics. At this moment, when it seems to me that a great many people are anxious to damage me, and a whole intrigue has been set on foot to give color to reports that are as stupid as they are wickedly calumnious, I ask you to be so good as to do me the essential service of ordering him to rejoin the army within twenty-four hours. I would like it to be the Army of the North.[55]

In August 1796, Lucien ended up with the Army of the Rhine and a desk job; Christine and their daughter were with him. Christine was pregnant but miscarried. On September 14, Lucien wrote directly to Barras: "My campaign in the Rhine and Mosel begins under most unhappy circumstances. My wife's state of health is alarmingly dire and requires me to take her back immediately to her family, the only refuge for her given her condition." Lucien informed Barras that he was petitioning the minister for a change of post to Marseille: "[I]n case of any difficulty, we count on your friendship to overcome it."[56] If this petition failed, he wrote, he would have to resign his job.

Christine's condition—which Lucien did not specify was due to a miscarriage—clearly did not strike Napoleon as a legitimate excuse for his brother to leave his post once again. When Carnot forwarded Lucien's request to Napoleon, the latter, at the end of his tether, replied to Carnot:

> I have received your letter of [October 8, 1796]. You must have seen by merely reading his letter how hare-brained this young man is. He got himself into trouble many times in '93 notwithstanding the good advice that I never ceased again and again to give him. He wanted to play the Jacobin, so that it was lucky for him he was only eighteen, and his youth could serve as his excuse; otherwise he would have found himself compromised along with that handful of men who were the disgrace of their country. To let him go to Marseille would be dangerous, not only for himself, but also for the public interest. He would be sure to fall into the hands of intriguers, and besides his former connections in the neighborhood are very bad. But Corsica being now free, you will greatly oblige me by ordering him to go there, if his disposition will not allow him to settle down with the Army of the Rhine. In Corsica he could be of service to the Republic.[57]

It was a heavily paternalistic letter. Napoleon was putting down his brother, describing him as a weak young man who should obey his elders. It was true enough that Lucien's behavior had been anarchic, that he had tried to play the Jacobin and plunged into politics rather irresponsibly. But in his letter, Napoleon seemed to reproach Lucien principally his idealism and lack of cynicism—evidently faults in the mind of a man ready to sacrifice everything and everyone to the gigantic tasks history had bestowed on him.

He acknowledged that his brother had talent, but he preferred to ignore it, instead trying, rather uselessly, to impose dry military discipline on the restless humanist, pushing him around according to his whim and disregarding the fact that Lucien was not one to accept orders.

But this time Lucien simply had no choice, principally because he had no means: He had to go back to Corsica. He knew it would hardly be a triumphal or heroic return. At most he could delay his fate, by taking his time traveling. He stopped in Marseille for as long as he could and managed to arrive in Bastia—with his family—only in March 1797. Lucien found out he was to be stationed in Ajaccio. Soon after his arrival, Letizia left for Italy with Pauline and Caroline, on Napoleon's request: He was expecting them in Milan, for he had decided that Pauline should marry Adjutant Général Charles Leclerc, with whom he was fighting the Italian campaign. Pauline's romance with Fréron had to be broken off for good: The Persian viceroy had been politically disgraced, charged with embezzlement and other misdemeanors. Joseph also went to Italy—he had been elected ambassador to Rome, no less.

Everyone had left Corsica. Lucien was lonely and had little to do—in effect, the modest post he was assigned to was a demotion. He was living as a kind of guest in the old family home, which Joseph had restored up to a point, assigning the running of the place to an agent when he left for Italy. It must have been a strange situation—at home but in a virtually new house, in the city of his youth but desperate to make something out of his adult self. At least Christine and little Charlotte were with him, and Christine was pregnant again.

One day in 1797, Lucien decided to take a short break from the drudgery of his job; deserting his post, he sailed to the town of Hyères, on the mainland. A celebration of Napoleon's Italian victories was about to take place, and representatives from the town presented themselves on deck as Lucien arrived, formally inviting the "young warrior," as they called him, to be their guest of honor. It was an unexpected and attractive invitation, but this time, Lucien knew better. His military exploits were close to nil—he had been working as an army bureaucrat, not fighting on the field—and it would have been rash, if not plain dangerous, for him to speak on behalf of the Army of Italy and thus of his brother. In any case he was supposed to be at his post in Ajaccio, not in Hyères; all the more reason not to draw attention to himself. So he declined the offer to speak, by means of a letter at once honest and official:

> *In a republic, glory is purely personal. She covers with her laurels the defender of the homeland, without extending such fame to the members of his family. If I accepted the honor you offer me, I should be violating this sacred principle, the very basis of democracy. I should also be acting in opposition to the positive wishes of my brother, who recognizes no festal laurels unless they are gathered on the battlefield. Accept then my thanks in my own name, and that of my brother, and include among your toasts our invariable toast, "Honor to the generous sons of liberty, Vive la République!"*[58]

Then he sailed back to Ajaccio; the break from tedium was over.

In June 1797, Letizia returned to Corsica and set out to finish restoring the house. She came with Elisa, just married to Felice Baciocchi, a rather insignificant Corsican nobleman whom Napoleon had made a colonel and posted as commander of Ajaccio (mainly because he was too mediocre as a soldier to be sent anywhere else). It was a chance for Letizia and Christine finally to get to know one another. Lucien had not been on good terms with the family since his wedding, and his subsequent lack of discipline and direction had not helped to improve relations.

As it happened, Letizia did warm to Christine, endeared to her natural grace and good character and touched by her loving devotion to Lucien. Christine called her *maman*. The two women had more in common than either might have expected—intelligent but uneducated, straightforward and earthy. Christine believed she expected a boy this time. On August 1, she penned a letter to Napoleon—Lucien had taught her how to write by now—in the hope that the brothers would finally make peace: "Allow me to call you brother," she began.

> *My first child was born at a time when you were irritated with us. How I wish that she might soon be able to caress you, so as to compensate you for all the trouble my marriage has caused you.*
>
> *My second child was not born. Fleeing Paris on your orders, I aborted in Germany.*

In one month, I hope to give you a nephew. A happy pregnancy and many other circumstances give me the hope it will be a nephew. I promise to make him a soldier; but I would like him to bear your name and for you to be his godfather. I hope you will not refuse your sister.

Please send your procuration to Baciocchi, or to anyone you wish. The godmother will be maman. *I await impatiently this procuration.*

Do not despise us because we are poor; for, after all, you are our brother: my children are your only nephews, and we love you more than fortune. I hope one day to show you the tenderness I have for you.

Your most affectionate sister,
Christine Bonaparte

P.S. Please do not forget me to your wife, whom I would very much like to meet. In Paris it was said that I looked a lot like her. If you remember my face, you should be able to establish the truth of this.

Napoleon seems to have accepted the olive branch sent by Christine. Soon afterward he appointed Lucien Commissioner of the Republic in Bastia. It was a good post, with a good salary, all expenses covered.

The baby was born at term. It was not a boy. The couple called her Victorine; a baby of "singular beauty," she lived only briefly. Lucien wrote, "Her death, as painful as it was unexpected. Shining with health, she dies in my arms, aged seven months—a true little angel in heaven."[59]

Napoleon's life during those months could not have differed more from Lucien's. Exceptionally busy on the Italian battlefields, Napoleon won eighteen battles, collected unprecedented glories, and garnered the spoils of war as his due, self-consciously marching in the footsteps of Caesar and Alexander the Great, conquering swiftly and crushing any enemy that tried to stop him. Thousands died, civilians suffered, but no matter. He was becoming France's most heroic defender at a time when the country was under attack from all sides—ever since the death of the king, in fact,

France had been living under a perpetual menace, and wars had been raging on all its borders.

In December 1797, at the end of his victorious campaign, Napoleon returned triumphantly to Paris. He was immediately offered the command of the army against England. It was a thorny position, which he turned down, explaining to the Directory the strategic reasons for which it was impossible to engage England in a frontal struggle. Instead he set out to organize a grand expedition aimed at undermining the British Empire in the Orient, but he kept his plans secret from everyone, including his family. His goal was to create obstacles to the British access to India, eventually joining with Indian Muslims against the British so as to gain the upper hand in trade and thus complete the economic war France was already waging against Britain, beginning a new French colony in the East.

Away from the centers of power, Lucien did not witness any of Napoleon's great exploits. But after four years of virtual absence from the political stage, he was eager to be part of the action again. By now he was twenty-three and had honed his natural skills with systematic readings; over the lonely months in Corsica he had accumulated energy, updated and improved his ideological language, thought through his political principles, and even campaigned to obtain suffrage for the Corsicans. He had matured and understood how vain could be the enthusiasm for one's own speeches. He was ready to reenter the political fray: He would stand for election to the Council of the Five-Hundred.

Lucien left Bastia with his family and returned to the continent. While he traveled to Paris, Napoleon was on his way to Toulon: A large fleet under his command was ready to leave its port for Egypt—though the destination was undisclosed to those on board. On May 19, 1798, Napoleon wrote to Joseph: "If Lucien is not elected a *député*, he can come with me. He will always find many opportunities on this trip."[60] There would have been many opportunities indeed, but Lucien did not accept his brother's invitation. His only contribution to Napoleon's adventure was symbolic: His daughter Christine had been born in Corsica a little while before, and now she received the well-wishing middle name of Egypta.

Lucien was the last family member to move to Paris. They all lived close to each other, in today's Eighth Arrondissement (it was then the

First), re-creating the sense of a small community in the big capital. Lucien, Christine, and their two daughters stayed with Elisa and her husband Felice Baciocchi at first, in a house on the corner of rue Verte. Joseph and his wife Julie lived with Letizia and Caroline in rue du Rocher, while Madame Pauline Leclerc took up residence in rue de la Ville-l'Evêque. Jérôme was still in school and Louis, ever the obedient brother, had followed Napoleon to Egypt.

In June, Lucien was successfully elected *député,* that is, representative, to the Council of the Five-Hundred. At twenty-three he was once again underage, and so, once again he availed himself of Joseph's birth certificate to qualify. Nine months earlier, on September 4, 1797—a date remembered as the 18 Fructidor—there had been a military coup d'état, when the Directory took power away from the two councils. Napoleon, together with a majority of the five directors, subsequently suppressed counterrevolutionary movements that arose in response to the coup, banishing many deputies. But corruption gradually set in, and by the time Lucien assumed his public functions, the Directory's power was on the wane. Over the next eighteen months, he actively contributed to weakening further that ineffective governmental body, fighting numerous legislative battles to undermine it. He put his fiery rhetoric to work, peppering his speeches with an imposing array of artfully used classical allusions, displaying an impressive, authoritative grasp of the subjects at hand. He spoke clearly and well, with esprit and poise. Over time, high-pitched emotion had given way to measured passion.

Finally entrusted with an important role, Lucien was giving his all to the tasks that came his way. He was particularly proud of the part he played in helping to secure the independence of the press by rejecting a project of law that would have accorded the police the right to censor or censure newspapers; it would have constituted a profoundly unwelcome return to the restrictions imposed under Robespierre. As a result, on June 5, 1799, a legislative plan that would have authorized the Directory to preventively inspect newspapers was shelved. This was an important moral and political victory, essential in staving off the state of emergency that in recent French history had cost so many lives and that the government was threatening to reimpose, pompously proclaiming "dangers to the homeland."[61] But Lucien paid a price for that victory, in the shape of a mortal enemy: the sinister, cunning Joseph Fouché, soon to become minister of police.

❧ ☙

Meanwhile, Général Bonaparte was fighting in Egypt. At first he defeated an army of Mamelukes at the pyramids; he imposed French rule on Cairo, successfully repressed the population, and initiated cultural missions that would result in significant advances in Egyptian scholarship. There were also disasters: a plague in Alexandria, the defeat of the French in the Battle of the Nile by Horatio Nelson's British fleet at the cost of many more lives, and an insurrection in Cairo. Napoleon's subsequent entry into Ottoman Syria and Palestine, to confront a coalition of Turkish-led troops, was catastrophic: The French committed a massacre in Jaffa, brutally pillaging and raping for days, after which a plague epidemic broke out; there was a bloodily failed siege at St. John of Acre, where the English navy assisted the Turks—the departing French burned everything in the area, and Napoleon asked an army pharmacist to administer an opium overdose to the living wounded who were too sick to go on. Back in Egypt, impressive victories alternated with dreadful setbacks. The final Battle of the Nile (July 25, 1799) was enough of a win for the French that Napoleon decided the campaign was over.

All along, Napoleon had been taking care to ensure that the news slowly filtering into France reported the campaign in the most positive terms possible—and as the personal accomplishment of the heroic Général Bonaparte rather than as the collective deeds of the Army of the Orient. He even composed some of the dispatches himself. He was also keeping abreast of the news from Paris, where the political situation was fast deteriorating. He wrote to Joseph and Lucien, asking them to speak strongly to the Directory and get it to pay serious attention to the shining army in the East, but neither of them took up the subject in public.

Instead, Napoleon received a letter from his brothers urging him to return to Paris. It confirmed the entreaties he also received from the Directory, and specifically from Barras, urgently demanding the general's secret return: There was an increasing threat from Austria and Russia, and Bonaparte was the man to deal with it. These dispatches had been sent from Paris in late May, and by the time Napoleon received them, in mid-July, the very governance of the country was in jeopardy, in large measure thanks to the liberalization of the press that Lucien had helped guarantee, and which made room for ferocious criticism of the Directory. The French wanted change. They were disgruntled with the 1795 constitution, which caused the government to function as an oligarchy where conflict reigned between the Jacobin left—a majority in the Council of the Five-Hundred—and the royalist right, rendering it incapable of attending to the needs of a nation at war. The only solution seemed to be to strengthen the executive, so as to allow a revision of the constitution; but the legislature would never vote in such a resolution. The crisis came to a head when the abbé Joseph Sieyès, until then ambassador to Berlin, obtained a seat in the Directory. He was a moderate, neither Royalist nor Jacobin, and so was above the current political fray—a conservative who had coolly voted for the death of the king; a secretive, melancholic, brilliant, and authoritative man who rarely smiled but always imposed his views. He determined that a coup was necessary to change the constitution; and he was the man to whom Lucien and Joseph rallied.

After sixteen harsh months in the Middle East, Napoleon abandoned his tattered army—on the pretext of real enough defeats in Italy and Switzerland—and began to make his way back to France. He sailed incognito, as had been planned in Paris, stopping in Ajaccio, where he met his uncle Fesch and gathered some cash, and departed again once the contrary winds lifted. On October 9, 1799, he landed in Fréjus, a town on France's Mediterranean coast—and there was nothing covert about this homecoming: He was welcomed everywhere with an electrifying explosion of enthusiasm; the streets were filled with cries of "Vive la République! Vive Bonaparte!" The savior of the *patrie,* it seemed, was already synonymous with the state. Joseph and Lucien met him in Lyon, where a troupe of actors rapidly improvised a piece they titled *The Hero's Return,* and which an exhausted Napoleon obligingly attended.[62] Throngs crowded the hall and the surrounding lanes. The cheers were so loud that no one could hear the words, but that did not matter. Napoleon arrived in Paris on the morning of October 16. He rushed to his house on rue Chantereine (which in 1816, after his fall, would be renamed rue de la Victoire). But, to his dismay, his wife was not at home.

WORDS AND SWORDS

The general had been having deeply troubling private concerns. Two years earlier, Joséphine had started a liaison with a dashing, irresistibly charming officer, Hippolyte Charles. It began when Napoleon was away leading the Italian campaign, pining for his new wife, sending her desperate, sultrily romantic love letters in which he requested her presence by his side and threatened his return to Paris if she did not join him, even at the cost of his military glory, telling her that "I have always been able to impose my will on destiny."[63] She had taken a long time to arrive in Milan, and when she did, he fêted her extravagantly, despite his suspicions. While he was in Egypt, a stream of reports informed Napoleon that her affair was ongoing; Joseph and Lucien reinforced the message. The Bonaparte family, including the two brothers, were furious with Joséphine, who did not have the heart to break off the affair completely for another year or so, although she repeatedly tried to put a stop to it, aware that she risked her marriage. Napoleon had begun to distrust Joséphine; his ardor had certainly cooled by the time he returned from Egypt, where he had an affair of his own with a certain Pauline Fourès.

But the coquettish Joséphine wanted to be a good wife and even started longing for Napoleon. Intent on romantically celebrating his return after such a long time apart, she decided to surprise him by meeting him on the road he was taking up to Paris; she missed him because her hostile brothers-in-law had maliciously misdirected her. According to the *Mémoires* of gossipy *salonnière* Madame de Rémusat, Joséphine returned that very evening in a panic, only to find the bedroom door slammed shut. She started crying and begging for forgiveness, to no avail. It was four in the morning when the wounded general finally deigned to open the door. He had clearly been weeping, though he affected a stern air as he reproached her "with her conduct, her forgetfulness of him, all the real or imaginary sins of which Lucien had accused her" and announced his firm decision to divorce her. Joséphine's twenty-year-old son by her first marriage, Eugène, was there with his mother; he had accompanied Napoleon to Egypt, and to him Napoleon enjoined: "As for you, you shall not bear the burden of your mother's faults. You shall be always my son; I will keep you with me." Eugène bowed out of the offer: "I must share the ill fortune of my mother, and from this moment I say farewell to you."[64] Bathing in the bathos of this dramatic moment, the three weeping characters fell into each others' arms; Joséphine and Eugène knelt at Napoleon's feet and embraced his knees. Joséphine explained away the deeds Lucien had accused her of. Napoleon believed her, and called for Lucien to be ushered into their bedroom at seven in the morning, ensuring that he found them together, the couple enjoying the pleasure of a heartfelt revenge.

Joséphine understandably bore a grudge against Lucien and promised herself that sooner or later he would have to pay for attempting to destroy her marriage. In the meantime, she tried to steer Napoleon to side with her close friend Barras and against Sieyès, because the latter was close to her brothers-in-law. When Napoleon arrived at the Directory the next day, theatrically and rather oddly gotten up in half-civilian, half-military dress— wearing a round felt hat, an olive green greatcoat, and a Turkish scimitar at his hip held up by a silk cord—he proceeded to read out a lengthy report about Egypt. He was intent on justifying his supposed desertion of the Army of the Orient (the defeats at home were such that he could not stay away, he argued), for which members of the Directory wanted him punished. And he ended on a dramatic note: "Citizens Directors!" he cried with a swagger, putting his hand on the pommel of his scimitar, "I swear that I will never draw it except in defense of the Republic and its government!"[65] The assumption that he would be part of that government was implicit.

Sieyès was irritated by his insolence. Worried about the unexpected popularity of the returning general, who had blatantly shunned him, he entreated Lucien to approach Napoleon at once in order to arrive at an agreement. When it came to political convenience, Napoleon always had the instinct to choose what was best for him. His political allegiances were purely instrumental, as he saw nothing in men but "means or obstacles."[66] After his first few days back in Paris, he realized that Barras was no longer the center of the action and that Sieyès had taken over. He decided to disregard Joséphine's advice and to meet with Lucien, without letting her know. "Sieyès is right," he told Lucien, "France needs a more concentrated government. Three Consuls are better than five Directors. . . . Act without fear. Thank Sieyès for his confidence."

"Where and when do you wish to meet him?" asked Lucien. "He is longing to do so."

"It is useless for us to meet anywhere other than in public, at the Luxembourg Palace. Things are not yet far ahead enough. Let him devise his plan of action. When everything will be agreed upon, we'll meet secretly, at your place."

"Can I assure him of your consent to be one of the three Consuls?"

"Certainly not! Don't even think of it; I don't know if that would suit me. I've only just gotten here, I need some breathing space. I don't want to risk my glory. Would France gladly see me exchange my sword against a robe? I don't want to engage myself personally. If by any chance we fail, he is a man to repudiate. I wish to be master of my own actions, and to have no ties with anyone."[67]

On October 23, 1799, Lucien was elected president of the Council of the Five-Hundred. It was a very timely appointment; Napoleon had had his first meeting with Sieyès on that same day. The encounter was lukewarm, full of mutual distrust, but each of the players knew that he somehow had to rely on the other to achieve his goals, and they began to discuss the coup. On October 28, Général Bonaparte was summoned to appear before the Directory to discuss his desertion and his next army assignments, but he showed even more defiance. Instead of letting the directors speak, he aggressively denied rumors that he had embezzled funds during the Italian campaign; his outraged tone forced Barras on the defensive, and Napoleon did not respond to the Directory's request that he leave Paris because his military genius was needed elsewhere. Two days later, he had a private meeting with Barras. When the director, known to the public as "the swine," agreed that something had to be done to achieve the regime change, but suggested to call on the sword of another general who had been mildly successful in Saint Domingue, Napoleon wrote him off: Any respect he had left for Barras vanished. On November 1, the decisive secret rendezvous with Sieyès at Lucien's house took place.[68] The plot was ripe, and all the most ambitious and influential figures were called on board: Charles-Maurice de Talleyrand, the intriguer for all seasons; Général Jean-Baptiste Bernadotte—now married to Désirée Clary, Joseph's sister-in-law and Napoleon's former fiancée—and the shady, ruthless Joseph Fouché.

The date for the coup d'état was fixed for November 9, 1799 (18 Brumaire), exactly one month after Napoleon's landing at Fréjus. Lucien left his home on rue Verte very early in the morning and made the base of operations the house of the president of the Council of the Elders. Everything went according to plan. By evening an extraordinary session had approved of the two joint councils at the Orangerie at the Château de St. Cloud, outside of Paris and far from the Luxembourg Palace, seat of the Directory. On the next day, the 19 Brumaire, the ratification of the dismissal of the directors was up for a vote. To ensure secrecy, Fouché ordered his people to filter all information regarding the activities of the legislative bodies, and he detained Barras in his apartment. Bernadotte kept the troops in Paris under control. Napoleon's rushed entrance into the Council of the Five-Hundred threw off the rest of the plan, but thanks to Lucien's presence of mind and swearing on his brother's sword, Napoleon emerged as first consul. Sieyès laconically summed up his disappointment by saying "I made the 18th Brumaire, but not the 19th."[69] As for Lucien, he had no reason to be disappointed: His brother owed him a favor.

TWO

DIPLOMACY

1800–1802

I did not understand much of the Brumaire events, which occurred the evening I arrived

in Paris, and I was delighted that young general Bonaparte became king of France.

—Stendhal, *Life of Henry Brulard*

PORTRAIT OF THE MINISTER AS A YOUNG MAN

When France awoke on the morning of November 11, 1799—the day after the famous 19 Brumaire—the tottering Directory government was gone. Général Napoleon Bonaparte was now first consul and the effective ruler of revolutionary France. Without Lucien's intervention, Napoleon might have been killed or incarcerated. Riots might have broken out in the capital. Instead, Lucien's composure had brought the remarkably bloodless coup to a successful end.

The Brumaire plotters were elated; and in their conviction that they had acted in the name of the republic and the Revolution, they were at once sincere and self-interested. They genuinely believed they were perfectly equipped to rescue the French government, and their conviction paid off.[1]

Within the victorious Bonaparte clan, roles now had to be defined. Napoleon and Lucien had been apart almost always throughout their childhood and adolescence—there was a six-year gap between the two—and their relationship lacked intimacy. Lucien was deeply aware of this, and regretted not having enjoyed Joseph's closeness with Napoleon. The dramatic, fraught circumstances of his brother's return from Egypt did not give either of the siblings much time to work out how to share the limelight. Both were eager to seize the opportunity of this historic moment and establish themselves firmly at the center of the political arena, but with different if not opposite agendas: Napoleon wanted to stay at the top; Lucien was keen to defend the republic. Now they had to learn how to live side by side.

In the frantic process of rewriting the constitution—the latest version had established the Directory, in 1795—Sieyès was overwhelmed by Napoleon's superior strategic skills: The first consul made all the changes that gave him leeway to build, in time, absolute power. Napoleon and

Joseph spent one long night at the Luxembourg Palace convincing Lucien to pledge his silence regarding Napoleon's exclusive conception of shared power. Lucien had just been nominated a member of the Tribunat, one of the four assemblies that constituted the new government, and an independent body that conceivably could be the breeding ground for the opposition; in such a position, Lucien too would be independent from the first consul. Napoleon sensed that this would be dangerous for him; Lucien himself was capable of heading the opposition. Napoleon had to keep his headstrong brother at arm's length. And so he offered Lucien the Ministry of the Interior.

Lucien accepted the offer that night. Upon taking office, at the end of December, he expressed his fervently democratic views before the government. He declared that, as minister of the interior, he aimed to "preserve in all their purity the liberal and tutelary principles of the revolution of the 19 Brumaire" by resorting to a "practical philosophy" that would ensure the happiness of all citizens. One does not govern "with or through a party, but by the general will, and by the practice of justice." Experience and knowledge were needed, not systems. Lucien made a point of making clear how aware he was that "an ardent patriotism may have led to excesses," and he did not disguise his ambition to transform Paris into the Athens of the 1800s: Philosophy might be necessary, he said, but "a republic is not entirely made of philosophers, and the principles by which one may govern Sparta do not apply to a great people for whom commerce, luxury, the arts, have introduced a host of needs and pleasures that must be fulfilled: because a truly free government is not for the few, but for everyone."[2] This was not just rhetoric: Justice truly mattered to him.

Lucien, who had no experience of governing except the little he had acquired in Saint-Maximin and Bastia, was aware of the immense responsibilities that had fallen on him. The job entailed control over the country's internal administration—including the placing of prefects and mayors—the national draft, agriculture, trade, arts and manufacture, artistic and scientific institutions, public works, mines, bridges, roads, prisons, schools, archives, and statistics. What the minister of interior did not control at that time was the police, which was under Fouché's firm grip. The time would soon come for Fouché to embarrass the young, vulnerable minister. Napoleon trusted Fouché, though he did not actually like him.

The man Napoleon did not trust was his own brother Lucien: He disapproved of his passions and feared his independent mind, despite Lucien's active support of the consular cause and even as he fulfilled his duties as minister. Lucien performed another noticeable service for the first consul when, in early 1800, he announced the results of a general plebiscite called to approve the new constitution and therefore legitimize the new government. Three million voted yes, and just 1,562 no. It was a surprising landslide in favor of the Bonaparte government. (In 1793, during the Terror, 1.2 million fewer people had supported Robespierre and his gang.[3]) Suspicions of vote-rigging were immediately raised; and it is very likely that the calculations were manipulated, perhaps by Fouché. Lucien effectively upheld his belief in universal suffrage, but in this instance he was again a tool, probably unwitting this time, in the undemocratic establishment of his brother's rule.

Lucien took seriously his ministerial tasks, performing well despite the pressures of the office. And there was no denying the attraction of the rewards and perquisites that came along with his new responsibilities. He took advantage of his new position to live lavishly, as if overcompensating for the previous years of hardship and enforced humbleness. He was now as spendthrift as he could afford. Passionate about art, he started acquiring artworks. He rented and moved into a splendid private mansion—an *hôtel particulier*—the Hôtel de Brissac, near the Luxembourg Palace and Gardens. He also bought a country house in the vicinity of Neuilly, outside Paris—Le Plessis Chamant, complete with its elegant park. In short, he was happily settled, living comfortably with his wife and two daughters, Charlotte, whom he called Lolotte, and Christine-Egypta. But life in Paris was distracting and its women dazzling. Lucien had never enjoyed such power. It was all rather heady, and exhilarating. As he admitted later in life, chastity was not one of his qualities; nor did he bother to maintain the appearance of it. And when the chances at romantic trysts presented themselves, he did not necessarily hesitate.

There were many such chances. Lucien's looks were far from perfect, but he managed to be very seductive. Laure Junot, the Duchesse d'Abrantès—wife of Général Junot, who had fought with Napoleon in Italy—was a Corsican with close ties to the Bonaparte family. She painted Lucien in lively colors.

> He was tall, ill-shaped, having limbs like those of the field spider, and a small head, which, with his tall stature, would have made him unlike his brothers had not his physiognomy attested to its being from the same die from which the eight children were, if I may so express it, struck like a medal. Lucien was very near-sighted, which made him half shut his eyes and stoop his head. This defect would have given him an unpleasing air if his smile, always in harmony with his features, had not imparted something agreeable to his countenance. Thus, though he was rather plain, he pleased generally. He had very remarkable success with women who were themselves very remarkable, and that long before his brother took power.[4]

Christine knew about his escapades. She chose not to reproach him, although she evidently did suffer. Lucien's infidelities could be understandable in a man of his energy and charm who had married at such a very young age and who appreciated female beauty as he did. But he never made much effort to conceal his erotic adventures. And, combined with his lack of economic restraint, that very energy and seductive prowess, that very indiscretion, soon made Lucien an easy target for those like Fouché who, under the invisible baton of Joséphine, wanted him out of power. The chief of police spread all sorts of rumors about Lucien's financial and romantic life. The minister was said to have embezzled funds—he was called an "Italian Jew"[5] by the customarily unreliable and prejudiced Madame de Rémusat, who wildly exaggerated his patrimony of 5 million francs, claiming he had 500 million.[6] Yet according to the generally not-so-flattering Secret Memoirs by Andrea Campi, Lucien's Corsican secretary, "the interior arrangements of Lucien's house displayed the utmost refinement of luxury, although there was nothing very magnificent in the appearance either of his servants or equipages: taken together, his table, the purchase of a country house near Senlis and expense of keeping up that establishment, did not exceed the emoluments of his office."[7] Lucien enjoyed the good life; but he was not dishonest. Equally, although he was a romantic and something of a philanderer, he did remain an affectionate family man.

Juliette Récamier, the great beauty and *salonnière* (salon hostess), famously depicted in a portrait by Jacques-Louis David on a chaise longue that is now still called a récamier, became the object of Lucien's romantic longing. She was married to an older man, a banker; the marriage remained unconsummated, and Juliette happily, perhaps compulsively, seduced everyone with her large dark eyes, her alabaster skin, her delicate mouth and rounded cheeks, the combination, carefully cultivated, of childlike innocence and womanly self-possession—but without conceding her favors. She teased and demurred. As a result, countless men were passionately enamored of her.

Lucien was the first of her many hopeless lovers to actually declare himself to her, and he never made a secret of his infatuation with that "very remarkable" creature: Madame d'Abrantès, who knew Mme Récamier (though the two were not close), was surely referring also to her with these words. In the summer of 1799, before Lucien's triumph at St. Cloud, he had become the talk of the town for his obsession, and rumors circulated that the two were having an affair. (Apparently, chastity prevailed.) Fouché, the cold-blooded archmanipulator and seasoned backstage operator, was puzzled by Lucien's seeming ability to maintain his political energies while devoting himself to his passion, and claimed quite absurdly that Lucien had planned the 18 Brumaire at Juliette's country house.[8]

Lucien's courtship of Juliette at first consisted of a literary exercise of sorts, where he was Romeo writing to his Juliet. Although this Juliet was not untouched by Romeo's verbal ardor—by the passion he expressed in the romantic style of Goethe's *Werther* and Rousseau's *La Nouvelle Héloïse*—she met his devotion with studied indifference. She even returned to Lucien his first letter as Romeo, publicly complimenting the author while advising him to concentrate on his higher, more useful destiny as a politician. From then on, Lucien wrote in his own name, with increasing passion. She showed the epistles to her husband, who thanked his virtuous wife for her confidence and advised her to cultivate the brother of the first consul to the extent that her dignity allowed, for the sake of his business and their fortune. Lucien's flame burned for about a year, during which time he saw Juliette as much as he could. He knew perfectly well that he was unlikely to obtain his prize; but that was not the point. His feelings alone sufficed; as lovely as she was, his wife, Christine, could not be the object of such a fashionable, elaborate *amour-passion.*

Lucien wrote over a hundred letters to Juliette. This display of romantic bravado set off a keen sentimental and literary rivalry with the writer François René de Chateaubriand, the only man to whom, some years later, Juliette would open her carefully sealed heart—and boudoir. In his masterpiece, the *Mémoires d'Outre-Tombe,* he quoted indiscreetly some of the letters by Lucien, whom he identified not as a minister but as "the author of *La Tribu indienne ou Edouard et Stellina"*—an oddly prophetic novel Lucien published in 1799—and he commented mockingly: "[I]t is *piquant* to see a Bonaparte sink into a world of fictions."[9] Little did he know that Mme Récamier preserved two batches of love letters in a trunk inscribed "papers to be burned without reading": one batch of letters from Lucien Bonaparte, and the other of letters from Chateaubriand, her actual lover.[10] That literary Bonaparte had not left her so indifferent after all.

Chateaubriand nevertheless captured an important aspect of Lucien's character, which Mme d'Abrantès described with insight and sympathy

With respect to understanding and talent, Lucien always displayed abundance and variety of both. In early youth, when he met with a subject that he liked he identified himself with it; he lived at that time in a metaphysical world, very different from our little intellectual world. Thus, at eighteen, reading Plutarch carried him into the Forum and the Pyraeus. He was a Greek with Demosthenes, a Roman with Cicero; he espoused all the ancient glories, but he was intoxicated with those of our own time. Those who, because they had no conception of this enthusiasm, alleged that he was jealous of his brother, have asserted a willful falsehood, if they have not fallen into a most egregious error. This is a truth for which I can pledge myself. But I would not with equal confidence assert the soundness of his judgment at this same period, when [Napoleon] Bonaparte, at the age of twenty-five, laid the first stone of the temple which he dedicated to his immortality. Not naturally disposed, by the grandeur of his genius, to view things in a fantastic light, and attaching himself solely to their reality, Bonaparte proceeded direct to the goal with a firm and steady step. He had in consequence the meanest idea of those who traveled, as he put it, in the "kingdom of fools."[11]

Lucien might well have been the dreamer, the lofty idealist of the family, and Napoleon the ruthless realist who imposed his will as forcefully as his earthbound passions directed it. But Lucien certainly did not live in a "kingdom of fools": It was just that he had a responsive sensibility and a creative mind, fed by his vast humanist culture. In society he was as sharp as a whip. At a party hosted by the wealthy arms dealer Gabriel-Julien Ouvrard, later lover of the *salonnière* Madame Tallien, Lucien sat across from Juliette. One of the guests started toasting the present beauties; toasts followed to all the absent ones. Suddenly—and unexpectedly since he was notoriously abstemious—Lucien raised a glass of champagne and proposed a toast to the most beautiful of women. All eyes turned toward Mme Récamier, who blushed demurely. Lucien paused for effect; a suspenseful silence filled the room. Everyone expected Lucien to recite a pleasant couplet. But instead, he simply said: "Let's drink to Peace! Don't we all long for her?"[12]

It was an elegant and witty vendetta: and it is not surprising that, in her later *Souvenirs,* Madame Amélie Lenormant, Mme Récamier's niece, sketched a rather negative portrait of the whimsical, failed lover. The twenty-four-year-old Lucien was quite good-looking, certainly, she conceded; taller than his brother, endowed with an agreeable gaze despite his much-noted myopia. But "the pride of novel greatness transpired in his manners, everything in him was aimed at creating an effect: there was contrivance and no taste in his style, pomposity in his speech and self-importance in his whole being." According to her, even though Lucien inspired "gaiety" in Juliette, she did not particularly like him; nevertheless, he wanted to believe he was the most favored of her lovers, indeed was encouraged to believe so by his "courtiers."[13]

One person who was decidedly unhappy about this affair, and the rumors around it, was Christine. She was also uncomfortable with her husband's new lifestyle: The material lavishness, the intense sociality alarmed her. She had simple tastes and did not enjoy the duties that befell her as the minister's wife—she missed the modest, ordinary life she had always known. She often went to see Mme d'Abrantès's mother, confiding her distress and asking for all sorts of practical advice. For his part, Napoleon, who had never paid attention to Christine, suddenly began to warm to her and appreciate her qualities. This delighted her. One day she showed her confidante a beautiful set of jewels that Joséphine had given her—on orders of Napoleon, and against Joséphine's own will, since her dislike of both Lucien and Christine had not diminished.

Nor were Joséphine's feelings toward them in any way confined to the private sphere. Lucien regularly entertained in the Hôtel de Brissac. His impressive parties took place inside a gallery that its owner, the Duke de Brissac, had added to the building specifically for such events. Mme d'Abrantès recounts how, at one of those parties in the winter of 1800, Joséphine

> took her seat at the upper end of the gallery, assuming already the attitude of sovereignty. The ladies all rose at her entrance, and when she retired. The good and simple Christine followed her with a gentle smile upon her lips, and the remark was frequently made that if the one was the wife of the First Consul, the Chief Magistrate of the Republic, the other was the wife of his brother; and that Madame Bonaparte might, without derogation of dignity, have accorded the courtesies of society and family intercourse, by giving her arm to Madame Lucien, instead of requiring her to follow or precede her.[14]

Joséphine was as good at humiliating her sister-in-law as she was at keeping up the appearance of friendly relations with Lucien and Christine. Lucien realized perfectly well what game Joséphine was playing, but Christine hid from him the extent to which it upset her, reluctant to have Napoleon find out from his brother how Joséphine was behaving. Family tensions were high enough.

It was in the country that Lucien and Christine could relax, with their daughters and in the company of friends. Mme d'Abrantès described Joseph's house at Morfontaine, where guests spent their time in various activities, such as "excursions upon the lakes, public readings, billiards, literature, ghost stories more or less mysterious," all in an atmosphere of "perfect ease and liberty." And at Lucien's house, Le Plessis, she did "not remember in my whole life, even in its most joyous seasons, having laughed so heartily as during the five or six weeks I spent among a numerous party of guests at that villa." Christine was "very amiable," and no doubt preferred staying in the country, where she felt much more at home than in Paris. Lucien's moods varied rather more, but "that did not lessen the amusement to be found at Le Plessis; perhaps in some measure it contributed to it."[15]

❦ ❧

At the height of spring, Christine fell gravely ill with a pulmonary disease. She died at Le Plessis on May 14, at age twenty-eight. She was pregnant; the unborn baby died with her. Charlotte was six, and Christine-Egypta, two.

Lucien was devastated. He buried Christine in the park of Le Plessis and erected to her memory a monument of white marble, surrounded by an iron palisade. There he spent hours in deep despair. He wrote to Mme Récamier:

> *I received your letter, Julie. I am back in the country. I have only come here for the funereal and deep pleasure of sitting on the tomb of the best of women, of reading and crying over those words I've had inscribed on her tombstone: "amante, épouse, mère sans reproche" [lover, wife, irreproachable mother]. I needed this trip: I shall make it each month. If, Julie, you had known well the one who rests at Plessis, you would have loved her like a sister. She was without faults. . . . All my private happiness has, I believe, vanished with her: I was loved too much to be loved again.*[16]

This was the "first immense sorrow" of his life. He had her death commemorated by a painter he admired, Jean-Antoine Gros, a pupil of the great Jacques-Louis David. The picture represents the funerary garden and Christine's tomb, before which her daughters stand, the elder near the grave, in apparent meditation, while the younger is captivated by a birds' nest, in which a mother is feeding her chicks. The inscription on the tombstone is visible—though the word "amante" is prudishly covered by leaves.[17]

Lucien's sister Elisa, younger than him by just two years, helped him in the funerary garden. Her presence greatly comforted the mourner. She took assiduous care of the girls and effectively became their surrogate mother.

PARALLEL LIVES

The day Christine died, Napoleon was crossing the Alps to engage the Austrians in his second Italian campaign. It was to be swift and much less sweeping than the first. The decisive battle against the Austrians was fought at Marengo, in northern Italy, on June 14, 1800. Initially it looked as if the French were losing; but at the very last minute, Général Louis Desaix, one of Napoleon's best officers, arrived with reinforcements. He won the day for Napoleon but fell in battle. Napoleon, distraught by Desaix's death, wrote to the Austrian emperor to negotiate a peace on his own terms: "On the battlefield of Marengo, amid grief and pain, sur- rounded by fifteen thousand corpses, I implore Your Majesty, it behooves me to give you an urgent warning. You are far from the scene, and your heart cannot be so deeply moved as mine is on the spot." A show of humane diplomacy followed the brutal battle—a plea for life after the bloodbath: "Let us give our generation peace and tranquility. If the men of later days are such fools as to come to blows, they will learn wisdom after a few years' fighting, and will then live at peace with one another."[18] In truth, Napoleon was pugnacious to the last. But he did need the peace, not so much because of the death toll as because he felt he had to take hold of the reins of power in Paris.

His instinct to return was right. Paris was stirring with the makings of yet another coup d'état. Talleyrand, Fouché, Sieyès, Carnot, Lafayette, and others were painstakingly preparing themselves for the aftermath of Napo- leon's possible defeat. This was the so-called Auteuil plot (Talleyrand lived in the neighborhood of Auteuil). Sieyès met at length with Talleyrand to deter- mine what to do in such a case: They knew a debacle would signify the end of the First Consulate and that the Bonapartes would end up in jail.

Lucien knew about the plot. As soon as news of the Marengo victory reached him, he wrote to Joseph, who was in Italy with Napoleon, informing him of what was going on; and he appended a request in his letter that Joseph should read it to Napoleon and then reseal it carefully. He also asked Joseph that he (Lucien), and he alone, should be confidentially notified twenty-four hours in advance of the city gate through which Napoleon was to pass—he wanted to organize a celebratory welcome.[19] But upon being informed of the plan, the first consul requested instead a discreet homecoming, aware as he was that disaster had nearly struck on the battlefield and that, yet again, it had been averted at the very last minute and thanks to someone else, just as had happened on 19 Brumaire. "I have no desire for triumphal arches or any kind of ceremonial," he wrote; "the only genuine triumph is public content."[20] This show of calculated modesty was proof that Napoleon was learning how to hone his demagogic instincts.

Napoleon returned on July 2 and went straight to the Tuileries, where a crowd gathered spontaneously to cheer the returning hero.

Lucien had absented himself from government for some weeks after Christine's death, and he was slowly preparing himself to return to the ministry. Joseph knew how important it was that Lucien and Napoleon finally get along. He advised Lucien to make a show of submission to the first consul—to behave less provocatively, not to demonstrate his independence or express his personal opinions too forcefully, and not to react impatiently to Napoleon's provocations. Lucien was willing enough to respect the authority of the head of state, but he demanded that Napoleon treat him with proper consideration—or, indeed, with fraternal affection, since he seemed unable to summon the respect Lucien was owed as minister in a representative government. In any case, Lucien could not help thinking of Joseph as the elder of the family to whom all deference was due; and Napoleon's becoming head of state did not change that in his mind.

Soon afterward, Lucien paid his first visit to Napoleon since Christine's death. He would never forget the welcome: "You [Vous] have lost an excellent woman. An excellent wife is of utmost importance to a husband. I am lucky in that respect. I hope never to have to summon the courage you need to bear such a misfortune. You [Vous] are going to get back to work now, aren't you?"[21] Napoleon had never before used the *vous* rather than the *tu* form of address with Lucien: Customarily, the elder used *tu* with the younger sibling, who in turn used *vous*. This sudden shift to the colder, formal address was not auspicious. Lucien felt as if he were being ordered back to his duties by the supreme leader—roughly told to forget about his emotions and concentrate on the state.

Lucien did go back to work, and put his best efforts into organizing the Fête de la Concorde, which was to be celebrated on July 14, the eleventh anniversary of the taking of the Bastille. He renamed it Fête de la paix intérieure (interior peace) and decided it should be city-wide and more meaningful than had been the "ridiculous processions" favored under the Directory.[22] On the day, Lucien headed a group of ministers, prefects, and government administrators to the Place de la Concorde, where he laid the first stone of the new national column. The first consul presided over solemn military ceremonies.

In the early afternoon, Lucien gave a speech to the consuls. It was an occasion for him to reflect on the traumatic and transformative legacy of the Revolution. The setting was grand and the timing well chosen: Lucien spoke in the Mars temple in the Hôtel des Invalides, the great military monument and hospital that Louis XIV had founded over two centuries before.

"Violence is always the main element of revolutions," he began. "Whether due to the excess of tyranny or a desire for liberty, it is a terrifying tempest." Philosophy fed the revolutionary movement; it inspired "all souls prepared by an excess of ills," until "the sacred fire shoots through the veins of the political body; millions of arms are raised; the word 'liberty' resounds everywhere . . . the Bastille is taken." But the initial impulse was quickly derailed. "Why is it that, in deploying its powers, the human spirit does not always know how to control them? Philosophy, which had predicted the revolution, wanted to lead it." As a result, "liberty was travestied, disfigured, and became either the toy or the plaything of various factions." Death and mourning, civil war and chaos prevailed inside the nation, while heroes fought enemy armies on its borders. "Yet no revolution was ever exempt of furies and madness, for which no individual can be held responsible; and today, it was time to forget the errors and divisions, and to celebrate concord." He ended on a high note: "O France, Republic cemented by the blood of so many heroes and so many victims! Let liberty, all the more precious for its high cost, and concord, which repairs all ills, forever be your tutelary deities! The 18 Brumaire has accomplished what the 14 July 1789 began: all that the latter destroyed must never reappear; all that the former has built must never be destroyed."[23]

It was in this spirit of constructing a peaceful, solid future that Lucien ordered the erection of national columns throughout the country. Napoleon too began to understand the importance of turning his military successes into lasting monuments. Two days after the festival, he asked Lucien to commission five paintings of great French victories—not only his own.[24] The first consul also decided it was high time that Jacques-Louis David, the visual mouthpiece of the Revolution, execute a portrait of Napoleon. Many artists had done so before, but David was the greatest.

The first consul summoned David to come see him, in the presence of the minister of the interior; he asked the painter what he was working on. "*The Battle of Thermopiles*," replied David. "That's a shame," retorted Napoleon, "you are wrong, David, to waste your time depicting losers." When David objected that those three hundred losers were heroes who had died for their country and that, despite their defeat, they had managed to keep the mighty Persians away from Greece for a hundred years, Napoleon replied: "No matter. Only the name of Leonidas has reached us. All the rest is lost to history." David argued back, to no avail; and when Napoleon finally announced his desire for a portrait, David was delighted. He told the first consul that he was ready to start immediately and asked when Napoleon would be able to come sit for him. "Sit?" exclaimed Napoleon. "What for? Do you think that the great men of antiquity whose images have come down to us ever *sat?*" David replied that he was painting him "for your century," for those who knew him, and who would want the image to resemble the man. Napoleon said that resemblance was not a matter of physical detail but of character; one had to paint what animated the physiognomy, not some "mole on the nose." David surrendered gracefully, quipping that the first consul had taught him something new about the art of painting and promising to execute the portrait without the sitter.

When the interview was over, Lucien, who had silently witnessed the exchange, accompanied the puzzled artist on his way out and said to him:

"You see, my dear David, he loves only the subjects of national history, because he can play a part in them. It's his weakness: he's rather fond of being talked about."[25]

Lucien's attitude to art could not have differed more from his brother's. A couple of years after Napoleon's commission, Lucien acquired David's portrait of Belisarius, the defeated and blinded Byzantine general. That the picture was unrelated to him was of absolutely no importance to him (although Napoleon would later confess to his mother how disturbed he was by this dramatic depiction of defeat).[26] Lucien was not obsessed with his own legacy as a politician and never thought of art as a vehicle for his self-image. He was an aesthete; he also had an excellent eye and great confidence in his own taste. Like his brother, but without Napoleon's self-interest, he was a great admirer of David, who ever since the coup had played a role as a chief artistic advisor of sorts to the first consul, overseeing commissions and funding artists. But when Lucien nominated him "first painter of the Government" in February 1800, the politically savvy artist, although eager to be given an official position, refused the honorary title on the grounds that it "looked as if it would profit only me."[27] Lucien, headstrong and sure of his opinions—perhaps more so even in the art realm than in any other—did not accept David's refusal; there was a fight. David won the day.

Lucien's desire to take the lead was motivated by his deep love for art—not only the visual arts but also music and letters. As interior minister he was in a position to act on his passion and idealism. The arts should be encouraged, he said; not just those that are useful to politics but those that "beautify life and strengthen the ties that bind people together." They were the "most pleasant fruit of civilization"; they enhanced benevolence and gentleness.[28]

After Christine's death, he needed such consolation. He remained in mourning for a long time, although Elisa remained a great support, running the household efficiently. (A nasty rumor—never substantiated—even spread that the siblings took baths together.) Lucien put a stop to his brilliant soirées and restricted himself to one or two gatherings a week, mostly with intimate friends, all men of letters by either profession or vocation, with whom he could share his passions. He was especially friendly with Louis-Marcelin de Fontanes, who, exiled in England by the Directory, returned to France after the 18 Brumaire. He made his name giving a much-praised eulogy for George Washington in December 1799. Lucien helped Fontanes by entrusting him with the direction of the *Mercure de France,* a fine newspaper that he also supported financially.[29] As the lady of Lucien's house, Elisa hosted these small gatherings and was delighted by the presence of Fontanes—who had become her lover. Other close friends were the senator Count Pierre-Louis Roederer, one of the finest minds and ugliest men of his time—he was dubbed "the specter of the Revolution"—Adrien Duquesnoy, adviser to the minister and director of the bureau of statistics; and Antoine-Vincent Arnault, a well-known writer and dramatist who served with Napoleon in Italy.[30] These friendships helped ease Lucien out of the painful daze into which his mourning had thrust him.

Work helped as well. He threw himself into it, and his tenure as minister was brilliant and dynamic. He put forth a large number of enlightened policies, from guaranteeing adequate pay for museum employees to suggesting the creation of a Musée de l'Ecole française in Versailles that would house the works by French artists (living and dead) among the many works of art that Napoleon had plundered during the Italian campaign of 1797 and 1798. He commissioned buildings from architects and projects from artists for the decoration of the national column in Paris. He was very good at discovering and patronizing talented young unknowns. He surveyed and enriched art collections, exchanging and rationalizing holdings, buying works for the country but also for his Paris residence and for Le Plessis—paintings, drawings, sculptures, objects, precious furniture. He was attentive to their conservation, upkeep, and cleaning and passionate about the scholarship pertaining to them. He supported the project to reestablish the Académie française, the august body of scholars in charge of regulating the French language that had been suppressed in 1793 during the Revolution. He proposed as members his friends Arnault, Fontanes, and Roederer as well as Napoleon and himself; in fact, the Académie would be reinstated in 1803, with Arnault as a member. Lucien was just as concerned with education. He lowered from twelve to seven the age at which indigent pupils in public schools could begin receiving financial aid, dismissed unnecessary school employees who "slow down public instruction," ensured that libraries throughout the country became richer in holdings by decentralizing the budget for book transportation. He was pragmatic as well as visionary.

The first shock of loss abated; and, engaged and energetic as he was, his spirits began to improve after a few weeks. The public realm was no refuge for sad souls. Lucien needed his wits about him, especially in his dealings with the first consul: indeed, according to Roederer, Lucien and Napoleon were not getting along very well. Roederer was a trusted advisor of Napoleon but always wrote with fairness and equanimity about his dealings with all the Bonaparte brothers. He described a family gathering at Joseph's villa in Morfontaine on July 28, 1800.[31] Lucien came directly from Le Plessis, where he had been hiding away for ten days. He stayed only two hours and, as he was leaving, on the road he met Napoleon, who was just arriving. They did not exchange a word. Even the subtle Roederer could not put his finger on what was going on. He spent the whole afternoon with the first consul, took a walk with him in the handsome Morfontaine park, but not a word was uttered about the minister of the interior.

August went by, and in September the new revolutionary year was once again inaugurated with the Fête de la République, organized by Lucien. In his speech, the minister celebrated the republican consulate, enjoining all to forget the hardships that had given birth to it. The French monarchy was gone. Neighboring monarchies were trying to seize the nation's provinces, but the French republic was stronger than them all and, "with giant steps, is recapturing the borders of ancient Gaul." Ever since the 18 Brumaire, the grandeur of France was at its apogee: All divisions had disappeared, factions had vanished and "all that is French has can be shown."[32] Unity had triumphed over partisanship. Order was reestablished within the country's borders, the freedom to worship was finally a reality; the new, enlightened century beckoned in which would prosper freedom, peace, the sciences and arts, liberal ideas; France would fulfill its destiny as a great republic. It was a fervently optimistic speech, a vision of splendor and grandeur, matched later that day with the launch of a hot-air balloon over the capital; spectacular fireworks completed the celebration, as they had in the previous Fête de la Concorde.

But just as the balloon ascended into the skies, so Lucien's political career was crashing to the ground. However successful he was at his job, and however popular his public persona, by that festive September day, his reputation already had been seriously damaged. Fouché's zealous agents had been tirelessly recycling and spicing up rumors of all sorts about the interior minister's alleged financial embezzlement and moral bankruptcy, and their efforts paid off. Despite his good work, Lucien admittedly had been lax with regard to the administration of his ministry—bureaucratic details bored him, and he tended to delegate the day-to-day execution of ministerial matters as much as he could. He had assigned his ministry's accounts to an old friend, under whose rather careless watch were committed serious financial irregularities, particularly in the minister's absence. Lucien had no choice but to fire the man as soon as he realized what had happened. But it was too late, and nothing Lucien did to control the damage helped: Napoleon's trust in him reached a nadir, and the minister's reputation plummeted to a depressing low.

One day in late October, the first consul summoned Lucien to his rooms at the Tuileries and criticized him in the sharpest terms, his tone furious and condescending: The minister put far too much faith in his unreliable collaborators, and he would no doubt be let down again. Lucien, ever mindless of Joseph's repeated advice to him that he should control his reactions to Napoleon's provocations, responded vehemently to the unfair accusations, albeit in a jocular tone: "Jupiter, you are getting angry, therefore you are wrong!"[33]

The joke was lost on Napoleon. He exploded with rage, telling his brother he had a bad character. Lucien replied that Napoleon had a bad heart. The first consul snapped back, "[T]alk as much as you like: you will never be anything but a Jacobin!" and threatened to arrest him.[34] Lucien threw his minister's portfolio onto Napoleon's desk. It was one of the most embarrassing, uncomfortable, and painful moments of his life.

Napoleon had long wanted to dismiss his brother. The official pretext he found to finally do so was the unexpected publication of an anonymous, incendiary pamphlet advocating the need for the first consul to climb to the dictatorial height of absolute power. The booklet circulated among all the top administrators and bore the seal of the Ministry of the Interior. It was entitled, so explicitly it could have seemed a spoof, *Parallel between Caesar, Cromwell, and Bonaparte*, or also, even more insidiously, *Parallel between*

Cromwell, Monck and Bonaparte. Fragment translated from the English—the obvious implication of the subtitle was that it had been produced by the archenemies of France, the British, who would have good reason to compare Napoleon both to Oliver Cromwell, the infamous Puritan parliamentarian who led the antimonarchist side in the English Civil War and instigated the beheading of King Charles I in 1649, and to the Scottish general George Monck, who turned against Cromwell after supporting the antimonarchists. These were two egregious examples of ambitious men who had reached power by military means and ended up promoting themselves at the expense of their supporters. The pamphlet was explosive, then, not because the claims it made were untrue but because it made them in a dangerously untimely manner; and Lucien's enemies were quick to point to him as its author.

It is possible that Napoleon encouraged Lucien to write the *Parallel* at some earlier stage, only to disavow him when it appeared. It is also possible that it was the work of Fontanes, Lucien's friend and literary protégé—it does bear an elegant style that could be his. The first consul's gossipy secretary Bourrienne—Joséphine's confidant—gave a colorful albeit not entirely trustworthy version of the events. Asked by Napoleon what he thought of the pamphlet, Bourrienne replied: "I think it is calculated to produce an unfavorable effect on the public mind: it is ill-timed, for it prematurely reveals your views." At this point, "the First Consul took the pamphlet and threw it on the ground, as he did all the stupid publications of the day after having slightly glanced at them." The various prefects of Paris also "sent a copy of it to the First Consul, complaining of its mischievous effect. After reading this correspondence he said to me, 'Bourrienne, send for Fouché; he must come directly, and give an account of this matter.'"

Fouché was summoned to the Tuileries, where an impetuous Napoleon proceeded to question him: "What pamphlet is this? What is said about it in Paris?" Fouché, as cool and sardonic as Napoleon was fuming, replied: "Général, there is but one opinion of its dangerous tendency." "Well, then, why did you allow it to appear?" fretted Napoleon. "Général, I was obliged to show some consideration for the author!" "Consideration for the author! What do you mean? You should have sent him to jail." "But, Général, your brother Lucien is the patron of this pamphlet. It was printed and published by his order—in short, it comes from the office of the Minister of the Interior." "So what! Your duty as Minister of Police was to have arrested Lucien, and sent him to jail. The fool does nothing but contrive how he can commit me!"

Upon these words, Napoleon left the room, slamming the door behind him. Fouché had been suppressing a thin smile all along. He now told Bourrienne: "Send the author to jail! That would be no easy matter! I was alarmed at the effect which this *Parallel between Caesar, Cromwell, and Bonaparte* was likely to produce, and so I went to Lucien to point out to him his imprudence. He didn't respond. Instead he fetched a manuscript and showed it to me: it contained corrections and annotations in the First Consul's handwriting."[35]

When Lucien heard how Napoleon had expressed his displeasure at the pamphlet, he went to the Tuileries to reproach his brother with having abandoned him after petitioning it himself. "It's your own fault," said the first consul. "You have allowed yourself to be caught! So much the worse for you! Fouché is too cunning for you! You are a mere fool compared with him!" Joseph described the pamphlet to Roederer as "a work for which Napoleon himself had given the idea, but the last pages were by a fool."

The last paragraph of the *Parallel* was indeed incendiary, and it was the one that stirred the scandal. It read thus: "French, these are the dangers in which stands the *patrie:* every day you may fall under the domination of the Assemblies, under the yoke of the S . . . or of the Bourbons. . . . At each moment your tranquility may vanish. . . . You sleep on the edge of an abyss! And your sleep is tranquil! . . . Fools!"[36]

It is hard to believe that Lucien would resort to such cheap scare tactics; rather he was the perfect scapegoat for those whom such tactics served. Indeed, after accusing him of distributing this intolerable pamphlet behind the first consul's back, Napoleon (or Fouché) reissued it. The second edition was identical to the first, except for one slight but critical change: the phrase "yoke of the S . . . ," which clearly referred to Sieyès, the Jacobin constitutionalist who had been pushed aside after Brumaire's coup, was replaced with "yoke of the military."

Joseph tried to discredit Bourrienne and to defend Lucien, but Napoleon had firmly made up his mind: He kept his secretary—his wife's close ally—

and kicked out his younger brother with no further ado, making a point of not allowing him to celebrate the first anniversary of Brumaire while still minister. Joséphine, evidently briefed about the heated exchange between the brothers, told Roederer: "Joseph is an excellent man, but too indifferent to affairs. Lucien is full of *esprit,* but he has a bad character—there is nothing to do about it."[37] She could finally enjoy her long-awaited revenge against him.

AMBASSADOR IN MADRID

As soon as he learned the news in Morfontaine, Joseph, eager to broker peace between his two younger brothers, rushed first to Paris to meet with Napoleon. The next morning he went straight to Le Plessis, where Lucien had retired immediately after tendering his resignation. It was early, and Lucien was barely getting out of bed. Joseph began by telling Lucien that he should have heeded his advice to control himself before the first consul. Lucien answered that Joseph had "only heard one bell," that is, one side of the story, and that as soon as he heard the other one he would realize that he too would have lost his patience with Napoleon; and he proceeded to tell him his version of all that had happened.[38] Joseph listened and conceded that their "illustrious brother" could indeed have highly irritating manners but, unwilling to take sides, also reminded Lucien that their brother was a great man whom one could forgive for having to humor. Lucien disagreed vehemently: He would never accept that he should not react to mistreatment at the hands of the great man. Moreover, as far as he was concerned, as a Corsican Joseph was and remained the *pater familias;* nothing would ever make Lucien obey anyone but him.

Joseph revealed that the first consul wanted to give Lucien some time to think things over and was delaying the nomination of Lucien's successor; in fact, for the moment he did not finalize Lucien's dismissal. However, he had set one condition for Lucien's return: that he be less touchy. This seemed acceptable enough to Lucien, who in exchange requested that Napoleon should promise never to mistreat him. Joseph, the diplomatic factotum for Napoleon and ever the messenger between the warring factions, brought Lucien's response to Napoleon, whose further demand was that Lucien obey him always and without objection: In such a case he would accede to Lucien's request. The implication was that Lucien would have to buy his peace of mind at the cost of political independence.

Lucien finally realized to what extent Napoleon wanted his ministers to submit like slaves to his every caprice. He still thought of the government as a representative body, and so Napoleon's latest, most blunt request was immensely distasteful to him, not only as a proud brother but also as a politician who was not ready to give up his ideals for the sake of a puppet position. He turned down Napoleon's offer.

Letizia, who as matriarch had been paying close attention to this feud, started to become worried about the worsening situation, whose political consequences were still unclear and might become serious. Fearing for Lucien's safety and well-being—she believed he was surrounded by countless enemies—she recommended that he leave Paris for a while and journey in her company to Italy, where he had long wanted to travel. The first consul got angry with his mother for suggesting such a plan. Letizia assured him that if he were in Lucien's place, he would be the one she would protect.

Now it was the turn of Talleyrand, minister of foreign affairs, to intervene, playing the role of mediating apostle. He went to see Lucien and suggested confidentially that he demand the embassy of Russia or Spain. Lucien appreciated Talleyrand as the master of diplomatic silence—"less treacherous or less perfidious than Fouché"—and he was not so inexperienced that he didn't realize where such a proposal came from.[39] He had no choice but to accept. Twenty-four hours later, he received his nomination to the Spanish embassy.

Lucien was fully aware that this was a demotion. He even listed, with typical self-deprecating humor, the reasons why his enemies quickly insinuated that he would never succeed as a diplomat: because he was not loved by the first consul for his republicanism; for his myopia, which constrained him to wear spectacles; for the stiffness in both his posture and his character; for his lack of conciliatory qualities and French graces, the surest guarantees of diplomatic success in gallant courts like the Spanish one. In short, Lucien knew he was the "antipode of that world"[40] of professional liars, but his natural resilience and combative spirit pushed him to prepare himself for the task; he read the bible of French diplomacy, a tract by Monsieur Abraham de Wicquefort, which he considered poorly and flatly written and which put him to sleep.[41]

The newly appointed ambassador left Paris on the first anniversary of 18 Brumaire. He did not fail to see the irony of his situation: The man who had put the first consul in power was being ruthlessly removed from the stage he had built. On November 10, 1800, he stopped in Orléans on his way to Spain. Just outside his inn, he encountered a pleasant-looking local man who was standing in the strong wind and laughing at the sight of a hat floating on the Loire River. Lucien was inspired to exchange a few words and approached him by talking about the wind. Without revealing his identity, he casually mentioned that today was the 18 Brumaire and asked if any festivities took place in town.

"What is the 18 Brumaire? There are so many holidays one cannot remember them all."

"What do you mean? It is the St. Cloud holiday."

"Oh yes, against the Jacobins. Well, who cares. . . . May they celebrate. Nowadays one doesn't force anyone to celebrate—some celebrate Sundays, some decades, and some the 18s. . . . I don't like celebrations much."

"Are you happy with Général Bonaparte?"

"Happy enough. They say he is a good man. All is well and we hope for better still. But one needs peace, you see, for commerce, for the artisans, for everything."

"Well indeed! We will have the peace. . . ."

"Yes, God willing. We await it. Greetings sir; have a good trip."[42]

This brief conversation was sobering for Lucien: For all his advocacy of republican glory, he had to admit that the 18 Brumaire had gone unnoticed by the vast majority of the country. And while the Bonaparte regime change had been useful insofar as it helped avoid another civil bloodshed, the average people were far more concerned with their own business than with the business of politics—as long as they paid few taxes and lived safely and comfortably. Lucien too felt he could finally leave politics behind him for a while, despite a pang of regret—gazing at the swollen waters of the Loire, he thought of all the projects he would not be able to finish, such as works on the Quai d'Orsay or the Jardin des Plantes bridge. But it was a brief moment. He decided to concentrate on his journey, enjoying the landscapes he traveled through, reading a lot, and devoting much tender, affectionate attention to his little Christine-Egypta, three years old by now. (He had left the seven-year-old Charlotte in the care of Elisa.)

Lucien traveled incognito for the first time, writing missives to Elisa on the way, expressing to her the desire to return to being a "simple citizen": "I am cured, dear sister, of the weaknesses of ambition, radically cured. All the better for me, I shall live more happily.—All the better for my friends, I shall live more for them."[43]

Lucien arrived in Madrid in early December 1800 and went to the Escorial Palace before the carriage containing his official wardrobe had reached the city.[44] He had to practice, coached by his predecessor Charles-Jean-Marie Alquier, the ridiculous curtsy that court custom required of an ambassador: It consisted in delicately bending the knees without leaning forward, a movement that struck him as rather feminine ("to deck myself out in a skirt, that's all I need").[45] It was all very distasteful to him: There he was, the staunch republican, having to literally bend before the famously formal Spanish royals. He considered disregarding the formality, but he could not afford a diplomatic scandal. And so he presented himself at court, in boots and without having announced his arrival. This was a breech of etiquette. But, cursing and unwilling, he did curtsy effeminately, just as Alquier had taught him, before the king and queen. His effort met with approval, though he could barely suppress his hilarity.

The absurdity of this out-of-date protocol was matched by the persons of the monarchs. King Charles IV was devout, generous, naive, and supremely ineffective; he spent his days hunting and his evenings playing the violin.[46] His wife, Maria Luisa (with whom he never shared a bed), was a frivolous coquette who, having lost all of her teeth, always ate alone surrounded by her servants; but she was also the actual ruler and devoted much more time to the business of governing than Charles ever did. She had a long-lasting and, so the rumor went, intimate relationship with Prime Minister Manuel Godoy; her children purportedly looked very much like him, except for the firstborn, Ferdinand, the Hamlet-like prince of the Asturies, who had threatened to send his mother to a convent and to behead her lover. (This melodramatic character was to be the next king of Spain.[47]) The great painter Francisco Goya portrayed this set of characters with ferocious truthfulness. He also painted young Maria Teresa, the Condesa de Chinchòn, Godoy's neglected, hapless wife, in an extraordinary portrait that captured her poignant vulnerability and transparent fragility, married as she was to a potent, self-assured pachyderm of a man whose supremacy in Spain was unquestioned and whose appetite for women—other than her—unbounded.[48]

Godoy was a self-made man, arrogant and astute; he shamelessly exhibited his mistresses around the court with sadistic pleasure, humiliating in public both his wife and the queen. In private, he received hundreds of women and then complained that the pleasures they provided were too easily accessible. In response to his chauvinistic charm, Maria Luisa adopted a passive-aggressive strategy: She would push Godoy away one day and draw him back the next, constantly sacrificing the interests of the state to her personal whims, fancies, and eccentricities.

It is not hard to see why the twenty-six-year-old ambassador from France was perceived as a breath of fresh air at this stuffy, corrupt court. Not only was he a young, elegant, polite, clever, entertaining Frenchman, but he had an aura about him as the brother of the hero of the Italian campaigns; and the queen was in awe of the first consul. That first day at court, Lucien ended his presentation speech to the monarchs on a note of amused flattery: "I would be very happy to be the subject of Your Majesty, if I did not happen to have the honor of being French."[49]

At first Godoy received Lucien coldly: He feared that the new ambassador would drive a deeper wedge between himself and the queen. But eventually he warmed to the French envoy. They had much in common: They both came from humble backgrounds and had made their way to the top through their personal skills. Lucien was much less power-hungry than his Spanish colleague, but he shared with him a keen political sense and a reluctance to obey the dictates of hierarchy. They were near contemporaries, Godoy just seven years older. And both had a passion for art, music, letters—and women. A friendship soon blossomed between the two.

Meanwhile, Lucien tried to understand his new official role. Napoleon sent brief, uninformative messages, while Talleyrand, the minister of foreign affairs, gave him lengthy, garbled, and confusing instructions. Upon Lucien's departure, Talleyrand had treated him with disdain; but he then allowed Lucien to write directly to him. The minister even congratulated Lucien for having been welcomed so warmly into that difficult court: No less regard was due to "a great name and distinguished talents."[50] (This was an anodyne expression, typical of Talleyrand: It was unclear whether the talents in question were those of Lucien or of his brother.)

Talleyrand wrote that letter on the morning of 3 Nivôse, December 24, 1800. Little did he know what would be happening on that Christmas Eve. Napoleon was due to attend a performance of Joseph Haydn's *Creation* at the Opéra (the second performance ever in Paris—the first had been received with great enthusiasm). At eight-fifteen that evening, his carriage was passing with his retinue through the rue Saint-Nicaise, near the Tuileries, when the coachman sharply veered to the left to avoid a cart and horse—held by a young girl—that were blocking the street.

Just then there was a sudden, massive, deafening explosion. Napoleon shouted: "They're firing on us! Stop the carriage, César!" (The coachman's real name was Germain but Napoleon called him César.) The first consul jumped out; he was unharmed. He first feared for Joséphine—but her carriage was a few seconds behind his, and she had not been hurt either. Nonetheless, she fainted as she stepped down. Ladies in another carriage were also in shock. Caroline was eight months pregnant of her husband, Général Joachim Murat, and managed to keep her calm on the spot but would be deeply affected by the incident; Joséphine's daughter Hortense's wrist was wounded, and blood was splattered over her dress. The street was reduced to rubble, houses had collapsed, the carriages' glass windows were shattered; two or three bodies lay on the ground. The total tally of victims eventually exceeded fifty (including the young girl paid by the assassins to hold the horse). The bomb had been powerful enough for the explosion to be heard miles away—even inside the Opéra itself, where the orchestra had just begun to play the first bars of Haydn's great work, the Prelude, entitled "The Representation of Chaos."

On the cart that was blocking the street, there had been a barrel, closed with an iron hoop at either end; this barrel contained explosives that a man had ignited before fleeing the scene. The news traveled through Paris as fast as the spark that lit the gunpowder. Napoleon rushed to the Opéra as soon as possible, to show Paris that he was alive and well, that he was the leader, dependable, indestructible, above any assassination attempt. Exclamations resounded when the first consul entered his lodge, poised as ever, seemingly calm and in control of himself—and by extension, of the nation. Joséphine, by contrast, was in shock, pale and agitated, in tears and barely recognizable. She virtually hid beneath the cashmere shawl that in fact had saved her life: She had delayed her departure by those crucial few seconds over the choice of color for that evening's shawl. Cries, sobs, indignation all round greeted the couple. It was a collective manifestation of national anger and love for the leader. But Napoleon could not keep his calm for long. He left after a quarter of an hour, to vent his anger at home. He did not hear the world being musically re-created.

Despite the fact that Napoleon was "adored" by Parisians, according to Mme d'Abrantès, who was at the Opéra that night and heard the explosion, a dozen conspiracies against the first consul had already been discovered and unraveled. One involved a contraption much like the one that exploded on the rue Saint-Nicaise that night and that quickly became known as the *machine infernale*. No one knew yet who was behind it. But the target of Napoleon's fury were the Jacobins, who represented his ideological enemy, the republican revolutionaries. Fouché was adamant that the actual culprits should be prosecuted, once found and proven guilty. When the investigation, ably led by an agent of Fouché, yielded the two perpetrators—Royalists, as it turned out—the first consul was uninterested, so intense was his desire to punish the Jacobins, regardless of their involvement in this plot. He found it politically convenient to round up his preferred suspects, all of them tainted with Jacobinism. He did free 200 or so of the prisoners but sent 130 innocents into exile in the desolate town of Sinnamary, in French Guiana, where other political prisoners had been shipped previously. The rule of law was subsumed under the now fully autocratic rule of Napoleon.

News of the infernal machine echoed all the way down to Spain. The profound shift it occasioned in Napoleon's mode of ruling alienated Lucien all the more from the French government, wrapped as it henceforth was into the person of his brother. When Napoleon arrested the men he wanted to find guilty, Lucien asked Joseph to convince their brother to behave fairly and lawfully, in the interest of his own glory, even of his safety—for public opinion was against this cruel, unjust deed of Napoleon's. Joseph passed on the message to the first consul, whose reply to Lucien, via Joseph, was: "Dear brother Lucien is and will always remain a Jacobin for his whole life, and so he must be aware that even if the battalion of his friends presently sailing to its destination isn't guilty of inventing the infernal machine, it is guilty of many other crimes, so the punishment is appropriate."[51] This was Napoleon's standard justification for his decision: Others who heard him make it were no less scandalized than Lucien, but they remained silent before the first consul. No one had any say in the course of justice.

To some extent, Napoleon was aware that he had behaved rashly, for apparently he was relieved when he learned that Joseph had not forwarded his sarcastic, if not downright aggressive, response to their brother. Eventually, Napoleon's attention to the law would yield the great civic code that bore his name (the Code Napoléon) and that remains the foundation of the French (and Italian) judicial system. But for now his conscience did not lead to action. And rather than helping Napoleon see the light of reason and justice, Lucien's passionate pleas on behalf of the wrongfully arrested men only damaged Lucien further. Fouché went so far as to try to pin on Lucien the guilt for the conspiracy, indeed for all conspiracies against Napoleon.[52] No matter that the infernal machine took place after his departure for Spain. As Fouché reportedly put it, "The air is filled with daggers!"[53] Real dangers abounded, perhaps, but then so did imagined ones—products of the zealous, self-interested paranoia of the secret police.

FASHION RULES

Lucien tried to defuse the air of political poison, even attempting to pacify Joséphine: When she requested, on the eve of his departure, that he bring back or send to Paris some fancy Spanish fans, he promised to do so. Lucien was not particularly interested in feminine fashion trends, but very soon after his arrival in Madrid, he found himself embroiled in a scandal involving Joséphine's private dressmaker, who was one of Paris's most celebrated fashion designers: the Citoyenne Minette.[54]

The Spanish queen had recently sent to the first consul eighteen prized Andalusian horses—elegant animals and excellent warhorses. In exchange, Joséphine sent to Maria Luisa an equally elegant gift: the latest, most enviably refined dresses from Paris. Citoyenne Minette accompanied the precious clothes on their journey to Spain, armed with a recommendation from Talleyrand himself, who called her in his letter of introduction the ambassadress of "French superiority." It befell Lucien, as the new ambassador, to receive Minette officially in Madrid and introduce her to court, where it would be her duty to stand at the service of Maria Luisa for whatever tailoring the dresses required. Given the status Talleyrand's support conferred on Minette, Lucien welcomed her with velvet gloves.

The priestess of fashion was stylishly dressed and pleasant-looking—white-skinned, rosy-cheeked, and delightfully plump—yet her common origins showed through her speech. She spoke uninterruptedly, and at one point she let escape a detail that caught Lucien's attention: She declared to have brought to Spain twenty-seven chests of precious merchandise, whereas Elisa, who was perfectly informed of the mission, had written to Lucien that the cargo contained no more than a dozen boxes. The ambassador immediately suspected a large contraband operation—effected under his watch and in his own name. He had often spoken against contraband, of which his predecessors tended to be guilty, and was eager to investigate this affair. He wrote to the Spanish secretary of state, Godoy's cousin Pedro Cevallos, requesting that customs inspect the chests. Cevallos, instead of writing back, paid him a visit on foot—although he was crippled—to ask him confidentially to turn a blind eye on the business and let the whole shipment through. Lucien stood his ground and had the extra chests sent back to customs.

The next day Lucien was invited to the palace of the closest friend of the king and his chamberlain, the Marques de Santa Cruz. He was a decrepit old bore; his wife was a much younger woman, the thirty-seven-year-old Maritana Waldstein, known as the Marquesa de Santa Cruz, and still beautiful. Lucien was welcomed with pleasantries and etiquette, but the meeting was awkward: While the marques droned on about the great impression Lucien had made on the king, the marquesa remained utterly silent. Endowed with lively eyes, thin lips, and a full bosom, she was unquestionably attractive, and seemed rather more Mediterranean than Austrian, with her dark, long curly hair and well-defined eyebrows—she even looked a bit like Christine, as many French ladies would notice a few months later, when she went to Paris. The awkwardness increased when the marques left abruptly, declaring that he could not be late for his daily visit with the king. Lucien now found himself alone with the mute marquesa; dismayed at her continuing silence, he managed to break the ice by asking her in a facetious tone whether he had the misfortune of being disapproved of by her.

She candidly answered: "Oh my God! Yes, Bonaparte, of course I approve of you, but I feel so embarrassed!"

The conversation had barely begun when the door suddenly opened, and there, unannounced, appeared the Citoyenne Minette—who had been eavesdropping all along. She stormed into the room and began to cry: "Sire, my father is dead!" and then, dropping to her knees: "Citizen Ambassador, I am ruined, ruined, ruined!"

Lucien was not insensitive to her tears, which, he found, enhanced her looks as much as her verbosity dimmed them. But he was irritated with her for ambushing him so officiously and for the lack of decorum with which she appealed to him as ambassador. He tried to leave; but just as he was grabbing his hat, the marquesa entreated him to stay. She then led Minette away from him; Lucien was close enough to overhear the marquesa quietly telling the crafty chatterbox that everything would be all right. Lucien was now furious with the marquesa for contriving this absurd charade of an accidental meeting—and all the more so when, returning to Lucien, she confessed that it was in fact she and the Duchess of Alba who were to blame for Minette's terrible situation and possible ruin.

The Duchess of Alba was Spain's wealthiest personage and grandest lady. Proud of her exalted status, she nevertheless felt a constant need to outdo the queen—the only woman in the country who outranked her. The most accessible tool at her disposal for competing with Maria Luisa was fashion, and she spent much of her time seeking out the latest outfits, carriages, and accessories. She made a point of wearing up-to-the-minute dresses before the queen had a chance for a fitting and would go to court so decked out, in one of her fabulously appointed carriages. The queen would understandably become irritated by these provocative shows of one-upmanship and on occasion had a guard politely have the duchess turn back and go home. The king laughed off these "little acts of female harassment," but when reports reached his ears of jokes by the duchess and her friends at the queen's expense, all laughter stopped and he exiled the duchess to her lands, where she grew bored after a few months. The queen would then entreat the king to recall the duchess, who, after a short lapse of time, would resume her usual performance.

This time, the duchess outdid herself. Upon hearing of the exceptional quality of the outfits offered to the queen by the first consul's wife, she sent to Paris one of her favorite ladies-in-waiting, who managed, via the banker Récamier—husband of Juliette—to inveigle Minette's favors for herself without incurring the suspicion of anyone and obtain duplicates of the extraordinary dresses. Minette, delighted at this new client's unlimited pockets and enthusiasm, even threw in a few extras that no one in Spain had ever seen; precious jewels completed the bundle. Minette thought nothing of shipping the duchess's goods along with the gifts to the queen— everyone was agreeable to the idea of avoiding a hefty customs levy. But by the time Minette arrived, there was a new ambassador, who, tolerating no breech of legality, stood in the way of a complete triumph. And so the marquesa tried to help the duchess, by offering to bribe a subaltern at the French legation. This failed miserably when the subaltern realized that the new ambassador was inflexible.

Lucien was quite eager at this point to forget about the whole affair; but he staunchly refused to be an accomplice to contraband, and so, with humor and flattery, he conveyed the thought to the marquesa that she and the duchess surely would not be ruined if they paid customs. That was fine, replied the marquesa; but Minette's reputation would be ruined. Lucien had no sympathy left for Minette, whose ruin, he said, would be fully deserved. The marquesa implored Lucien to let her appeal to Godoy on behalf of the *modiste*. Lucien acceded to the gracious lady's wishes, and the next morning, he paid a visit to Godoy, who mocked him maliciously: "You have a heart of stone, Ambassador! I would have been swayed by the tears of citoyenne Minette, who they say is rather pretty, which has never harmed a bad cause." Lucien at first did not listen, insisting on upholding severity and justice; but he was relieved enough when Godoy exclaimed, "Come on, let me take care of this business!"

And so, everything did eventually end well for everyone. The queen remained unaware of the role played in the affair by the rapacious Duchess of Alba; she was enchanted by the bounty and asked Minette to help with the fittings of the dresses. There was much to try on, as the outfits came in sets of three, each consisting of a morning dress, or "déshabillé," a daytime "promenade" dress, and an evening gala dress of the latest Lyon manufacture, along with a rich selection of accessories—shoes for each outfit, scarves, belts, mantillas, flowers, feathers, laces, ribbons of all sorts. These were all French goods of the highest quality and should remain the stuff of diplomatic triumph, not diplomatic scandal.

MAJAS AND MADNESS

Quite apart from its happy ending, this odd episode so early on in Lucien's Spanish career cemented the friendship between the ambassador and the prime minister. Godoy persuaded Lucien that he had to stop pretending to be incorruptible. With the Minette affair, Lucien had been successfully tested, standing the moral ground but remaining pragmatic enough to let go just in time and delegate a decision; and Godoy saw that he could involve Lucien in political dealings of a much more serious nature. This merry mess also enhanced their intimacy. By early January 1801, Godoy wrote to the Spanish ambassador in Paris that the doors of his house were always open for Lucien, who came unannounced at any time and was received warmly and without any concern for the otherwise strict protocol. Lucien confirmed to Napoleon that he had broken "the barrier of etiquette" and had free access to the royal family and their protégé.

It is most likely around this time that the ambassador was shown the most exciting artistic treasure that Godoy owned. In his private boudoir, probably hanging behind curtains, the womanizing minister had hidden the naked portrait of one of his sexiest mistresses, whose fleshy graces later became known to the world as the ones of the *Maja Desnuda,* or *Naked Maja.* At the time, only very few people had set eyes on her. Her name, according to art historians, was Pepita Tudo. The head is oddly askew, and does not seem to belong to the body; it was most likely repainted at some point.[55] Godoy might have had qualms about displaying an actual representation of his mistress in the palace—however concealed the picture, it would have been best for the subject not to be recognizable to anyone but him. Lucien probably was one of the happy few who saw the painting in its original form and knew along with Godoy whose lovely body it was.

Lucien had come to Spain along with his friends, the writers Laborde and Arnault and the painters Sablet and Lethière. Guillaume Guillon Lethière was the third illegitimate child fathered by a French officer to a black companion while posted in Guadaloupe. Monsieur Guillon eventually recognized his offspring, but only after Guillaume, age sixteen, had traveled to Paris to study art. From an early age he was a passionate artist—and also, like the young Lucien, a ladies' man, whose slightly exotic good looks and darker skin proved irresistible to the many French ladies he portrayed with natural skill. He had traveled to Rome and Naples in the years following the Revolution, perfecting his style, and by the time he returned to France, he was considered one of the most promising talents of the day. Lucien had met Lethière in Paris in the early days of his tenure as minister and had taken to him immediately. A friendship developed quickly, and Lucien invited him to come along to Spain, where Lethière, endowed with a good pair of eyes, picked some of the best paintings for his employer's rapidly expanding collection. He might have seen the *Maja Desnuda* too. At any rate, Lucien would one day, soon enough, ask Lethière to re-create a version of this extraordinary painting, where the Maja was not Pepita Tudo but the woman of Lucien's life.

No less exhilarating than the great art Lucien acquired was the complicity that Godoy offered him. Lucien was pleased with himself for winning the confidence of the court. Such confidence was necessary for Lucien to achieve the mission Napoleon had charged him with: The ambassador was supposed to convince Spain to wage war on Portugal, which was allied with England, France's archadversary. Napoleon had always regarded Portugal as an English colony, and he felt that to attack it was akin to assailing England. He also wanted Portugal to break its commercial relations with England and turn to France instead.

There was a serious family obstacle to this warmongering task: The daughter of the Spanish monarchs was none other than the Princess of Portugal, and this conflict was clearly eating away at Charles IV. "You will agree, dear Ambassador, that it is quite sad to be a King if political duty forces you to wage war on your own offspring," he told Lucien. Enamored of his little Christine-Egypta—nicknamed Lili—Lucien was sensitive to this feeling; and he became all the more circumspect about forging plans to execute the first consul's orders.

He was, in fact, more intent on leading a peaceful life in Madrid, enjoying the court and the social life, than he was on playing political power games. Soon Lucien rented and moved into a wing of the Santa Cruz palace, where he and his daughter became a constant presence in the household. A slight unease remained—the king and queen used the familiar "tu" to address Lucien, putting him on a footing equal to that of the old marques, an honor that, to the chamberlain, seemed rather undue—but they all got along very well.

Lucien often had chocolate in the marquesa's rooms. He was beginning to develop some feelings for her. She was graceful, witty, a good mother, and a sincere friend from a noble family; and she lovingly helped Lucien care for Lili. Lucien was still mourning—seven or eight months had passed since Christine's death. He had had a few affairs in Paris—with a couple of actresses who were still writing him hopeless love letters—but those were insignificant for him. The marquesa, however, was a mature woman; warm and caring, she had been forced into a loveless marriage with a very much older man. Her wits and charms came alive with the young Frenchman, her junior by over a decade. It was not the first time that the marquesa's appetites had been whetted by the charms of a foreign envoy. In 1787 she had initiated a flirt with the English lord and outrageous dandy William Beckford.[56] Despite her operatic insistence, he had not responded to her advances with great enthusiasm; he was much more interested in young choirboys. During the Directory, the marquesa had been luckier with Félix Guillemardet, a

dashing French ambassador who preceded Lucien and Alquier. Lucien was
an even juicier catch, since he was younger and more versed in literary and
artistic matters, and his posting came directly from the most powerful man
in France.

Affection between the two grew steadily. Lucien wrote to his sister Elisa
that the marquesa, a dilettante painter of some talent, was sketching a portrait of him. A letter from Elisa arrived soon after. Probably informed of
Lucien's affair by Arnault, who had just returned to Paris, she quipped to her
brother: "[Y]ou, in love . . . that's a great feat that was reserved for Spain."[57]
A few days later, she communicated her delight at his reported faithfulness:
"I would gladly embrace that marquise."[58] In his sister's eyes, it helped that
she was well born and well connected. Lucien, for his part, talked relatively
little of his passion for the marquesa; but the affair had a profound impact
on his psyche. There were clandestine rendezvous; the adulteress used a secretive and passionate language in her letters to her lover. It is not difficult
to see how taken she was with him, and he must also have felt strongly for
her. In the long run, the age and class differences would take a toll on their
relationship, but Lucien allowed his affections to mature. His need for a
monogamous, lifelong companion was growing; the time for lighthearted
flirtations was ending.

Another affair would nevertheless be attributed to the ambassador, causing him a spot of trouble. The fascinating Countess M——, terrified by the
threats of her jealous husband, had sought refuge at the French embassy.
While being pursued by her Othello, she conveniently fainted in the arms of
Lucien, who was stepping out of his carriage. The beauty, endowed with the
"sensuous perfume" that the sensitive diplomat declared Spanish women to
emanate, aroused his protective instincts.[59] The outcome of his noble gesture
was a writ from the count to the young ambassador, who responded that his
heart was actually occupied "better, or at least elsewhere" (evidently with the
marquesa).[60] It was not a pleasant situation. Lucien accepted the challenge
to a duel but demanded a delay. It would have to remain secret: Duels were
illegal. This was mostly an issue for the ambassador, whose diplomatic status
might be compromised. Lucien sent his great friend Lethière, on whose discretion he could count, to tell the count that Mr. Ambassador did not care

to kill him or to be killed, since he was at the point of closing the treaty for which he had come to Madrid; so he begged him to accept that, after he had achieved his goal, without tambourines and trumpets, he would be at the count's service.

Predictably, the count refused. He was eager to be rid of a rival and was not interested in waiting to fight him—he always fought when his passions were roiling; otherwise the duel might look like the worst sort of premeditated murder. Lucien continued to insist on the delay, and Lethière returned to the count with that message: The ambassador would fight "when the treaty is concluded, whether it is ratified or not."[61] If the count still declined to wait, Lethière himself was available to fight in the stead of the ambassador. This offer—Lucien tells us—was Lethière's unprompted initiative. It might have seemed an act of bravado if not for the fact that the painter, strong and fit at the time despite his corpulence (which would increase with age), was certain he would neither kill nor be killed: His plan was simply to put the young count out of business and, for courtesy's sake, without a wound. This, at least, was the assurance he politely gave the count who, an excellent fencer himself, merely smiled at him with a mixture of disdain and astonishment. Skinny, slender, and quick, he considered the large man before him, laughing at the clear advantage he found himself in, and offered another, elegantly aristocratic rebuttal: He would be very upset to force such a good painter to interrupt his work. It was a matter of etiquette: Surely, one of Spain's finest noblemen could not put his life at risk by fighting a painter.

The Marquesa de Santa-Cruz happened to be distantly related to the count. She saw fit to arrange for Lucien and the count to meet not as rivals but over an exquisite lunch. The two got off to a courteous albeit icy start, but as the meal progressed they warmed to each other, and by its end the count was waxing lyrical over the beauties of his lady and his passion for her. Lucien, touched by such emotional outpouring, convinced the count of his fidelity to the woman who reigned over his own heart. That evening at the theater, Lucien saw the Countess M——in the count's box; the reconciliation had succeeded. Lucien remained friends with the count and was saddened to learn of his untimely death a year later, apparently after having lost his mind.

SPANISH BULLS AND BRAZILIAN DIAMONDS

Lucien was becoming Spanish in spite of himself, even acquiring a taste for bullfights. At first he had found those "barbaric games" repugnant; but soon he would not miss a single one.[62] Yet he was also being dragged into another sort of bullfight in which he himself was unwittingly playing the part of the bull: Spain's rulers sent him messages he did not know how to decipher.

From one side of the arena, Godoy flatteringly kept insinuating to Lucien that he would one day become a head of state, perhaps of the Cisalpine Republic in northern Italy. Lucien was naive or vain enough to repeat this proposition to Napoleon, who understood that Godoy was toying with his brother's ambition. From the other side, the queen called Lucien into a private conference and entertained him for an hour about her beloved thirteen-year-old daughter Maria Isabella, who might—just might—be a perfect young wife for the first consul.

During this whole interview, the queen kept using the confidential "tu," putting a gentle but extraordinary pressure on the ambassador, who was both surprised and honored by the intimacy and confidence she expressed. In a letter of April 4, 1801, he carefully and skeptically wrote to Napoleon about the "overture" that Maria Luisa had made to him without apparently consulting either her husband (as was the norm) or Godoy (which was unheard of).[63] He added that he would perfectly understand if his brother remained silent in response. Instead, with devastating indiscretion, Napoleon went straight to Joséphine, reporting the letter as if Lucien himself were trying to force him to divorce his wife to marry the teenage princess of Spain. This malicious distortion resulted in a total breakdown of the already tense relationship between Lucien and Joséphine. From then on, she would cultivate hostility toward him both in her heart and in society.

Lucien was aware that Maria Luisa's confidential discussion with him also risked compromising his ties with the prime minister, if he were indeed ever to find out about it. Godoy's political friendship, which Lucien needed in order to fulfill his official mission, had never been assured. That moment of intimacy with the queen was therefore much more frightening for Lucien than it had been flattering.

But his main mission in Spain moved forward. The war machinery was gathering momentum, and Godoy had the troops gather in Badajoz, his hometown, just by the Portuguese border. Proud of his humble origins, he had his family house swiftly restored and redecorated in time for the event; the king and queen paid a ceremonious visit to it, declaring their enchantment; courteous words were spoken, while the courtiers sneered to themselves at the servility and grandiloquence of the occasion. Lethière, on the scene, painted Lucien meditating in the landscape of Badajoz. The invasion began just over a week later, halfheartedly, and lasted all of three days, after the Portuguese town of Olivenza was conquered. The brief skirmish was dubbed War of the Oranges, on account of the orange branches the Spanish military sent to Godoy on their way to Lisbon—the prime minister then sent them on to the queen.[64]

The resulting Treaty of Badajoz, signed on June 7 by Lucien and the Spanish and Portuguese parties, ceded Olivenza and another couple of towns to Spain, gave France a hefty 15 million francs compensation for having mobilized its troops, and guaranteed that Portugal's ports would thereafter be closed to the British navy. It should have been enough for Napoleon, but the first consul refused to ratify the treaty. He had full war on his mind. Lucien had practiced mere diplomacy, not a military mission, and it was diplomacy "à l'eau de rose" at that—rosewater diplomacy—as Napoleon sneeringly described it; he was furious that Lucien had not negotiated hard enough.[65]

Lucien, for his part, was content with the outcome of his mediation and convinced he had fulfilled his obligations. Talleyrand had even written him complimentary words. The ambassador was ready to leave and join the marquesa, who went to Paris in mid-June. Before her departure, and while he was in Badajoz, she had written him that "everyone in Madrid says that you've been named Consul of the Cisalpine Republic—since you once told me your thoughts on this matter, I am not worried by this rumor and I'm just enjoying letting it run its course, the better to hide our plans."[66] From Paris, she wrote him affectionate missives, describing how his family received her in the capital. Elisa said that she and other people found her "beautiful, very beautiful, and very lovely"—"truly charming, talented and graceful."[67] She added that it must have been painful for Lucien to part from her, and recounted how the two of them cried when the marquesa told Elisa of her belief that Lucien was unfaithful—a "calumny" Elisa was quick to dismiss, though she entreated her brother to reassure his lover.

But Lucien could not leave just yet. Napoleon still kept his army in Spain, and because of this Portugal was determined to demand some slight alterations to the treaty. Napoleon, on his part, demanded further concessions from Portugal. This situation kept Lucien under intense pressure, since the Spanish king refused to consider making any further demands on the Portuguese. To Lucien's mind, Napoleon's attitude risked starting a war between France and Spain, formal allies since the 1796 signing of the Treaty of San Idelfonso, which guaranteed that either country would defend the other in case of attack by a third party (in that case, England, the common enemy). Napoleon was treating Charles IV like all other monarchs he dealt with—as if he were a puppet—and sadistically enjoying the exercise of power over his ally. After countless protests from Lucien that he was making an enemy out of Spain, the first consul relented, signing the treaty in early October—five months after the initial negotiation. But still he refused to give Lucien license to return to Paris, despite the ambassador's repeated requests—which were met with an insulting silence, a clear signal to Lucien that the first consul wanted him far away.

Lucien finally lost his patience. The marquesa had returned to Madrid, and Lucien was of course pleased to see her; but her presence was not enough of a draw for him to want to stay on. Despite Napoleon's overtly rude behavior toward Lucien, the king and queen continued to receive him warmly; on their behalf, Godoy even offered him the Order of the Golden Fleece—which the ambassador had to refuse, in the name of his republicanism. Tired of political games and eager to return home, he would not await Napoleon's authorization any longer. He resigned his post and, exactly one year after his departure from Paris, on November 9, 1801, he left Madrid.

As reward for his successful negotiation of what amounted to a peace treaty between Spain and Portugal, each court offered Lucien a hefty sack of unpolished Brazilian diamonds. These stones were not particularly attractive, as they looked like unrefined sea salt, and Lucien was not aware of their potential value. He gracefully accepted the gifts, as was customary for ambassadors leaving their post on good terms with their royal hosts. The queen had grown immensely fond of his daughter Lili and had taken to calling her "jolie pouponne" (pretty child).[68] Lili too received from her majesty some lavish gifts—along with affectionate, tearful hugs. So did Lili's nanny, Madame Leroux, who, in a complete breach of etiquette, had been allowed free entry to the queen's chambers whenever she brought the child for a visit. Lucien's presence had clearly humanized the court, and his warmth was going to be missed in Madrid. The marquesa was in despair, but Lucien promised that they would soon see each other in Paris, where her husband, glued to the king as if he were his personal shadow, would never allow himself to follow.

When, sometime later, Lucien had his bags of diamonds appraised in Amsterdam, he found out, to his astonishment, that they were worth some 2 million francs—an immense fortune, which turned Lucien into an independently wealthy man. "If money were my passion, I would already be a millionaire," he had written to Napoleon back in April.[69] Now he effectively was a millionaire, free to make plans for his future.

Upon returning, Lucien paid a visit to Napoleon before going to Le Plessis, to pay respects to his wife's tomb and rejoin his older daughter Lolotte after the long separation. Only some weeks later did he go back to Paris— he dreaded seeing his brother again. Roederer, the sharp-minded and unattractive minister, reproached him for avoiding the first consul—rumors were building that the brothers had quarreled. Lucien told Roederer that he and Napoleon had spent three hours together upon his return from Spain and that Napoleon had assured him that he would show him due respect; but the first consul did not keep his promise, taking advantage of the fact that Lucien no longer had an official role and was in a vulnerable position. Lucien could not suffer how Napoleon treated him—taunting, mocking, humiliating, and demeaning him before his officers. Roederer reported Lucien's own account of his meeting with the first consul:

"When, and where, shall I be able to see you? I am not your minister anymore—nor am I or do I wish to be a state councilor. I have no more uniform. I can only come to your audiences as a brother."

"Come every evening to the salon; the mornings I lunch by myself, at eleven; come whenever you wish."

"Your salon—that is fine, but please, no more bad jokes—no more Citizen Lucien! The great Lucien! The grave Lucien! I don't want to be the laughingstock of your field assistants. Nor do I want any more functions, or missions. I want to live in Paris as a citizen of Paris, unless you want me to be part of something useful that will help consolidate your power."

Lucien uttered his wishes very clearly. He wanted Napoleon to treat him as a brother, not as a subaltern. Napoleon acquiesced. But the next day, when Lucien entered the salon, Napoleon welcomed him with these words:

"So, Citizen Lucien, what are you up to?"

"Citizen Consul, I don't do anything but little things of which I don't need to notify anybody, unlike you who do great things and report them gloriously to everyone."

Napoleon then asked Lucien, in front of everyone: "That woman who runs after you, Madame what . . . Madame Santa Cruz, is she still in Paris?" (The marquesa had indeed joined Lucien in early December.)

"Ah Citizen Consul, spare a woman who isn't made for brocades. I have no need to be talked of in such a way by my brother, and even less so by the First Consul."

"But we have no need for your approval."

"At least I don't have to hear it. Greetings to you."

Lucien took his leave. By the time he reported this unpleasant meeting to Roederer, Lucien had not seen Napoleon again. Napoleon sent Talleyrand to see Lucien and transmit that he would invite Mme Santa Cruz to dinner. Lucien responded that he should never see her again if she accepted the invitation.

Joséphine kept up a relationship of polite appearances with Lucien. A couple of days after the meeting with Napoleon, she told him that her husband did not always mince his words. To Lucien's complaint that he had not been allowed entry into Napoleon's apartments, she replied: "He doesn't receive anyone, not even me."

"With you it's different; you sleep with him."

Replying to Roederer, who thought this was all a bit too harsh, Lucien said: "No, I don't want to be humiliated. He sent his police against me, I am pursued by them more than ever, and I've been mistreated. I don't love him anymore. I honor him, I respect him, I admire him as the head of state, but I don't love him as a brother anymore. He tried to dishonor me in Madrid. I didn't let him. He thought he would downgrade me, and I let people know of his infernal Machiavellianism."[70]

Fully aware of what he considered his victory as a diplomat, of the power he had been able to wield in Spain and of the ferocity with which Napoleon had tried to undermine it, Lucien was furious with his brother for refusing to recognize his achievements.

TEMPEST IN A BATHTUB

Lucien's pride at having brokered a good peace rather than encouraged a useless war between Spain and Portugal was more than justified. And so was his pride at another major achievement: He had negotiated the smooth handing over of the vast Louisiana territories from Spain to France. Napoleon had told Lucien to hold on to that "beautiful mane" until he had convinced King Charles IV to let go of the "nice and good colony" he was so attached to.[71] (It made up almost half of what was then known as Northern America.) According to Lucien, the treaty, signed on October 1, 1801, in Madrid, had been the "thorniest"[72] of his negotiations; according to the sardonic Talleyrand, it was "the most brilliant jewel in his diplomatic crown."[73] It certainly was a huge conquest for France, achieved at no cost and without a single gun or cannon being fired.

One evening, Lucien returned to Paris from Le Plessis for the premiere of a play at the Comédie Française and stopped at his house to change into suitable clothes. He was surprised to find Joseph eagerly awaiting him in his living room. "Finally here you are! Quite a show it will be tonight," the eldest Bonaparte brother announced. "I've got some news for you that won't put you in the mood for fun."

"What's going on?"

"You won't believe it—but the general [as the brothers called the first consul to each other] wants to sell off Louisiana."

"But who would buy it from him?" scoffed Lucien.

"The Americans."

Lucien was flabbergasted. "Come on! Even if the general really had this wild fantasy of selling off Louisiana, after all he has done to get it—and despite his always broadcasting the necessity for holding on to our colonial interests as a matter of national dignity—he could not manage this without the authorization of the Chambers. As for the Americans, they would not want it without that clause."[74]

Lucien was outraged not only by Napoleon's unexpected plan but also, and especially, by the likelihood that he would consider acting on his own. Lucien's republicanism was all the more ardent as his brother's despotism increasingly affirmed itself. Napoleon claimed George Washington as a model, but Lucien wondered how the American hero would have defended himself if the bureaucrats, military, and politicians had agreed to substitute the presidential outfit with a royal or imperial crown.

Since early 1800 Napoleon's political interlocutor overseas was Thomas Jefferson, who as president in April 1802 wrote to the American ambassador in Paris that, until then, France had been a "natural friend" of the United States, but if France seized control of New Orleans "through which the produce of three-eighths of our territory must pass to market . . . placing herself in that door assumes to us the attitude of defiance." He continued: "Spain might have retained it quietly for years. Her pacific dispositions, her feeble state, would induce her to increase our facilities there. . . . Not so can it ever be in the hands of France. The impetuosity of her temper, the energy and restlessness of her character, place her in a point of eternal friction with us. . . . They as well as we must be blind if they do not see this."[75]

The two statesmen, like expert chess players, each saw that the long-term effects of a French Louisiana would be mutual and mutually detrimental enmity. Well aware of this, Napoleon was secretly preparing to sell the colony at the best price, while Jefferson, unaware of Napoleon's plan, was gearing up to controlling it if France did not let the United States have it. Lucien was not privy to either statesman's pragmatic calculations. His geopolitical grasp of the situation was not clairvoyant, and his outrage at Napoleon's proposal was all but strategic. He had, after all, beautifully negotiated the smooth passage of the territory from the hands of the Spaniards to those of France; he had acted on Napoleon's request that he make it clear to Godoy—confidentially—that ceding Louisiana to any country other than France would be considered a cause for war.

Lucien awoke to all these thoughts the day after Joseph broke the news to him of Napoleon's decision. Lucien returned to the Tuileries in the morning and found the first consul in his bath, its waters perfumed with eau de Cologne. Napoleon's welcome was unusually warm. The men began chatting amicably. Napoleon regretted that his two brothers had not met him at the play the night before, where the great actor Talma, whom he much appreciated, had been "sublime"; and the Parisians, he added, always seemed happy to see him.[76] Admittedly, seven years before, in Vendémiaire 1795, as a recently appointed artillery commander, Napoleon had not hesitated to have his well-positioned guns shoot the mob that was menacing the seat of the governing Directory right there, before the Tuileries—the very palace where he was now enjoying his warm bath; and he had not imagined he would one day be loved quite so much. That episode, the so-called whiff of the grapeshot, had opened a new era: It announced the grip that a tearless, if not fearless, military chief could exercise on the supreme symbol of French power. In fact, Napoleon repeatedly declared from that day on that "if Louis XVI had shown himself on horseback, he would have won the day." The king had been weak and lost his head—a lesson no leader should ever forget.

Lucien had shown himself fearless too on 18 Brumaire. His cold-blooded mastery of a pandemonium was such that, in the eyes of the great general, he already had shown that he could become a menacing adversary. Napoleon resented the fact that his younger brother had been publicly useful to him on that day, and thereafter he was ever more eager to keep him at bay and constrain his political actions, just as he controlled those of his other brothers.

Yes, mused Lucien, people so easily forget things, good and bad, as if "the waters of the Seine have the same properties as those of Lethe"—a poetic allusion to the river of forgetfulness that runs through the Greek underworld. Napoleon quipped in response: "Ah! You are still attracted to poetry! I much approve of this. I would be upset to see you renounce it entirely for politics." Lucien responded that the one activity had never impeded the other—witness King David, King Solomon, and, indeed, Napoleon himself.

The two brothers began reminiscing about their first literary exploits in their early days in Corsica. The conversation moved on to Paoli, to Corsican independence as hailed by Rousseau, and to Jacobinism—still a matter of upsetting divide between the two brothers.

These were all serious issues. But Napoleon was beating around the bush. The subject of Louisiana still had not come up. Lucien was disappointed. Napoleon's valet quietly stood, towel in hand, ready to wrap it around his master, who prepared to rise from the tub. At that very moment, Rustan, the tall Mameluk bodyguard Napoleon had hired in Egypt, scratched his nails on the bathroom door, like a cat, announcing Joseph's arrival. (The system, which replaced ordinary knocking, had been adopted as novel etiquette throughout the entire palace.)

"Let him enter," the first consul stated. "I'll stay in the bath another quarter of an hour." Napoleon loved his baths, and this was a perfect occasion for him to indulge in the pleasure. As soon as Joseph joined his brothers in the steamy room, Lucien discreetly gestured to him to signify that nothing of consequence had been said yet. Joseph seemed somewhat awkward, not knowing where to begin. But Napoleon jumped right in. "And so, my brother, have you not talked to Lucien?"

"About what?"

"About our Louisiana project, as you well know!"

"You mean about *your* project, my dear brother? You cannot have forgotten that, far from being mine. . . ."

"Oh come on, preacher. . . . But I don't need to talk about it with you—you're so pig-headed. I speak much more readily to Lucien about serious things; he might contradict me at times, but he is able to share my point of view, when I find it worth trying to change his."

In the midst of such brotherly bantering—they exchanged affectionate insults like "airhead" and "ironhead"—Napoleon announced his firm intention of selling Louisiana to the Americans without seeking the approval of the Chambers. To Joseph's sincere indignation and Lucien's feigned astonishment, he displayed cold irony. It was also inappropriate to discuss these serious state matters in the presence of a valet, as trusted as he might be. Joseph and Lucien were ready to take leave of Napoleon, who once again was about to exit the bathtub, when he suddenly addressed them in a harsh, ruthless tone: "And by the way, gentlemen, think what you will of this business, but you should both put your mind at rest about it, you Lucien about the sale itself, and you Joseph, because I will do without the approval of anyone—you understand this?"

Joseph was piqued. Approaching the bathtub, he replied forcefully: "Well, make sure you don't present your project in parliament, my dear brother, because if I must, I will place myself at the head of the opposition that will inevitably grow against it."

Napoleon's response was a gruff, loud, forced laugh that stopped as abruptly as it had begun. Lucien remained quiet, unsure of what to do. Joseph was being overcome by one of his legendary anger spells. Increasingly agitated, his face nearly scarlet, he exclaimed, in a near stutter: "Laugh, laugh, sure, go on laughing! That won't stop me from doing what I say I'll do, and much as I dislike going up to the tribune, this time they'll see me there." Napoleon, half raising himself out of the tub, responded in a solemn, energetic tone: "You will have no need to stand as speaker of the opposition, because I repeat, this discussion will not take place, since this project which happily does not have your approval, conceived by me, negotiated by me, will be ratified and executed by me alone, do you understand? By me, and I couldn't care less about your opposition."

With that, Napoleon plunged back into the sweetly perfumed bathwater. Joseph could not contain himself. Addressing his younger brother with the familiar "tu," he shouted: "Well, I tell you, general, that you, I, we all—if you do what you say, we may as well prepare ourselves to join those poor innocent devils you so legally, humanely and oh so justly had deported to Sinnamary."

A brief moment of tense silence followed. Then Napoleon shouted back, rising again from the tub: "You are an insolent! I should . . ." But his vocal threat was lost in the pandemonium that ensued when he forcefully sat back in the water, splashing Joseph from head to foot.

Lucien was standing far enough from the tub to stay dry. The scene was absurd—Napoleon was as pale as Joseph, entirely drenched, was red-faced. Lucien repressed his laughter though could not resist quoting the *Quos ego,* Virgil's lines from the *Aeneid* about Neptune unleashing the fury of the ocean's waters against the winds. Joseph, dripping, responded: "In any case, your god is quite mad." Napoleon turned to Lucien, ignoring their elder brother, and quietly commented, "Always a poet on occasion."

The wave had extinguished Joseph's ire. The valet, quite overwhelmed, tried his best to dry him. Having been in Joseph's service before passing into that of Napoleon, he had trouble handling this embarrassing situation, where his former master had been spectacularly splashed by his current one. It was all too much for him: He fainted then and there. Joseph tried to pick up the poor man, Lucien rang for help, and Rustan, the muscular body-guard, speedily entered the room; he was ordered to assist Joseph by the still-bathridden first consul, who called for another valet to help him out of the tub. Lucien offered to aid the new arrival, but Napoleon refused. Joseph was not quite dry, and Napoleon coldly suggested that he get changed in his *cabinet de toilette.* Joseph, nonplussed by the gesture, replied even more coldly: "Thank you, I'll change at home. Are you coming, Lucien?" Napoleon asked maliciously: "Has he also been splashed?" "No," replied Lucien. "Well then, do me the pleasure of awaiting me with Bourrienne. I need to speak to you; I'll be with you in a moment."

Out of this unlikely scene emerged the Louisiana Purchase, a crucial moment in the formation of the American nation: A little man played god in his bathtub, splashing his elder brother and manipulating his younger one. But Lucien was never going to be as easy to handle as Napoleon hoped he would be.

Lucien was shown into a room where he found the unbearable Bourrienne, that busybody of a secretary, who was close to Joséphine and infamous for his malicious gossip. Lucien decided not to address him at all—he had no wish to explain to him the noises from the bathroom that had certainly reached his sensitive ears and to have him gloatingly report to Napoleon's wife on the colorful disagreement among the brothers. So Lucien sat and hid his face behind a newspaper, waiting to be called. A good half hour later, Rustan showed him into the office.

As soon as he entered, Napoleon spewed his rage against Joseph. "Well, let me tell you, when something gets to Joseph, he's worse than you when you think you're right."[77] Lucien was bracing himself to resist the onslaught of his brother's anger and to stand up to the principles Joseph had gotten splashed for. Especially at this moment, he felt strongly allied with Joseph against Napoleon.

It had not always been so. After their father died, Joseph and Napoleon, the two eldest of the family, had made a sort of pact not to step on each other's toes. The right of primogeniture was of prime importance in Corsica, but Joseph had allowed Napoleon to have his way, often staying home with their mother while the younger and more ambitious sibling pursued his military career. The mostly peaceful arrangement was occasionally perturbed by the natural charisma and vanity of the third-born son, Lucien. He had an easier way with words and with women than either Joseph or Napoleon, and his gifts for eloquence and seduction were both prized and envied by his older brothers. But after Napoleon had reached an unquestionable position of preeminence, Joseph and Lucien often banded together to try to contain his overpowering tendencies, and this was exactly what was happening over the grave issue of constitutional power.

Lucien remained convinced that it was more dishonorable for France to give away Louisiana to the Americans for a low price than to let them gain it through warfare. France would be better off taking advantage of peace to send troops there instead, just as Napoleon had done in Saint-Domingue (today's Haiti; the eastern part of the island, Santo Domingo, is now the Dominican Republic). He shared these thoughts with Napoleon, who reminded him that he, Lucien, had not been an enthusiast of the Saint-Domingue expedition either. Its aim had been to take back from the slave rebel Toussaint Louverture, the "Black Jacobin," the sugar plantations the French had been handsomely profiting from. But the expedition was a debacle. The French army was decimated by yellow fever. Général Leclerc, Pauline's husband and

Lucien's friend, who was the governor of the island, was one of those who later would die in the epidemic.

Now, in response to Lucien's observation that Napoleon should have agreed to negotiate with a diplomatically willing Toussaint—who in fact could have determined the outcome of the French mission but instead was to starve to death in prison—the first consul mused that this expedition was one of his least inspired military ventures. He said that the French navy was far too weak to sustain the impact of the overpowering English fleet. It was therefore strategically wrong to pursue territorial conquest outside Europe (the Egyptian failure had also taught something to Général Bonaparte), and it made perfect sense to relinquish the huge Louisiana territory to the Americans.

The conversation proceeded along these lines, but military strategy was neither Lucien's forte nor his interest. For him, the matter of Louisiana was one of principle: If Napoleon got away with violating the democratic rules now, he would be free to impose his will or whim on anything else.

After a while, the first consul sat in an armchair and entreated Lucien to do the same. Lucien, taking his brother's hand and squeezing it affectionately—the squeeze was not reciprocated—said: "Believe me, my brother, it is impossible to have more fraternal devotion than I do." Napoleon responded that devotion was demonstrated by facts, and that given how much time had been wasted with Joseph on the important matter of Louisiana, Lucien could well dispense with all this talk. Lucien tried once more to be conciliatory, saying: "Allow me to assure you again that my devotion is profound enough to sacrifice everything to you, except my duty."

"Except, you mean, anything that you want to except."

"No, my brother, because if I believed, with Joseph, that this alienation of Louisiana without the assent of the Chambers could be fatal to me alone, I would consent to take all possible chances in order to prove to you this devotion of which you doubt. But it's just too unconstitutional."

Upon hearing the word "unconstitutional," Napoleon burst out into that forced laughter; it seethed with concentrated anger. When Lucien conveyed his surprise that Napoleon could be so mocking with regard to such an important subject, the laughter broke off abruptly, and the first consul said: "Oh please, leave me alone. And in any case in what way have I violated your constitution? Answer." Lucien repeated that the project to give away any annex of the republic was all the more unconstitutional that it came from the supreme representative of national sovereignty: "In a word, the constitution—" Napoleon now lost his patience altogether, shouting "Go to hell! Constitution! Unconstitutional! Republic! National sovereignty! Big words, big phrases! Do you think you are still at your Jacobin club in Saint-Maximin? We're well beyond that. Ah really! You show us a pretty face! Oh that's a good one, unconstitutional! Suits you well, you, mister the knight of the Constitution, to talk to me in that way! You did not show the same respect for the Chambers on 18 Brumaire."

Lucien replied, "You know very well, my dear brother, that no one fought more than I on your behalf when you entered the Council of the Five-Hundred. I was not at all your accomplice, but rather the man who undid the evil you had done to yourself, and this at my own risk, and with all the more generosity—may I add, since we're at it—that no one in Europe disapproved more than I that sacrilegious attack on national representation." Lucien remained calm as he spoke. He could detect the rising anger in Napoleon's gaze, but he insisted again: "Yes, unconstitutional, attack on national sovereignty—"

"Go on, go on then, it's too beautiful to be brief, Mr. the Orator of Clubs; but meanwhile rest assured, you and Joseph, that I shall do exactly as I please; that I loathe, without fearing them, your friends the Jacobins, of which not a single one will be left in France if, as I hope, it continues to be up to me; and finally that I couldn't care less about you and your national representation."

"I do care about you, Citizen Consul, but I know well what to think of you."

"What you think of me, Citizen Lucien, I am really curious to know. Tell me fast."

"I think, Citizen Consul, that after having sworn to the constitution of 18 Brumaire by my own hand, as the President of the Five-Hundred, and seeing you despise it so—well, if I were not your brother, I would be your enemy."

"My enemy, ah! in this case, I would encourage that! My enemy! That's a bit much."

Napoleon began lunging toward Lucien, as if to hit him; but Lucien's immobility neutralized the impulse, and there were no blows. Yet Napoleon's anger had reached its apex, and he shouted: "You, my enemy! I would crush you, you see, like this box!

As he exclaimed this, he grabbed a snuff box on which Jean-Baptiste Isabey had painted a miniature of Joséphine and threw it violently on the floor. The rug softened the impact and it did not break; but the portrait detached itself from the box. Lucien hastened to pick it up and, with a respectful look on his face, gave it back to Napoleon. "It's a pity," he said, "it's the portrait of your wife you broke, while waiting to break the original of myself."

Napoleon began picking up the parts of the snuff box, and as he tried to insert the painting back into it, Lucien left the room. When he told Joseph about Napoleon's explosion, the oldest brother laughed it off, saying "As you can see, I'm not the only one inclined to anger in the family." It was true that Joseph's rages were more fleeting and less deep than those of his brothers.

This episode soon became notorious in Paris and was retold in a variety of versions, embellished and dramatized. Years later Joséphine's daughter Hortense reported that her mother, being Creole and superstitious, was concerned that the accident might have been a bad omen. Immediately after Napoleon told her about it, she had gone to consult a card-reader, who advised her to discreetly replace the ruined portrait with a copy.[78]

THREE

LOVE
1802–1803

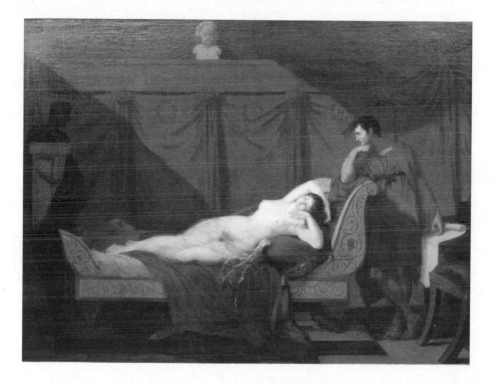

Napoleon must have been shy with the ladies. He feared their jokes; and that soul, impregnable to fear, took revenge on them when he became all powerful, constantly and crudely expressing his contempt, which he wouldn't have talked about had it been really present. Before he became grand, he wrote to a friend about a passion that captivated Lucien: "Women are muddy sticks; one cannot touch them without dirtying oneself." With this inelegant image, he was referring to the errors of conduct they lead to: it was a prediction. If he hated women, it was because he feared supremely the ridicule that they dispense. At a dinner with the Madame de Staël, whom he could have won to his side so easily, he rudely exclaimed that he loved only women who took care of their children.

—Stendhal, *Life of Napoleon*

THE MARVEL

In the spring of 1802, Lucien made his last appearances as a public figure, delivering two important speeches in Paris on religious freedom and on the creation of the Legion of Honor. These were worthy causes, and he put his usual eloquence at work to support them. But his heart was elsewhere by now. Thoroughly distressed by the authoritarian regime that Napoleon was creating, he wished to be far away from the capital.

Lucien's family and friends mistook his somber mood for studied dignity, but he was merely melancholy and in need of some intimate companionship, separate from that of his large, overly invasive family.[1] The recently widowed Marquesa de Santa Cruz sent him a note announcing that she was about to set out for Paris, and he found himself awaiting her eagerly: Her affection might help lift his spirits. Her arrival being delayed, he decided to meet her at the Spanish border. He had not had the chance to explore the Pyrénées during his trip south eighteen months earlier, and this was the perfect opportunity to leave the Parisian unpleasantness behind. Lucien's friend Alexandre de Laborde, a historian and politician who had been with him in Spain, invited him to stop by on his way at his beautiful retreat in Méréville, near Paris, and Lucien accepted gladly.[2]

He arrived after midnight; a sumptuous supper was still being served in the dining room, where a lively group of a dozen friends chatted away. Lucien took his seat at the lavish table and noticed that there was an empty spot across from him. He could not help wondering about the absent person. He understood from the other guests that it was a woman and that she had decided to go straight to bed, seemingly uninterested in acquainting herself with the new guest; this piqued his vanity as much as his curiosity. He heard from Madame Arnault, another guest, that she would be down soon, and he found himself looking forward to meeting her. But as the supper continued, the table setting remained vacant. The name of the absentee, he was told, was Alexandrine Jouberthon, *née* de Bleschamp.

Lucien knew that name: Napoleon himself had mentioned it to him as belonging to the most beautiful woman at a party that Talleyrand had organized for the first consul, a few days before Lucien's return to Paris from Spain. Lucien thought the absent woman must indeed be stunning; the first consul had a knack for noticing female beauty. But that was all Napoleon was able to notice: Female psychology was beyond his reach, and he was unable to take women seriously as intellectual interlocutors. The famously influential and assertive writer Madame de Staël, admired and respected by both Joseph and Lucien—as indeed she was by most contemporary luminaries, some of whom courted her—was deeply despised by Napoleon, principally because she combined cerebral power and fierce independence with less-than-average looks. His anti-intellectual stance, nicknamed at the time (probably by Mme de Stael herself) "ideophoby," or fear of ideas, mirrored his violent antifeminism.[3]

An otherwise praiseful Stendhal surmised in his *Life of Napoleon* that, as a very young man, Napoleon had been skinny, short, and poor enough that his beginnings in love must have been painful. At any rate he grew into an unrepentant misogynist intent on seducing all good-looking women. As Stendhal told it, the average amount of time Napoleon spent with any woman he had summoned to his private apartments was no more than three minutes, during which time he would barely take his eyes off his papers and rarely bothered even to remove his sword from his side.[4] Women were a territory to be conquered, and it was a territory that interested him less than the actual lands of his constantly expanding, embattled realm. In this too he could not have differed more from Lucien, who was as uninterested in conquering lands as he was in merely seducing ladies. Lucien was—or at least had been—a ladies' man, but he appreciated women's minds as much as their beauty.

That night at Méréville, his romantic longing fed on the gossipy conversation about the absent lady; as the others talked, he could not help staring dreamily at that empty seat in front of him. To the assembly he seemed tired. In fact, as the night wore on, he found himself becoming increasingly intrigued and disappointed, even resentful—absentees are always wrong, one says in French. It was early morning when the party dissolved. Laborde took Lucien to his room. Lucien's ever faithful valet, Pedro, who had come with him from Spain, volunteered some information while his master was getting ready for bed, saying that the lady who was absent from the table had also been talked about by the servants: "*Monsiou,* they say she is *una bella Señora!*"

Lucien's sleep was fitful and marked by an unusually intense dream in which he saw an unknown, beautiful woman to whom he was strongly drawn. Next to her appeared the marquesa looking old and sad; there was also a marble bust that resembled him, without actually representing him. A dramatic flourish of fire, water, flowers, and various noises completed the picture. He awoke briefly, and when he returned to sleep, the unknown woman appeared again. The marquesa was absent now. By the time he was fully awake, the day was ripe; he felt a strong need for fresh air and set out on a walk in the park of Méréville, in whose midst the château was set.

The park was a sumptuous retreat, at once studied landscape and exuberant heath. The legendary grounds had been designed by the landscape painter Hubert Robert some two decades earlier, commissioned by the owner of the property, Alexandre's father, Jean-Joseph de Laborde, who had been guillotined during the Terror. Chateaubriand visited in 1804 and described it in his *Mémoires d'Outre-Tombe* as "an oasis created by the smile of a Muse, but one of those Muses whom Gallic poets call learned Faeries."[5] And in those spring days of 1802, Méréville was a fresh marvel. Its botanical layout was exquisite, and Lucien particularly appreciated the rivulet that ran through it, which he thought he should copy for his own grounds in Le Plessis.

As he continued his walk, he suddenly caught sight of a woman ambling on her own among the trees. Although he had never seen her before, he thought he recognized her—from his own dream. She struck him immediately as the most seductive woman he had ever laid eyes upon. Tall and thin, in her mid-twenties, she moved gracefully. Her gaze was at once gentle and luminous; there was nobility and grandeur about her, enhanced by her fair skin. He noticed her lovely arms and hands and her well-shaped feet. She was simply ravishing.

Lucien had never experienced such an emotion of instant devotion before; he was at first speechless before this stranger. But he did not have to remain alone and tongue-tied for too long. Soon their host, Laborde, appeared with the rest of the group. In this age of conventions, it might have been awkward to be seen alone with her, even though everyone knew that they could not have planned an inappropriate rendezvous. And so everyone was formally introduced. For Lucien, the introduction was unnecessary; the feeling that he had seen her before, in his dream, remained powerful in his mind. She told him that he bore a striking resemblance to Napoleon, whom she had met. Many years later, she confessed in her *Souvenirs* to having felt a measure of impatience, even anxiety, at the prospect of the arrival of the famed Lucien, as if she knew the meeting would be momentous.[6]

The sound of a bell suddenly broke into the greetings. To Lucien's inquiry after its nature, Laborde, slightly embarrassed, replied: "It's nothing, that is to say it is . . . I believe it is the Mass." "How charming. Do you celebrate the Mass in Méréville? Ah! This is quite unique." Masses had been prohibited in revolutionary times and for a while after. Even marriage had lost its original sacramental value; unions had been sealed in simple civil ceremonies and were easily undone by divorce. But in reaction to this extreme ban on traditional ritual and to the libertinism that accompanied it, a new wave of religiosity was about to sweep the country. Just about a year before, in 1801, the Concordat had been signed between Pope Pius VII and Napoleon—with the active mediation of Lucien as interior minister—that restored the Catholic Church as the official church in France, and Mass was no longer a crime. But this was recent. And although Laborde's pious mother, as it turned out, had managed to hold a secret Mass throughout the Revolution, at Méréville the church was in disrepair and there was still no priest, so mere house bells were used to announce Mass.

Everyone was now enthused at the idea of partaking in the long-forbidden ritual—Lucien more than anyone else. He had last done so just before giving up his training to be a priest, a good decade ago. Mass took place in the simple chapel, which consisted of a room and a table that served as the altar, with a crucifix and two lit torches. Lucien managed to stand next to Alexandrine, and she did not seem displeased at all. The Mass was simple and solemn, the priest venerable. Lucien felt devout again. It occurred to him for the first time that the tomb of his late wife Christine should really be in a church rather than a garden; and he now contemplated building a church on his property at Le Plessis. In his mind, he was finally burying Christine; perhaps he was putting an end to his mourning.

At lunch, Lucien and Alexandrine sat next to each other. At last they could speak. He quickly realized that her charms were not only physical. She shared Lucien's staunchly republican, anti-Royalist sympathies; that was a good start. They began an engaging conversation about Chateaubriand, whom she esteemed; she had read his romantic novel *Atala*. Lucien recommended to her his just-published *Genius of Christianity*, a book that was already contributing to the renewal of Catholic tradition in France; he eagerly volunteered to get her a copy and to introduce her to the august author, a friend. She demurred, on the pretext that she was not able to lead a very social life these days. Lucien secretly rejoiced at the revelation, persuaded that she would make an exception for him.

Then the conversation casually turned to the subject of the first consul, for whom Alexandrine professed great admiration. Lucien did not refrain from telling her that she had caught Napoleon's eye and that he had even told Lucien about her. She blushed, telling him that she had had the "honor" of seeing Napoleon on a few public occasions but had not had the "pleasure" of speaking to him. This expression of polite enthusiasm angered Lucien—he was now irritated with her as well as with himself, and began talking about the weather to the lady on his other side, Mme Arnault—who was an old friend of Alexandrine's.

Not impressed with Lucien's brusque reaction, Alexandrine asked her friend whether she would not agree that the bust of Napoleon resting on the mantelpiece in her house might be easily mistaken for a bust of Lucien himself. Mme Arnault did agree. Alexandrine now added that the most precious object she had in her house was that very bust. Lucien was pleased, and he noticed a slightly mischievous smile on the face of Mme Arnault.

Soon Lucien met Alexandrine's three-year-old daughter, Anna, whom she had brought with her to Méréville. She quickly charmed Lucien, who found her the most graceful of children. The admiring guests showered her with compliments, though Lucien said nothing. When the child brought her mother a bunch of flowers she had picked in the garden, Lucien plucked up the courage to ask for one from the lady's hand; she gave him a carnation. Little Anna stared at him, broke into laughter, and threw her arms around her mother's neck.

MIRROR GAMES

A postprandial walk had been planned, but it began to rain, so the party stayed indoors and played trictrac (a French version of backgammon). Lucien was defeated by none other than Alexandrine. He felt too distracted to play the rematch. By then the weather had cleared, and it was decided to attempt the walk. The excursion included a game that consisted in chasing larks with mirrors. Lucien and Alexandrine sat near a bush, far enough from the others to enjoy some privacy. Their mirrors were not very active against the larks, but Lucien tried to reflect in his mirror the figure of his fellow huntress, and it seemed to him, although he pretended not to notice, that she was doing the same, discreetly turning her mirror toward him.

The moment was pregnant with possibility and romance. But Alexandrine was still the wife of Anna's father: As such she cautiously maintained her distance with Lucien. He made sure to remain as gentlemanly and respectful as was required, hoping to gain her confidence. At this point she confirmed what Laborde had already told him: She was eagerly awaiting the first opportunity to sail to Saint-Domingue, where her husband, Hippolyte Jouberthon, was working. In fact, she was glad to have met Lucien because she wanted to ask him to write a letter of recommendation on her behalf to his sister Pauline, the wife of Général Leclerc, the governor of the occupied island, in order to obtain a passport that would allow her to rejoin her husband.

Lucien did not welcome this declaration, of course, but he promised to write the letter—while wondering whether he would be capable of delivering it. That day, it became obvious to him that he could no longer contemplate meeting the Marquesa de Santa Cruz at the Spanish border, and he decided to cancel his trip to the South. He wrote her a note: "I cannot come see you because, besides having great preoccupations, I am a bit sick." He minimized his sense of guilt by telling himself that he was only committing a white lie, since he was effectively sick—in the heart. Entrusting a servant with delivering the note, Lucien returned to Paris along with the other Méréville guests.

Back in the capital, his acquaintance with Alexandrine deepened. He learned that she had had a neglected childhood caught between warring parents and an oppressed youth. She had been married off to an older, honest man at the age of twenty and had become rich thanks to him, but if she loved him at all, it was mostly out of gratitude, in spite of his subsequent misfortunes and financial ruin. Persecuted by his creditors, he had been forced to migrate to Saint-Domingue, in order to try to repay his suffocating debts. It was a touching story. Lucien tentatively offered his help; her situation in Paris was far from brilliant, her finances in jeopardy.

Meanwhile, the marquesa arrived in town. Now free and still in love with Lucien, she was intent on marrying him. Lucien faced one of the worst moments of his life when he sat down with her to tell her the truth; he could not pretend things were as before, and did not have it in him to lie to her. His love for her had been real enough, but with Alexandrine he felt renewed. He was sure there was no looking back. He tried to justify himself with the thought that since he was not the marquesa's first lover, he would not be her last either. She was surprised and pained by the end of their affair; but Lucien could not blame himself, and he sensed that she did not blame him either.

The marquesa was as well received in Paris—and by Lucien's family—on this visit as she had been earlier. Her social standing was certainly firmer than that of Alexandrine, and soon people began to consider her a victim of the latter. Lucien's courtship of Alexandrine was no secret in Paris circles, and his enemies soon became hers, even though Lucien was not yet sure that his love was fully reciprocated.

Elisa, ever the outspoken supporter of the marquesa, reacted swiftly. She called Alexandrine Lucien's "so-called mistress." Supportive and nurturing of Lucien as Elisa had been since Christine's death, she had also taken advantage of the wealth her brother acquired upon his return from Spain, spending his money without restraint and taking for granted their closeness. The appearance of Alexandrine on the scene set off a sharp competitiveness in her. She sensed immediately that her territory was being encroached upon—that Alexandrine was a powerful character who, by uniting herself with Lucien, would divide the close-knit Bonaparte clan. Although brother and sister continued to cohabit—both in Paris and in the country—a rift set in.

Elisa managed to overcome her resistance enough to request to meet Alexandrine. Lucien hesitated but thought it wise not to refuse. It was a matter of finding the right occasion. To encourage him, Elisa promised to obtain the letter of recommendation that would enable Alexandrine to travel to Saint-Domingue to see her husband—and thanks to which Elisa would have effectively gotten rid of the problem. Lucien was silently in despair. He saw his beloved every day, sometimes even twice a day, but never alone, for little Anna was invariably present. Still, this was better than not seeing her at all. He then came up with a politically ingenious plan: He asked Elisa to Le Plessis, entreating her to invite Alexandrine, along with other ladies. He himself could not honorably have asked Alexandrine. Elisa was happy with the plan. Alexandrine accepted the invitation, although she did set the condition that she bring her daughter along. Lucien admitted that, while Anna was charming enough, he was somewhat jealous of her.

***

The guests began arriving at Le Plessis. Elisa mocked Lucien for the care he took in having Alexandrine's room prepared. Rubbing her hands, she said disingenuously, "Oh! How happy I am to see you truly in love!" Meanwhile, Elisa's husband, Felix Baciocchi, arrived, equipped with the violin from which he was never parted. (Elisa, however, was still conducting her affair with Fontanes, who later would write unpleasant letters about Lucien's "coquettish and covetous" mistress.[7]) Alexandrine was the last of the party to appear, with little Anna, her servant, and Laborde.

It was a lively group. Joseph, who was there too, was very favorably impressed with Alexandrine, much to Lucien's relief. Another guest was Chateaubriand, to whom Alexandrine, in awe of the writer and eager to make a good impression, addressed studied compliments. Lucien himself had been the one to give her a copy of *The Genius of Christianity* after their return from Méréville, as he had promised; but the seductive, slightly exalted air she took while speaking to the great luminary, about Saint Augustine and much else, got on his nerves to some degree. Fontanes, who was a close friend of Chateaubriand, later informed the host that his colleague had been charmed by her.

Letizia—Madame Mère—sent a note announcing that she was about to arrive at Le Plessis, where she wanted to attend one of the family theater productions. Ever since his days as a Jacobin, Lucien had remained enamored of the theater and had become quite serious about the productions he put on at his villa. He was a talented actor and was on good relations with the most celebrated professional actors of the day. He was very keen on his home theatricals, especially as they competed with those Napoleon set up at his residence in Malmaison. Napoleon's were high-minded affairs; the costumes came straight from the Comédie Française. Participants admitted that one did not have quite so much fun there as at Le Plessis. Napoleon was incensed on one occasion when Lucien and Elisa appeared on stage there to perform Voltaire's play *Alzire* virtually in the nude, before an audience that included the first consul and the whole Malmaison court.

In order to deflect society's attention from his courtship of Alexandrine, Lucien thought it best now to show himself with other women, exploiting his reputation as the ladies' man he no longer was. He hired a beautiful actress to whom he gave a lavish costume to play the roles of Semiramis and Clytemnestra, two famously fatal queens. Alexandrine did not seem in the least jealous of the actress. Lucien noticed her cool: It struck him that she was sure of herself, and of him.

In the midst of theatrical drama, dramatic news kept arriving from Saint-Domingue: The epidemic of yellow fever had become an implacable enemy, killing soldiers and civilians by the thousands. The occupation of the island by Napoleon's troops was not unsuccessful; but at this point any news from there was news of death. Alexandrine was worried about her husband, from whom she had not heard in three months. The likelihood that she had become a widow was increasing. Lucien struggled against his hope, aware of how morally dubious it was, but he could not help wondering what might be going on in her mind. People around him were beginning to consider their marriage a real possibility. Still, he did not dare presume anything, and he remained wary of the potential suitors of this extraordinarily lovely young woman who indeed was capable of being "coquettish"—and not only with Chateaubriand. She charmed Dezerval, for instance, a rather good-looking friend of Lucien's, but not a man of much culture. By now Lucien understood that the sharp-witted Alexandrine had a penchant for intellectually impressive types.

The courtship progressed, on Lucien's territory, among this chosen, pleasant society. Lucien's feelings for her were unambiguous. Hers remained necessarily harder to devise: She had not declared her love, and he was kept on tenterhooks for a while longer, prudent enough not to dare be convinced of what, in fact, was inevitable.

NAKED PASSIONS AND SECRET PASSAGES

An ominous letter, sealed in black, arrived from Saint-Domingue for Alexandrine. She retired to her room to open it. A while later she called into the room her friend Mme Arnault, who soon emerged to announce the death of M. Jouberthon. The letter had been written by his banker in Saint-Domingue. The young widow immediately left for Paris with her daughter. Lucien joined her there the next day; most of the other guests left Le Plessis as well.

Lucien wrote to Alexandrine as a widow, following protocol as any gentleman would. She agreed to see him at home a few days later. In his eyes, her beauty was only enhanced by her black dress and tear-streaked face. She made it clear that she was mourning the father of her child more than her husband. Her widowed state rendered Lucien's manifest feelings for her legitimate; he promised to be a father for Anna. The rest remained unsaid, because it was so obvious.

Finally the time came to propose. Although she was not surprised by Lucien's talk of marriage, it was too early, and she first reacted with fear and distress. He tried to reassure her, determined to go ahead, despite the circumstances, knowing full well that his all-controlling brother would not make things easy, given his tendency to marry off his siblings for political advantage. But Alexandrine's resistance did not last, and it took her little time to declare herself in turn. She treaded carefully, however, keeping her reserve, and retiring from society even more than she had done since the death of her husband. She was clearly glad to abide by these widow's conventions, and must have found consolation in avoiding activities that distracted her from the work of mourning.

They were not yet lovers. But for Lucien, those days of platonic intimacy were embued with sweetness, with the promise of full possession and deep happiness. His romantic and sensualist nature came to the fore. His years as a womanizer were definitely over. Elisa remained skeptical; she could not believe that Lucien would ever be constant in his love for a woman. The siblings' relations were increasingly strained, until both agreed that she should move out; he would help Elisa and her husband Felix Baciocchi find a suitable home and even give them necessary household items. Mme Mère disapproved of Lucien's excessive generosity toward an ungrateful sister. And indeed, in spite of Lucien's willingness to assist Elisa, she turned against him and Alexandrine, revealing what she thought she knew of them to Napoleon and Joséphine. She had never liked the latter, but now a new alliance was forged between the two women.

This was the beginning of a long-term feud. A rumor that Lucien and Alexandrine had married reached Napoleon. The couple, now established as such, received anonymous, threatening, and vicious letters; defaming songs circulated, attributed to Elisa but of unknown origin. Lucien felt the need to defend himself against the first consul's predictably furious reaction to this piece of news, and he wrote him a long letter in which he denied having married or wanting to marry, or that his "beautiful and good mistress" would want to marry him without Napoleon's approval—if even Lucien himself were mad enough to want that.[8] However, he wrote, if he were to marry, nothing could make him repudiate his wife. Since he did not meddle with other people's love lives, he was entitled to hope no one would meddle with his. He was able to choose one woman over others because he had known many, but for the same reason, he was not susceptible to real passion. Indeed, if he were to be struck by that "illness," the first consul would be the first to know about it. It hurt him that Napoleon had believed him cowardly enough to deceive him; but the first consul's anger was dear to Lucien; it proved to him Napoleon's friendship.

Lucien also announced to Alexandrine that he was not going to let any one dictate how he should live his life. Despite the continuous pressures and unpleasant atmosphere, she took the situation in stride; and Lucien did not lose his cool, or his refined irony. He even managed to create a visual pun out of their situation. Sophisticated art lover that he was, he decided to celebrate his passion for Alexandrine artistically. The perfect man for the job was his good friend the talented Lethière, who had followed him to Spain and probably seen with him Goya's *Maja Desnuda* in Godoy's secret boudoir. Once Lucien met Alexandrine, Goya's daring picture would easily have been the inspiration for a similar one.

Lethière produced a canvas of such distilled eroticism that the *Maja Desnuda* itself, though resembling it in many ways, would seem tame in its company.[9] It depicted a sensuous, curvaceous woman—Alexandrine—languidly lying on a chaise longue, her milky nakedness and pubic hair barely concealed by a thin gauze. A dark, handsome man—Lucien—is gravely but covetously contemplating this sleeping beauty, his chin resting on his right hand, while his left hand rests on a partially unrolled writ. The names of the two lovers are inscribed in Greek under the chaise—Alexandra and Lukiano—their initials emblazoned together inside the far right laurel embroidered on the wall, while a wilted laurel wreath lies at his feet.

Lethière placed a half-bust in profile of a satyr gaping at the naked lady; its features recall those of Napoleon. The bust was akin to the one that had been in Lucien's dream in Méréville. Lethière also portrayed himself on a shelf at the top center of the picture. In the small cameo depicted on the right of the chaise, just between Alexandrine's head and Lucien's crotch and next to Neptune's trident, one can recognize another representation of the first consul in profile, a seeming reference to the "tempest in a bathtub," when Lucien had aptly quoted Virgil's lines about Napoleon acting as the angry sea god. This had happened only a few months earlier, so the memory of the defining clash between the brothers was still fresh.

The picture could not have been painted later than the autumn of 1802, when Alexandrine, whether she knew it already or not, was pregnant with their first child, Charles, born in late May 1803. Retrospectively, Lucien's decision to marry Alexandrine seems to be sealed by the fate depicted in the picture. He could have made up his mind this early in their relationship—but there is no way to know for sure. Mystery surrounds this picture, which the couple would have had to hide away.

Since his return to Paris from Spain, Lucien lived in high style—higher even than when he had been minister of the interior—surrounded by his extraordinary art collection, in an imposing *hôtel particulier,* known at the time as the Hôtel de Brienne. The building, typical of Ancien Régime grandeur and elegance, was located on the Place du Corps Législatif. (Today the building houses the Ministry of Defense.) Lucien rented it until July 1802. Then, all of a sudden, he purchased it, for 300,000 francs, and it was rumored that he spent a staggering 1 million francs on renovations—a sum that, even by today's standards, was extravagant. At any rate, Lucien meant to make this his primary, official residence, which would compete in luxury with Napoleon's own home at Malmaison. But there was also a hidden agenda to this purchase and renovation. He had Alexandrine move, very discreetly, into a nearby building. Then he hired one trusted worker and charged him with the most secretive of missions: to build an underground passage to connect his palace with her apartment, so that they would be able to meet freely, without being noticed, disturbed, or menaced. This was done remarkably fast, in less than a month. Lucien affectionately dubbed the passage "*souterrain conjugal.*"[10] And the provocative, sexy picture by Lethière might well have been displayed in Alexandrine's clandestine residence, perhaps in an appositely furnished boudoir.

The door to the passage was next to Lucien's celebrated gallery of paintings, in which was displayed the artworks he had begun to purchase in Spain and that he continued to acquire steadily with such zeal and passion that he was running out of space for their display. One day Joseph, who was visiting him, saw him emerge out of a fake wall. Lucien, a bit frazzled, told him that he had a "cabinet," or little office, built in there. Luckily, Joseph did not inspect it. Lucien was eager to remain as discreet as possible, and so he made a point of averting the family's curiosity about Alexandrine. When his sister Pauline—who had become a famously beautiful woman—returned from Saint-Domingue, after Général Leclerc's death, she asked insistently: "What is she like? Blonde? Brunette? White? Petite? Big?" "Not bad, not bad," he answered vaguely. Their mother, though, knew much more. She was on Lucien's side, and was the only person besides the two lovers who had a key to the secret passage. She knew so much, in fact, that she warned him of "certain little things" that might prevent him from living his great love affair.

Despite his discretion, Lucien's mistress was no secret in Paris. Napoleon did not hesitate to put his best man on the case: Fouché, the notoriously devilish minister of police. He had already managed to shove Lucien out of the public eye by slyly suggesting to Napoleon that Lucien was too vocal about his brother's ambition to become France's one and only leader. (Until 1804, Napoleon formally led the country, though hardly shared the power, with two other consuls, Jean-Jacques-Régis de Cambacérès and Charles-François Lebrun.) Lucien now looked like a potential danger to the first consul, who charged Fouché with interfering with his brother's private life, a task the minister professed was not worthy of his skills. Nonetheless, he set himself to pursue it and, in a preventive move, sent an official notice to all of France's mayors stating that the wedding of Lucien could not be lawfully celebrated.

Because Lucien and Alexandrine wanted to establish themselves as a married couple, this was troublesome. Now that a secret civil ceremony would not be feasible, they settled for a religious benediction, satisfactory enough as a temporary solution, especially for Alexandrine, who felt strongly about her Catholicism. The secret nuptial blessing was celebrated by the abbot Perrier, in Le Plessis, on May 25, 1803—the day after Alexandrine gave birth to

Charles, christened after Lucien's father.[11] (Napoleon had married Joséphine in similar circumstances, thanks to a papal dispensation.) Alexandrine finally abandoned her black mourning clothes for white garments. She did not take Lucien's name but renounced her married one: Mme Jouberthon was now Madame Alexandrine de Bleschamp. And it was as Mme Alexandrine that Lucien introduced her to his two young daughters, Charlotte and Christine-Egypta. He told them they must love her, since she was his best friend.[12] Alexandrine was overjoyed to adopt them as her own. And so she and Lucien, living together as wife and husband, were now the parents of three girls—and their first, infant boy.

"THE BEST CATCH IN EUROPE"

A period of quiet domestic life was beginning for them, focused on the children and a small group of friends, including the Arnaults, Dezerval, the abbot Perrier, doctors Paroisse and Corvisart (who was Napoleon's personal physician), his friend Briot, and Lethière. Lucien decided he should help further Alexandrine's education—which had been brutally interrupted by the Revolution—especially in history and literature. She was sophisticated but there were gaps in her knowledge, and he thought it a good idea to fill them as much as possible. At twenty-four, she believed herself too old to study, but he insisted, adamant that a woman should be as educated as a man and that parity of education made for happier marriages. So they spent their days poring over books and their evenings with their children and friends.[13]

They went out seldom, attending the theater, a passion of theirs, as often as they could but as discreetly as possible. They were living under siege, oppressed by the asphyxiating air of Parisian politics. Simply being together felt like a honeymoon, but Alexandrine thought it was time to get out of the city for a few weeks, to take a break in a countryside where they would be entirely anonymous.[14] Lucien agreed that the time had come for them to take a breath of fresh air, far from the capital. He too looked forward to an idyll of quiet with his new wife, and to escaping the attention of the police spies who surrounded them.

Alexandrine suggested a place near the Thibouville River, in Normandy. Ten years before, as a teenager, she had stopped with her father in that undiscovered, bucolic area; she remembered a peaceful landscape, pure air, bird-song, flowery meadows, clear water and plentiful fish, warm peasants, and pretty women who offered the visitors baskets of crayfish. Her handsome father (an ex-navy officer) had reveled in the compliments these women showered upon him and the young Alexandrine, and she dreamed of returning. Lucien could not stop himself from laughing at this vivid recollection. But the place sounded charming; and he had never been to Normandy.

They decided to leave the very next day, a Monday, on the strength of Alexandrine's precept that the only way to ensure the success of a useful or pleasant project that presents difficulties was to execute it as rapidly as possible. Preparations were made. Lucien visited his mother to announce his departure, without giving further details or mentioning their destination. She warned him he should not leave his wife alone in Paris, and he reassured her that they would be traveling together. The new baby was in good hands, with the wet nurse.

At that moment a post carriage was heard in the courtyard and Joseph entered the room, announcing that he and Lucien had been summoned to lunch at the consul's table in Malmaison on the following Wednesday, June 1. This summons was an imposition on their time. Lucien now had to call off his vacation with Alexandrine; and Joseph, an inveterate hunter, had to forgo a hunting expedition. Letizia told them to beware, with a particularly suggestive gaze: "Perhaps the consul is trying to have a new law passed at the Senate, and would rather you were not present there," she said.[15]

Lucien had been made a senator in July 1802—it was a way for Napoleon to give his brother an honorary title without having him involved in politics. Lucien had not participated much in the works of the high chamber, although he had planned on announcing to Citizen Laplace, the chancellor, his leave of a few weeks—artificially prolonging his leave of sickness that followed an earlier bout of Indian flu. That would be unnecessary now, sadly. And it turned out that the first consul had no new law to pass at the Senate that day. Instead he wanted his brothers present at his home for a very precise purpose: a conversation. It would be a lengthy, important one. Lucien recorded it word for word, complete with the spirited rejoinders, humorous tone, and underlying tension that no amount of jesting, quipping, or bantering could hide, simply because Lucien was withholding the crucial fact of his secret marriage throughout.

Lucien and Joseph traveled to Malmaison together. After a brief exchange with Napoleon, they were shown to the dining room. Rustan entered solemnly, followed by the valet de chambre, bearing a platter with the first consul's coffee.[16] Napoleon explained to the brothers that he could have only coffee for lunch and so would not sit with them; as for Joséphine, she had been suffering from toothache the whole night, so she would not join them either. The brothers were left alone and served an excellent truffle pâté along with bad wine; they hungrily gulped down the pâté. Since Lucien was abstemious, only Joseph tried the wine and sent back one bad bottle for an equally poor one. Despite the delightful—albeit skimpy—pâté, the brothers complained about their forced detention.

Napoleon must have been eavesdropping behind the door while the two were eating: They heard some noise from the other side for a few minutes before he appeared. Upon entering the room, he mocked them for taking so long to eat. Joseph replied that "the First Consul does not remember often enough that one doesn't get old at table."[17] Napoleon responded: "Bah! Bah! Glutton's talk! Only good enough for the code of constitutional kings that I allowed myself to call you-know-what." Joseph and Lucien completed the sentence together: "Yes, pigs in manure." "Exactly," replied Napoleon. "So, am I wrong?" "I don't really think so," said Joseph, and Lucien added: "It's up to the English to decide this question, since we French haven't yet properly tasted a constitutional king." Napoleon said: "Whether this is a good or a bad thing, I say that, if it is up to me, you shall never taste one. It is a hollow idea, nonsense, stupidity. But follow me."

Napoleon led Lucien and Joseph to his office, where the three brothers sat down. Napoleon immediately announced why he had convened this meeting: It was for the sake of "a family project of some importance," one that had been preoccupying him for some days and that pertained to Lucien. But it took a while longer for Napoleon to come to the main topic. He be-

gan by insultingly referring to Alexandrine by her first husband's name—he
would never desist from doing so, in order to provoke his brother. "I am
afraid that the eyes of your lady will cost you very dearly, Citizen Lucien.
How do you call her? *Mame Jo . . . Mame . . . Jou . . . Mame Joubert*—a devil
of a baroque name, which one can never recall." Lucien did not take the bait,
saying: "If I knew whom you were talking about, I would help you recall it."
Napoleon went on: "I can easily believe that you don't know it. I do, though.
A beautiful woman indeed! I don't disagree. I think I told you about her
some time ago, praising her even. Oh well! I don't deny it, she's an attractive
person. Does Joseph know her?"

Joseph pretended not to know about whom Napoleon was talking.
"Don't be so reticent," said the first consul. "You know very well whom I
am talking about, and Lucien even more so than you. Well! That he love
the lady, that is fair enough, and natural. Let him idolize her, if he finds her
worthy; but not to the point of blinding himself, or of being so childish as to
let the best catch of Europe slip through his fingers." Joseph asked who that
would be. Napoleon replied: "It is a catch that all marriageable princes have
set their eyes on; one according to which they adjust their aim, as does the
hunter of a beautiful prey, with their diplomatic rifles."

Lucien quipped, "Well, these poor princes, why would one want to go
after their game? Especially me, since I'm not even marriageable."

"And why is that?" asked Napoleon.

"I am not marriageable," Lucien declared, "because I have neither the
desire nor the will to marry, and that would seem to me rather necessary to
do anything about it, in particular to take a wife."

Napoleon exclaimed: "Here we go with our rhetorician! What sophistry!
But I won't be discouraged. You have too much spirit not to hear the voice
of reason, and too much heart not to be moved by what I want to do for
you. You see, I also became a hunter, for your sake. I don't want to miss this
beautiful shot, which, at the end of the day, will obtain for me nothing more
than to see you join the ranks of the reigning families. Don't you think this
quite superb? . . . Ah! really, you seem so above it all, don't you."

Lucien replied: "I certainly believe I am, as brother of the victor of
Marengo." "Fine!" said Napoleon. "[B]ut let us not puff ourselves up too

much; and if you wish, ask our older brother Joseph, isn't it the case that this is an occasion not to be missed?"

Joseph said: "How times have changed! Republicans like you and me, Citizen Consul, proposing, pressing the alliance of a republican like Lucien with the reigning families! Oh, what would the Jacobins say!"

Napoleon retorted, "You *coquins* (rascals)! They'll see that there's more to come, I hope. Their reign is over. It is time to reorganize society."

Lucien said: "Thanks to you, my brother, society is being reorganized, and I don't see why dynastic alliances of French citizens should be able to consolidate our republic, which, like any other republic, does not care for what enslaved peoples revere in monarchies."

Napoleon called these "empty sentences, neither true nor appropriate to this case," and continued: "I only need to tell you the choice I've made, and Joseph and you will agree with me that what is happening to us is quite extraordinary."

Joseph attempted to put an end to this charade: "I shall probably agree with you, since you find it so excellent; but why are you beating around the bush for so long?" "Don't you know that the First Consul has fun keeping us hanging?" said Lucien. They both entreated Napoleon to get to the point. But Napoleon continued taking his time, playing cat-and-mouse with his brothers. He patted Lucien on the shoulder after menacing to pull his ear, assuring him again that he was free to marry whomever he wanted, that a good many high-placed, powerful lords would want to be in his shoes. Lucien responded that he considered himself to be even higher-placed than any of those lords and that what appeared good to them would not suffice for him.

Finally, after another irritating round of mischievous banter, the first consul revealed who the great catch was: the queen of Etruria. The king of Etruria had died just a few days before, on May 27, and Napoleon had wasted no time trying to arrange the new dynastic alliance. Etruria, the ancient region of Italy, encompassed Tuscany and its surroundings. In 1800, Lucien himself had made the region into a kingdom, when he had met, in Paris, the princess Maria Luisa Bourbon, the daughter of the king of Spain, married to the Duke of Parma and ruler of Etruria. Madame Georgette Ducrest described her in her memoirs as "short, ungracious and ugly, with brusque, common and unpleasant manners."[18] As soon as Maria Luisa was widowed, she took over the reign. Napoleon was eager to multiply his connections with Europe's royal families, and here was an available queen: an occasion not to be missed, indeed.

Lucien knew about marriage intrigues from his time in Spain, when he had conveyed the queen's proposal about the union of the *infanta* Isabella with Napoleon. Since the deal would have entailed the first consul's divorcing Joséphine, it had been a moot one, serving only to strengthen Joséphine's animosity toward Lucien. Now Napoleon was turning the tables and trying to force his brother to marry another Spanish princess who controlled a hefty part of central Italy. The memory of the *infanta* episode changed Napoleon's mood. He somberly marched to and fro in his cabinet, arms crossed on his chest. Now he spoke again: The queen of Etruria was not after his own hand. Lucien was the candidate this time.

"Do you hear, Citizen?" he said. "Lucien is available. I have charged Talleyrand with negotiating the affair, and he has queried the queen on this matter."

Lucien was taken aback. "Let me say without mincing words that I should have been queried in the first place. This would have saved you the rest of the negotiation, since I would have told you with no hesitation what I have been repeating over and over again, that I will marry only a woman chosen by myself."

Napoleon replied: "We could have proposed her to one of your choice, monsieur. Moreover, this is not the way one treats affairs of such importance. I have followed the usage adopted in similar cases. The queen's response was as flattering as could possibly be. She has said, and these are her own words, that Senator Lucien is one of the most distinguished gentlemen she knows, for whom she even has the strongest feelings. . . ."

"But what folly this is!" exclaimed Lucien. "The strongest feelings!"

"Why not?" asked Joseph. "Since she knows you."

Lucien replied: "This is very honest of you, my dear brother, as they used to say at court; but—"

Napoleon interrupted: "Let me finish! If you deign to allow me, you will see, messieurs, that these very strong feelings the queen has for Senator Lucien are simply feelings of gratitude. He is the one who signed the treaty that created a kingdom for her husband, and therefore for her son. As a result, her heart and hand must be, and are more than ever, at the First Consul's disposal. Is this clear?"

Lucien replied: "Very clear, Citizen Consul, so clear that I now see better still what I had only suspected before: that her gratitude undoubtedly must be stronger for the direct and supreme founder of the kingdom than for his representative."

Napoleon told Lucien he was "really the most opinionated sophist of France and Spain." Joseph intervened, trying to defuse the tension: "Lucien, I think you shouldn't treat this business too lightly. One should coolly evaluate its advantages and disadvantages and then, after careful deliberation, decide to accept it or not. For instance, I believe, and the consul will agree with me, that the fact that the queen has a son who is already the King of Etruria is not a very happy circumstance for the children who could be born to her and Lucien."

"Regardless!" responded Lucien. "I can tell you that no son of mine will ever be born to that woman."

"Why do you say this?" asked Joseph. "Is it because she isn't pretty? And why should that matter?"

Napoleon winked at Joseph, pretending that Lucien did not notice. "Undoubtedly! Why does that matter? There are so many other advantages. I admit that the little king is what I least like about this union; but so many events can take place, and anyway, one can't have everything in this world."

Lucien said: "Oh my brothers, how I admire you! What? You know me little enough to actually believe that I would ever marry an ugly woman?"

Joseph responded: "An ugly woman, no; but a queen."

"That's even worse," said Lucien.

Napoleon tried again, this time with a tender expression on his face and a mellifluous voice. "And Lucien, believe me: It isn't necessary for our wives to be beautiful. With our mistresses, that's a different matter. An ugly mistress is a monstrous thing. She would essentially fail in her main or, better, her only duty."

Joseph added: "And would make us seem all the more guilty in the eyes of the wise, since her appearance would not provide an excuse."

Napoleon said: "That's very true. Do you agree, Lucien?

Lucien responded without blinking. "Completely, and that is exactly why, I believe, a woman must be beautiful, so that she can always remain her husband's mistress."

Napoleon replied: "One could not offer a more morally sound reasoning. If I remember correctly, you haven't always spoken this way."

"I have never changed my mind," said Lucien, "and now less than ever."

Napoleon intoned a fanfare: "Ta, ta, ta! Ta, ta, ta! . . . Since when are you so exemplary? There was a time when you would have disliked even appearing to be exemplary."

Lucien replied: "Certainly, if you believed anything that our common enemies have spouted against me, at a certain time, I would be nothing less than a lying libertine. However, the truth is that I am no more of a libertine than any others, and perhaps am even much less of one."

Napoleon said cheerfully: "To whom is this addressed? To Joseph or to me?"

Lucien answered in an equally cheerful tone: "To neither the one nor the other. Please note that I said 'others' in the plural."

Joseph said: "I understand. To both."

Lucien was laughing. "Perhaps; but I refrain in any case to blame my venerable elder brothers."

Napoleon turned to Joseph. "Anyone who were to see or hear us would certainly consider him the wisest of us three, although he is the youngest."

The three Corsican brothers began to muse about female beauty, and in particular about the graces of the actress Mademoiselle Georges, much appreciated by both Napoleon and Lucien, who might both have been her lovers. A few salacious remarks later, the first consul returned to the main question at hand: "By the way, Citizen Lucien, what instructions should I give Talleyrand regarding Queen Maria Luisa?"

"Do me the favor, Citizen Consul, of not following up on this business."

"What? You want to make me dance this pantomime? After having welcomed her advances and responded in the way I have. . . . You are mad!"

"I would in fact be, if I—"

"Have you decided to test my patience? . . . I count on you, Joseph, to make him become reasonable. Come on! . . . the queen has nothing abnormal about her, I know her well, and I ended up finding her quite pleasant. She is a very proper lady. . . ."

"Ah! Ah! Ah! 'A very proper lady!' Ah! Ah! Ah!"

"I don't understand what is so laughable about pointing out such qualities in a marriageable woman."

Lucien had a hard time containing his hilarity. Joseph joined in the laughter but soon tried to regain his composure, fearing the consul's anger with Lucien (not so much with himself), and interjected that the queen was absolutely not deformed.

Napoleon brusquely dismissed the brothers: "As for Lucien, I give him three days to think and tell me whether he wants to take advantage of my intervention or refuse it; but in this case, I would rather that he not regret it." On these words, he shut the door to his cabinet. The two brothers were left alone in the antechamber.

BETWEEN BROTHERS

On their way back to Paris in Joseph's carriage—Malmaison was about an hour away—Lucien expected to be lectured on the subject that Napoleon had brought up. The allegedly superb marriage plan annoyed him on many levels. Napoleon's offer was unacceptable not only because it positively irked his liberal views but also because, for Lucien, there was no more degrading position than that of husband to a reigning queen, since, ordinarily, a man was supposed to be his wife's protector. It would be humiliating to be the first courtier of one's wife: The king-in-waiting, the adventurer who had married a queen was not the role he had in mind for himself. Especially if that queen was a Bourbon, the dynastic nemesis for the convinced republican that Lucien remained. So he went on, attempting to convince Joseph on these highly principled grounds that his refusal could not be countered. Lucien was sure that Napoleon would be pushing him off the scene forever, thus getting him out of the way by forcing his marriage plan upon him. Joseph listened and acquiesced, even though he had not been opposed to the notion of Lucien marrying a queen: It was desirable that a Bonaparte should use marriage for social elevation. Lucien might want to consider Talleyrand's niece, for instance, or perhaps Lafayette's daughter—Washington's friend certainly would not have turned down the offer of Lucien as a son-in-law, if he had received it.

As Joseph went on outlining all the marriage options, Lucien decided that it was time to tell his eldest brother the truth and explain his circumstances more concretely. Alexandrine—Mme Jouberthon, as he prudently referred to her—was no obstacle. Joseph was at once startled and relieved, until Lucien added that she made any of these marriage plans impossible, for "I am no longer free. We married secretly, but as legitimately as can be, before the Church." To Joseph's initial disappointment and hurtful denial of the significance of a moral and religious marriage, Lucien could only exclaim "Ah! my brother! my brother!" after which Joseph, sensitive as he was to his brother's predicament, admitted not only that Lucien was right but also that their mother had already told him everything. She knew, as did Joseph, that Lucien and Alexandrine were now awaiting the death certificate of M. Jouberthon: that seemed to be the only impediment to the civil ceremony, which, given Napoleon's plan, was now urgently necessary.

Once the brothers had reached the Hôtel de Brienne, Joseph was not ready to continue on toward his home: He wanted first, and without delay, to be introduced to Lucien's wife—in formal terms, as her brother-in-law. They had already met once, at Le Plessis, but things had changed since then and, more important, he had not yet met their infant son. When he saw little Charles, he embraced him tenderly, and impulsively decided that his elder daughter Zénaïde, still an infant, should eventually be betrothed to him.

꧁ ꧂

Lucien was aware of Napoleon's stature as a great statesman. But stature certainly did not put him beyond the reach of criticism, and it was not only as a republican but also as a husband that Lucien profoundly reproached his brother for his stubborn, cold-hearted unwillingness to accept Alexandrine into the family. Napoleon was not alone in this view. After inviting himself back to the Hôtel de Brienne with his wife, Julie Clary, Joseph told Lucien what was already clear to him—that, besides their mother, Julie was the only woman in the family who did not disapprove of Alexandrine. Joséphine, who knew exactly how to influence Napoleon and to steer his emotions, objected in particular. Older and less attractive than Alexandrine, she resented Lucien's headstrong independence, which she thought posed a threat to her husband. In fact, she had made a point of telling Lucien of Napoleon's recurrent nightmare in which Lucien was coming after him at the head of an angry, terrifying rabble of the revolutionary populace, or *sans-culottes,* to violently chase him out of the king's Tuileries Palace. Whether this was a way for Joséphine to manipulate Napoleon's brothers or whether the first consul really did have such a dream, it is true that he would never forget a similar moment that he had witnessed as a very young man: the mob's storming of the same palace in 1789, as King Louis XVI was being seized. And all this, as Lucien said to Joseph, even though he had never offended Napoleon and had always reacted rather mildly to "his aggressions and the cloying perfidies" of Joséphine.

Once Joseph had left the Hôtel de Brienne, Lucien decided to keep all these troublesome thoughts to himself and not to tell Alexandrine about Napoleon's royal marriage proposal, since she might have felt he was sacrificing himself for her. The tensions were so high among the Bonapartes at the time that, even though Alexandrine was strong enough to bear them, he would have had no desire to make her position any more uncomfortable and insecure than it already was. Moreover, his painful tête-à-tête at Malmaison was about him, his freedom, and his relationship with the first consul; it was not about her, and it was not about love. It addressed matters of personal honor, principle, and political choice; and it enacted yet again the old pattern so familiar in the Bonaparte family history, in which Lucien's will was firmly set against Napoleon's.

In any case, he had made up his mind about Alexandrine the day he had met her, and was not about to change it. And so, four days after the meeting at Malmaison, Lucien grudgingly set out to take his response to Napoleon; a longer delay might have seemed like hesitation on his part. The first consul was returning to the Tuileries, and cannons thundered throughout Paris to announce his arrival there at nine in the morning.

Lucien presented himself at the palace before noon, arriving at the consul's cabinet to witness him sipping a large, strong lemonade, prescribed to him by his personal physician, Corvisart, to temper his acrid humors. Lucien found Napoleon in excellent mood, merrily teasing Corvisart, a favorite by now, about the impotence of medicine. The doctor took his leave after amusedly stating his full agreement with the consul's judgment. Without wasting a minute, Napoleon addressed his brother. "So, Lucien, have you thought about your important business?"[19] Lucien replied that he had purposely come to talk about it, as they had agreed, since Napoleon had not wanted to accept what he had said the first time round. However, he was no more inclined now than then to marry anyone suggested to him, although he was nevertheless very grateful for Napoleon's good intention.

Napoleon's initial reaction was disingenuous: He feigned surprise, as if Lucien's refusal were entirely unexpected. But soon the consul's features drew into a look of intense fury. Lucien remained quiet at first, aware that an outburst was sure to follow; then he reminded his brother that he should have expected this response, given all that had been said between them in the presence of Joseph. At that point, Napoleon's countenance changed radically: The lines of his severe, usually calm face contracted into a menacing grimace, and he exploded: "But you really are very fond of that woman, aren't you?"

Lucien did not dignify this rhetorical question with an answer. Napoleon was now spewing horrific invective and crude insults against the woman he hated so much. Lucien could not remain calm any longer; his self-control vanished. In a tone that was as provocative as was Napoleon's, he burst out, giving vent to his exasperation and outrage at his powerful brother's dishonesty and unfairness.

"That woman? You know very well the opposite of what you say about her, yes, you know it better than anyone!"

Napoleon stuttered and blushed, visibly embarrassed. "Me? Me? Me? I don't know her, that woman. I've never even spoken to her, and—"

That was a half-truth, or half-lie: Napoleon had indeed never spoken to Alexandrine, but he had seen and coveted her enough to invite her to a party that she had deliberately not attended. Now he chose to pretend that the woman of whom he had once spoken to Lucien, whose great beauty he had admired so much, was an entirely unknown entity, a loose woman unworthy even of the lowliest consideration. Lucien did not need to hear any more; he stormed out of the first consul's office.

ᘒᘒ ᘒᘒ

For some weeks after this, the two brothers did not communicate at all. One day in July, Joseph told Lucien about Napoleon's plan to institute regional senatorships, nominating senators to represent the government throughout the French territories. He was willing to name Lucien senator of Treviri, a German town near the confluence of the Mosel and Rhine rivers, occupied by the French since 1794. Lucien was surprised at first by what seemed an unexpected favor, but he soon realized that Napoleon had found a new way of removing him from the capital and of attempting to pull him away from Alexandrine. He told Joseph he was flattered enough to be one of Napoleon's chosen, given how cold the first consul had been with him and the extent to which he kept him away from political affairs—so much so that Lucien was disgusted with politics altogether. The offer was attractive to him: Much as Napoleon wanted him out of town, Lucien too wanted to get away, and if Napoleon was serious about this offer then yes, the senatorship of Treviri would be his first choice: He loved that part of the world (which he had seen when he had been sent north with Christine).

Joseph conveyed Lucien's response to Napoleon—but only its last, enthusiastic part. Napoleon summoned Lucien to see him. Lucien thanked him for the opportunity he was being offered with sincerity and even a measure of affection. He could not hide his astonishment at the offer, however. Napoleon asked him: "Did you not say to Joseph that you preferred this senatorship in Treviri to all others?" "I must admit I am very surprised." Napoleon proceeded to explain to his brother his cynical plan to take advantage of the ambitions of elected senators and prefects, in a move to replace aristocratic hereditary titles. Lucien smiled: These senatorships sounded like sinecures where talent would play no role, he told Napoleon, who agreed with the judgment. But he hastened to add, "There are exceptions—like yourself; I will pick some of my old buddies, their splendid obsolescence will ensure that the sacred flame of hope keeps burning in the hearts of your colleagues."[20]

This last sentence was pronounced with an ironic tone that reminded Lucien of an actor of the time known as Fleury (his real name was Abraham Joseph Bénard), who made his name playing patrician con men. Lucien was disgusted but kept his thoughts to himself, smiled, and managed to take leave of the first consul without a fight. He went straight back home, to tell Alexandrine the good news. She was no less stunned by this sudden change in Napoleon's disposition than Lucien and was delighted at the prospect of living far from Paris, away from its spies and intrigues. She started daydreaming about the trip they had never been able to have—the Rhine would be their Thibouville. But Lucien would have to leave before her to set up their residence in a château he had found near Bonn. This first separation since their meeting, albeit only a few weeks long, was going to be painful.

Having made all the necessary preparations for his departure, Lucien went to say a perfunctory good-bye to his brother and to his sister-in-law Joséphine, who was pleased at the prospect of Lucien leaving. Back at the Hôtel de Brienne, he bade tearful adieux to his wife, his daughters and son, and his mother Letizia, the only family member allowed to use the secret passage connecting the palace with Alexandrine's apartment. Letizia, who was eager for her son to declare his marriage publicly, was upset that Lucien was leaving without Alexandrine; he reassured her, promising that he would soon be in touch with good news. In the meantime, he made her promise to visit his wife and baby regularly, with the pretext of seeing the girls and using the *souterrain conjugal* to which she had the key. Everything was set now. But just as he was about to leave, he received a frantic visit from his friend Briot.

Pierre-Joseph Briot, a republican whom Lucien had met in his early days at the Council of the Five-Hundred, went out of his way to help Lucien, because he owed him his life. At the time of the "machine infernale"—the failed terrorist attack on the first consul—Briot, a former Jacobin, had risked being included in the group of men sent by Napoleon to starve in the desolate heat of Sinnamary. Lucien, ambassador in Spain at the time, had tried to save as many of his friends as he could from deportation. Although he had not succeeded in convincing Napoleon of their innocence, he did manage to ensure that Briot became chief of police of his native eastern department of Doubs. (By 1802, he represented the French government on the Italian island of Elba.)

That day Briot was joyous: He had finally managed to obtain the death certificate of Alexandrine's husband. The missing paper had been the main obstacle to the civil marriage of Lucien and Alexandrine—the only marriage of any legal value. Lucien wanted to arrange a hasty ceremony before leaving for Germany, but Briot dissuaded him, promising that he would make sure that upon Lucien's return, all the logistical details would be worked out for the couple to marry at Le Plessis. When he told Lucien of Napoleon's order that all mayors of France be forbidden from officiating the marriage, Lucien was incensed. His first, impulsive response was to say he would test the ban and Napoleon's commitment to treating him with such temerity. But Briot insisted that the ceremony should and could wait, and he left for Le Plessis to arrange things.[21]

Lucien departed right away for Bonn, traveling in the company of old friends—the painter Lethière, his doctor Paroisse, and a few others.[22] The trip was swift and the July weather pleasant. The ancient castle overlooked the Rhine. It was located in a picturesque village near Bonn and surrounded by a beautiful park that Alexandrine would appreciate. The building was of a simple, noble architecture. He and Lethière visited its every corner. It was extremely run down and would require extensive renovations, costing, an architect told him, at least half a million francs. This was far too expensive an undertaking, and Lucien decided against it. Instead he put away a few old pieces of furniture from the dilapidated manor and some pictures that Lethière noticed in the attic. He then received the various local authorities and met with a few of the town's attractive ladies, promising himself to introduce them to his wife—he was already imagining a social life that might replace to some degree the brilliance of Parisian salons.

But while Lucien was busy setting up his new residence, he received a letter from Briot, who, in a postscript, wrote that his mother was urging him to return as soon as possible.[23] No explanation followed.

Lucien was distressed by this cryptic message. He rushed back to Paris immediately, with his entourage. It was a pleasure to greet his wife and children after those weeks away. Alexandrine informed him that Letizia had sent her the family's faithful Corsican servant Saveria to reassure her, but that she and his mother would see each other only from the safety of her carriage, where she would use the usual hand greeting. She had not given any explanation for this either.

Letizia was visibly relieved to see Lucien. They sat down in the palace, and she told him what was afoot. As fearless as she thought she was, she had experienced a big fright—in the secret tunnel that she had been using to see Alexandrine and little Charles. She had never liked it: It was dark and humid, and she often found herself startled by her own shadow in that narrow passage. One day, as she was carefully walking behind Saveria, who was holding a candle, she saw from the corner of her eye not the usual flickering shadows but the silhouette of a man, wearing a round hat and a cape as dark as the walls, against which he leaned, clearly in order not to be seen. It was terrifying. Saveria had already passed the shady figure, and Letizia found herself alone before him. She stopped and decided to engage him, believing that, in such a narrow space, she would be able to negotiate a way out, especially if he was a thief. But she was soon reassured—the man was more frightened than she. He desperately tried to hide his face behind the cape and fled, like a hare, nearly extinguishing Saveria's candle. Just then Saveria caught sight of the intruder. She was convinced this was a ghost, whom she dubbed Babbo Taddeo di Bastia, the name of her godfather, who had died a few days earlier. Letizia watched the "ghost" flee through the courtyard overlooked by Alexandrine's apartment and went straight home. She told no one about the incident but decided never to use the tunnel again, and prohibited Alexandrine from doing so as well.

Lucien knew his mother as a courageous woman and took what she said seriously. This piece of news deeply upset him: It meant that Fouché's spy knew everything and that the tunnel was no longer secret. He called upon Paroisse to shut it down and, removing the security locks on either end, seal the doors. When Paroisse, along with the owner of the passage, ventured into the tunnel to do the job, he tripped over an object that lay on the dirt.

In the darkness he could not see what it was. He casually picked it up, doing his best not to attract the attention of the owner, and saw that it was a silver spur. He pocketed it and brought it at once to Lucien. They examined it: It had evidently fallen off the boot of the mystery man. It bore initials that they could not decipher at first. Eventually, the letters emerged: "L. M."

Lucien told the whole story to Alexandrine, who became alarmed. If the "ghost" had run into her rather than Letizia—they reasoned together— he might have hurt or kidnapped her. His plan might have been to take her away on a horse left in the vicinity. This was a dangerous situation and called for urgent measures. Briot made some discreet inquiries about the man Letizia had seen in the passage, whom she described as tall and athletic. There was a servant in the Hôtel de Brienne whom Briot suspected of spying, a short and fat man nicknamed La Jeunesse. Briot had kept an eye on him and determined that he could not possibly have stolen any of the keys to the passage. But he quickly figured out that the mystery man was Jean Le Marois, one of Napoleon's most trusted aides. This intelligence work had been ordered straight from the top.

Fearing that this turn of events might delay their much-awaited marriage proceedings, Lucien drove with Alexandrine to Le Plessis, where Briot had managed to organize the clandestine ceremony. Letizia stayed behind in Paris. The couple remained in the country long enough to drop out of sight of the consul's gossipy court and zealous police. The civil marriage was celebrated on October 26, 1803. The only witnesses were the inspector of the local forests, two peasants, and one doctor. Sometime later, Lucien wrote a letter to Napoleon announcing the act, keeping his earlier promise that he would notify his brother of any marriage he undertook.

> *My very dear brother,*
>
> *I would be failing in my duty if I did not hasten to inform you, as I do our mother and our brother Joseph, of my marriage at the municipality with the widow Mrs. Jouberthon de Vambertie, daughter of Mr. de Bleschamp, commissioner of the marine at St. Malo.*
>
> *Given that this union, forged over a year ago at the foot of altars, according to the rites of the Catholic religion, was not able to be legalized on account of circumstances that I offer, my dear brother, to explain to you if you so wish, it has had to remain*

secret. I dare and have reason to hope that this sacred and indissoluble tie will provide
a thoroughly legitimate excuse for my not accepting the marriage proposals you had the
goodness to effect on my behalf. That it was impossible for me to do so has not prevented
me from feeling deeply the gratitude I owe you for them, my dear brother; do I need to
assure you that my wife, filled as I am with the admiration that is owed you, is extremely
eager to have the joy of expressing to you and to my sister-in-law the feelings of a sister
who is as wholly devoted as she will always be.

Your brother Lucien[24]

Lucien enclosed this letter in another one addressed to Duroc, the field commander he most liked of Napoleon's close collaborators. Then he jumped
into the carriage with his wife and moved straight into their Parisian palace,
where the girls were eager to welcome Alexandrine as their new mother and
the servants to welcome her as the mistress of the house. There was no more
talk of settling in Germany for the senatorship, although Lucien kept his
title—and its income.

SLEEPLESS IN PARIS

Lucien and Alexandrine were fast asleep when, at around three o'clock one
November morning, they were rudely awakened by a loud knock on the
door. It was Pedro, their faithful valet de chambre, announcing Général Murat, who had arrived in great haste from Malmaison, on behalf of Napoleon,
of course, and had to speak with *Monsiou* right then.[25]

Alexandrine, startled by the visit, was at once apprehensive and reassured
that the visitor was the friendly Murat. Lucien got up, wide awake, and went
to meet him in the antechamber, in his nightshirt. Murat was in high uniform. "Well, here you are," Lucien told the visitor. "What in the world do
you want from me at this time of night?"

Murat grinned rather oddly, in that way he had when he was about to
say something unpleasant. And as he took Lucien's hand, more affectionately
than usual—as if he were about to express condolences of some sort—he
began, "I'm not bringing any news, actually. Rather, a response to the one
you gave to the Général. A commission . . . How shall I put it? Goodness, it
is rather disagreeable that he ordered me to convey it, since I gather it isn't

worth anything. . . ." "Hm, are you sure?" replied Lucien. "We'll see. But, please, first sit, we must sit."

Murat composed himself. He now would have to speak in Napoleon's stead. "First of all, how is my sister-in-law? Ha, ungrateful brat that you are! Not worthy of your secrets am I? Bad, very bad of you—I've shared all my secrets with you! But, well, I forgive you. Anyway it has hardly been a well-kept secret—you don't imagine I didn't know? And I certainly wouldn't be one of those who don't congratulate you! I want my sister-in-law to know that, all right?" Lucien replied, "Fine, in any case she is already sure of it since your name alone did not trouble her in the least, even at this time of night. But let's get down to business: What is your heavy burden?"

Murat said, "Yes, well, I have to tell you, don't I. Hm. The Général— sorry, the First Consul, the old habit you know, so, he says that, in matters of congratulations, he is not sending you any. . . . You do understand?"

"Not really, no—not if you don't speak more clearly. Please speak up, no fear!"

"Well. My dear Lucien. He means—he wants me to tell you that he does not acknowledge your marriage."

"Well, my dear Joachim! How do you think I ought to respond to *this?*"

"You are certainly smart enough not to need me to dictate your reply! This is trouble enough, breaking the news to you like this. Why the devil does he want me to mix in, what possessed him to ask me to do this? Look, I am just fulfilling a commission, that's all, what more can I say."

"Yes, indeed—right. But isn't this a little complicated? How did he tell you to tell me? You have to tell all. Do."

"You must be joking. But as for me, I assure you very sternly, this is truly unpleasant. What you ask me, I have already told you. And since you wish me to repeat it to you, he would like you to know that he does not acknowl-edge your marriage."

"This is just as clear as the first time around and to this, my dear Joachim, I respond no less clearly that I will do without his acknowledgment as much as I do without his permission."

Murat grinned unpleasantly again. "Ouch! It would be rather hard for me to repeat that. That devil of a man, you see. I'm not afraid of him, but he imposes himself terribly. I did not even dare refuse this commission, if you only knew how much it costs me. . . ."

"Console yourself, my good Joachim, because I would rather that he chose you over someone else I would not have received as well as you. It would have been unjust on my part, since in the end, with you military people, your first and only duty is to obey."

"It is, damn it! True. And it is not the most beautiful profession. On the battlefield, it can work. *À la guerre comme à la guerre,* it goes. But in the family . . . Because in the end, Lucien, you are my brother just as much as he is . . . always my good brother, you. Oh! It's very painful to think about."

"Come on, come on! Don't get all teary on me, my dear Joachim, give me a hug, and tell me in detail how it happened. Was he furious?"

"I'll tell you. But let's begin from the beginning, to avoid confusion. I will be sincere, I warn you, and then you will tell me what I should tell him."

Murat passed his hand over his forehead a few times, and recounted what had happened. "Just imagine" he began,

the concert was at its climax at Malmaison. The First Consul, who until that moment had seemed not to make much of the music, had perhaps taken a little nap. (It's simple: he never sleeps when the others do, so sleep takes its dues whenever it wants. . . .) Anyway, he had woken up for the *allegro* of the horn and harp concerto—and he had a good reason to, since it is such a gorgeous piece—when Duroc, who was standing at the door, was given a letter by Rustan, opened it and passed it into the hands of the Consul, who sat next to his wife. I was seated behind them. I could see that the letter he had opened and returned to Duroc contained another one which the Consul ripped open. He had hardly read the first line, than to my great astonishment and to that of the general public, but mostly that of his wife, he stood up and shouted with a booming, commander's voice, as if to be heard by all his legions: *Stop the music! Stop!*

The silence of the musicians had preceded the end of his antimusical shout and everybody was stupefied, as you can easily imagine. *Entre nous,* my dear, the Général looked like a madman. He was marching around the room, rotating his arms, which he never does, like a telegraph, repeating, with a lower voice: *Betrayal! Betrayal! It is a true betrayal!* The scene was becoming tragic, so comic it

was: Madame Bonaparte, her face pale despite the red and white on it (you know
that she makes herself up with white and even with blue), became painfully rigid.
She approached her husband and said: *My God, Bonaparte! What is going on?* I, as
everybody else, was frozen. The whole family, that is, our wives (Madame Mère
had excused herself) barely dared to move or lift their eyes. A dozen other ladies
with their husbands were equally aghast. You have no idea what it was like. The
musicians should have been painted, their instruments mute, their mouths and
eyes wide open, some with glasses, some without, some looking down at the floor,
tightening their lips in order not to laugh, depending on how they interpreted the
situation. Can you picture this? It's impossible. And it's not the best of it—or the
worst of it, as you'll see.

We were still left wondering in silence what extraordinary matter could have
caused all this, and the ladies kept asking "O my God! What is going on?" when the
Consul, crumpling violently the letter he held in his hands, and with a voice made
jerky by his fury but loud enough to be heard by everyone: *"What happened? What's
going on? Well . . . Know that Lucien has married his . . . his mistress!"*

Lucien later heard from another person who had been present that evening
that Murat had the delicacy of sparing him the word Napoleon had actually used to designate Alexandrine—not "mistress" but "*coquine,*" or "bitch."
Murat pranced nervously around the room, muttering that he would have
given up anything for this not to have happened. "Really, the Général behaved very badly. And the worst is that I don't know how it's going to end
between the two of you." "Don't worry about me," said Lucien. "If he wants
to persecute me, I am still capable of resisting him." Lucien told him briefly
about the ways in which Napoleon had tried to terrorize Alexandrine, the
nasty anonymous letters, the spies, the silver spur, its initials. Murat knew
well the "ghost" and was shocked by these stories. He told Lucien how Joséphine had reacted to the news of Lucien's marriage: The beautiful widow was
not the woman she had in mind for him, and her aversion to Alexandrine
could only be explained this way. But given Napoleon's extreme and sudden,
public outburst, she had feared some tragedy had happened. When she realized that it was merely a response to Lucien's letter, she looked as if she were
about to exclaim "What? That's all? That's the reason for the fright you've

given us?" After this, Napoleon and his entourage left the theater. Back in his office with Murat, the first consul sat at his desk; he began writing a letter, tore up the page, exclaimed, "No! No letter!" And addressing himself to Murat, he said: "I prefer to send you; but tell him on my behalf . . ." "But to whom?" "What do you mean, to whom? To Citizen Lucien, my dear brother, and your friend; that's why I've chosen you. So, go tell him that—" "But it's very late." "Good, you'll wake him up, and you'll tell him everything I've told you."

And that was the message Lucien had heard at three in the morning. "Did he say anything else besides what you've already transmitted?" Lucien asked. "Oh much more, accusing you of betrayal, lying, ingratitude, what do I know. Especially insisting that I tell you your marriage was invalid, that he'd prove that to you, that he had good reason to be sure of it. I've never seen him so frenzied. I left without saying anything else, I didn't know what to answer." "That was wrong," replied Lucien. "You could have asked him why my marriage was invalid." Murat said: "You're funny, Lucien. Do you think one can contradict him in any way? If I'd asked him that, he would have understood perfectly well that I did not believe a word of what he was saying. And you're undoubtedly even more convinced than I am. But I warn you, he's riding on this invalidity business in such a way you'll have trouble having him dismount."

Lucien suddenly realized that Napoleon could be so confident only if he was unaware that Lucien had gotten a hold of M. Jouberthon's death certificate, despite the obstacles the first consul had set against his obtaining it. Murat thought that might indeed be the case. Napoleon was wrong—everyone knew that the general was wrong, he said, but no one would dare tell him so. Nor would Murat himself. "Really," replied Lucien. "Well then, my dear coward, I pity you. So tell him that I am sincerely sorry—" "Excellent, yes, go on" "—sorry that a marriage I have judged necessary to my happiness should not be to his liking." "Very good, very good, thank you, thank you." "—to his liking. But—" "No but! Please Lucien, no but!" "Well, let me finish. But that my wife and I—" "Ouch." Murat grimaced. Lucien continued: "Listen up: My wife and I nonetheless express our feeling of the most tender and devoted fraternity. Happy now?" "Not bad, not bad. Tender and devoted, that's good. But if he asks me what you said about the invalidity of your marriage, what do I answer?" "To that, my dear, you will tell him that I don't believe there is any cause of invalidity in my marriage since I've had ample time to think about it, given the zeal of his police." "But, Lucien, I can't say that," Murat replied. "As you wish; but you can't not tell him the main thing, that if by chance he were to seek and find cause to invalidate my marriage, then I would hurry to marry again, ensuring that nothing is missing from the ceremony." "Ahi ahi!" exclaimed Murat. "You are compromising my status as ambassador; seriously, you know I can't say this." "But you know that I cannot answer in any other way. Come on, pick your fight. *Ambassadeur ne porte pas peine.*" (Ambassadors are not at fault.) Murat, defeated, shrugged. "Yes, that's true. But you pity me, don't you? You're right. I hope my sister-in-law won't hold it against me. My respects to her, and let her know this is not my fault. Good-bye then."

After two hours of intense conversation, Lucien went back to bed. Alexandrine awaited him there, quite calm about the situation. They spent much of the rest of the night talking about their position in the world as a couple, now that Napoleon's disapproval was known so publicly.

PUPPET THEATER

Later that morning, Letizia rushed to see Lucien and Alexandrine, whom she adamantly supported.[26] She was deeply unhappy about Napoleon's public opposition to a marriage she found no reason to disapprove of and encouraged Lucien to be indifferent to his brother, urging Lucien not to dramatize the situation. She was sure that, sooner or later, the first consul would come to his senses and realize that he had no more right to influence Lucien's marital choice than Lucien had to influence Napoleon's own. (Letizia herself had disapproved of Joséphine mainly because of her age—she was six years older than Napoleon—but would not have done anything to prevent the marriage.) Moreover, Alexandrine was well enough born, educated, and not deserving of Napoleon's ill will. With enough prudence and patience, eventually Letizia would overcome those who thought they would benefit from a rupture between the two brothers: She was their mother and would arrange it all. For Alexandrine, still an admirer of the great man and sorry to inspire such hate in her brother-in-law, Letizia had simple words: "Console yourself. Once he will know you, he will love you."

Just before noon, another visit was announced: the lawyer Jean-Jacques-Régis de Cambacérès, second consul in the government. Letizia had no desire to see the man, who in any case would surely speak more freely without the presence of Mme Mère, so she swiftly departed, whisking Alexandrine away with her. The great Mlle Georges was performing that night at the Théâtre des Français, and Lucien and Alexandrine would finally be appearing there. It was to be a grand event—their first public appearance as a married couple—and Letizia, who had agreed with Lucien it would be best for her not to attend, was eager to see her new daughter-in-law's outfit.

Lucien therefore received his visitor alone. They sat on the very sofa where Lucien had talked with Murat just a few hours before. It had been a long night. And it was stretching into the day, Lucien realized as Cambacérès began to speak. "I've come charged by the First Consul," he declaimed, with a majestically mannered tilting of his head, "with a mission important enough that he thought it necessary to entrust me with it." He was dressed as formally as he spoke: The first consul insisted on a strict dress code to receive, which consisted of white silk stockings, shoes, and buckles. (Lucien had established a contrasting code—trousers and boots—that suited his style better.)

Cambacérès was the author of the Civil Law Code, which would later become the Code Napoléon. Lucien admired his legislative talents while not forgetting that this moderate revolutionary had nevertheless voted for the death of King Louis XVI. (Cambacérès's brother, archbishop of Rouen, spent the rest of his life holding Masses and gathering alms to expiate the sin of his sibling.) Lucien knew that the magistrate's impressively well-trained tongue might trip him into some unforeseen trap. But he could not help finding him an annoying, comical character: Cambacérès was vain and self-important, a flamboyant homosexual accustomed to taking walks in the Palais Royal galleries, behatted and dressed to the hilt in his grand uniform of second consul, escorted by two humble aristocrats who flanked him on either side like courtesans, solemnly keeping pace with their companion, whose famously gourmet proclivities they shared.

As Cambacérès completed his sentence, he shook his head in greeting, to which Lucien politely responded. Cambacérès saluted again, seemingly embarrassed, and continued with some difficulty, avoiding Lucien's gaze: "This is a marriage that, if I may say so, does not have the approval of the First Consul." Lucien informed the grand magistrate that he had received that very message from his brother-in-law in the middle of the night. "I know, but the First Consul thought that, as a jurist and considering my devotion to him in particular and to all the members of his family, I could indicate to him the means . . . no, I mean the causes of the invalidity of an act that, for reasons of high politics, it is desirable you consider null and void." Lucien laughed sneeringly and described the second consul's mission as "shameful," asking him how he himself would respond to such words. Cambacérès vacillated for a moment, but his pedantry saved him: He talked of "goodwill," said that in Lucien's place he would do anything not to sadden the great man that was Napoleon, on whose shoulders weighed the destiny of France. Lucien, unimpressed, told him to convey to Napoleon the "sincere displeasure I feel at being unable to be happy without making him unhappy."

There was nothing left to say, or to hear. Lucien was about to ring a bell to adjourn the pointless encounter when Cambacérès gently and politely blocked his arm, promising the possibility of an agreement and requesting a moment of patience. Then Cambacérès rose and took from his pocket a wallet of green satin, with a pink lining. While he was fiddling with it, in search of the document that would resolve all disputes, Lucien looked at him, wondering what could possibly motivate the man's actions: How could this pompous character bear to subject himself to such embarrassment and to the risk of alienating forever a young man of his—Lucien's—political talents and promise? Lucien still believed he would again be helpful to his country, no less than was the refined regicide who stood before him.

Finally Cambacérès recalled that the paper he was searching for was in another wallet; after apologizing for having made Lucien wait, he asked for the formal permission to speak. He began a solemnly patriotic, legalistically baroque discourse, still not looking Lucien in the eye—as if he were arguing a case in court. "There is no point for any of us to resist the will of a great man whose genius has no equal, and whose power, I foretell, will only

grow each day," he said. Lucien replied that he was nonetheless determined
to fight tyrannical whims, especially when these impinged on his legitimate
affections. The lawyer tried to argue back that some family subordination
was due—if Lucien did not comply, his situation would become dangerous,
or at least uncomfortable. It was a diplomatic reprimand that sounded like a
scarcely veiled menace. Lucien was riled. To the magistrate's declaration that
Napoleon had felt "insolently duped" by his brother, Lucien replied that,
when the proposal to wed the queen of Etruria had come up, he had made
use of equivocal statements regarding his marital status in order to protect
himself until the obstacles Napoleon had put in place against his legal nuptials would be lifted—after all, his police had acted fraudulently by hiding
away the death certificate of M. Jouberthon. To himself, Lucien felt no need
to justify his white lies: He had legitimately defended himself from a brother
who made use of his superior power against him and Alexandrine simply because he had not obtained the favors of the lovely woman Lucien had had the
gall to win. Of that, Lucien was certain. Jealousy was a strong enough motive
for this mess. There was a long history of it between the two Bonapartes.

Cambacérès seemed surprised by Lucien's confidence that he had won
the battle of wits with his brother. But Lucien no longer cared. The exchange
had gone on long enough. He rose, in another gesture to dismiss the visitor,
boldly declaring that he felt fully justified in his behavior against the "unjust
and denatured adversary who doesn't fear exerting tyranny over a brother
who owes him nothing and to whom he owes a lot." Lucien had simply
protected the woman of his life from persecution. Courteously, Cambacérès
replied: "All this is unfortunate indeed, my dear senator, and I am sure the
First Consul has nothing to do with it; such a great man has other things
on his mind than woman hassles." Lucien replied: "Indeed, this is apparent
from the charming message you are bringing today on his behalf. What an
absurd conceit! To dare hope he'll be able to make me abandon my wife!! . . .
a wife no one imposed on me, who has brought with her neither dowry, nor
army command."

Cambacérès still showed no sign of relenting, or of leaving. Waving the
piece of paper he had been looking for, he said he would not depart until he
had submitted "this little project" to Lucien. "I must confess I had to work

hard to find a legal and honorable means . . ." Lucien immediately understood: This was a plan to unmarry him—and, he exclaimed, to find a way of doing so without his or his wife's dying was as much a feat as squaring the circle. Still, his curiosity was piqued. Cambacérès finally intoned his proposal: It was the adoption of a law establishing that all marriages contracted by a member of the consular family without Napoleon's previous approval would be considered null and void. Lucien's first reaction was to assert that he recognized no "consular family"; and he asked his learned visitor on what grounds the head of the republic should also be considered the head of the family—especially as it had always been Joseph who played that role. Such matters were established under the ancient kings of France, argued Cambacérès; Lucien countered that these were not the Middle Ages.

It was now clear to Lucien that his resistance was as much a matter of political principle as it was one of private self-preservation and preservation of privacy; or, rather, that his self-preservation had become a matter of political principle. But the exchange continued, becoming increasingly heated, with the seasoned lawyer and the young senator each trying to outsmart the other, the elder using a consistently courteous tone, the younger confidently impertinent, unwilling to hide his contempt for the man and his message. Cambacérès argued that Napoleon had the right to prevent either male or female persons he disliked from entering his family. Lucien rebutted: "I don't think you would have me believe, Citizen Consul, that politics, that is, the interests of the Republic, have anything to do with my marriage, or my marriage with the Republic; in a word, I swear I believe you don't think a word of what you say." Cambacérès seemed chastened for an instant, but he did not let go. He began to talk about the religious sacrament of marriage being preserved even once the civilian contract was dissolved. To his statement that his new law project could be applied retroactively to this case, Lucien jeered at the magistrate, telling him he was "becoming sublime" in his defense of a law he might want to consecrate as the first of the civil code he was devising with the first consul. He then suggested that they should apply the same project of law to American presidential families, so that no sibling of Washington or Jefferson be allowed to marry without their approval. To this witty remark the legislator blushed. Then—as if forgetful he had voted to kill the king—he pronounced America a different kind of republic from France, which, planted as it was in the heart of old Europe, would not tolerate being too isolated from the monarchic governments that surrounded it.

Lucien managed to preserve his sense of irony before this absurdly earnest man. But it seemed as if the painful conversation would never end. Under his polite exterior, Cambacérès was proving a determined but ultimately ineffective boa constrictor whose mission was to suffocate Lucien within the coils of arguments that fed on nothing but their own power. And despite their legalistic tone, Cambacérès was practicing the cheapest form of politics, with his legal training merely ensuring that no argument would defeat his for long. The man was brilliant, in his way. But while Lucien had felt some respect for him before this encounter, he now found Cambacérès vile, a snake indeed who crept close to the roots of power, and not a true statesman—for whom politics should be the art of governing rather than satisfying the passions of those who governed.

Finally Lucien extricated himself by getting hold of the bell and ringing it as loudly as he could. Excusing himself, he told his visitor that he would not want to delay any longer the delivery of his response to the first consul. Lucien opted not to tell his wife about the conversation, which he thought might distress her even more than it had him. He did inform his mother, who agreed with him that it should remain unmentioned.

Outwardly, the day proceeded as if nothing had happened. Friends came to pay their compliments to the newlywed couple. They decided to try to live as normal a life as possible and go to the theater that evening as planned. Lucien was determined not to let his brother run his life in any way; and he was convinced that Napoleon would never become powerful enough to persecute him more than he already had.

News about the rift between the brothers spread very quickly in gossipy Paris.[27] Lucien and his beautiful wife were immediately the talk of the town. Napoleon's popularity was at its apogee, yet no one quite understood what drove him to oppose so violently his brother's marriage to the lovely Alexandrine.

The first consul's reputation suffered somewhat from this strange, very public scandal over a private family matter.

Staging a spectacular entrance at the theater was an excellent way for Lucien and Alexandrine to start their new life as a legitimately wed couple, and Lucien was as eager as his mother, if not more so, for Alexandrine to look her very best that evening. All of Paris's elite would be in attendance. Many knew that Lucien and Alexandrine were to be present, including Jacques-Louis David, who at the time wanted to paint Alexandrine. He sat in the orchestra along with his favorite students and the whole of the Paris school of painting, all awaiting the arrival of the rebellious brother and his wife. In Lucien's box sat a handful of intimate friends and some family members as well as Général Casabianca, whom Letizia had sent in her stead in order to hear from him a blow-by-blow account of the effect produced by the couple's first public appearance.

And a discreet entrance it was not. As the door to their box was opened, a cheer resounded, loud enough for everyone in the theater to look up. Alexandrine looked ravishing indeed. She had opted for simplicity: an outfit "à la grecque," a classical style that had been all the rage in pre-revolutionary days, free of diamonds and of the finery that shone from other necks and ears in the theater but that was not popular by 1803, especially at the Tuileries. The taste for luxurious fashions of another Bonaparte sibling, Pauline, set the new tone in Parisian fashions. When she married the wealthy Roman prince Camillo Borghese in 1803 (after the death of her husband Général Leclerc), she had brought to Paris the wedding gifts she received from him. Lucien and Alexandrine were not invited to the celebration, but the rest of the family was. Pauline's young sister Caroline Murat was so impressed with the jewelry that she refused to wear her own. Joséphine, feeling the need to live up to Pauline's magnificence—and pressured to do so by Napoleon, who liked silks and satins—became the new fashion priestess. The advent at the consular court of bejeweled, luxurious glamour began. Even Alexandrine gave up the simple, elegant "Greek" style she had favored until then, much to Lucien's displeasure. But he succeeded in convincing her to return to it, so convinced was he that a natural beauty had no need for artifice or superfluous decoration. So with her understated outfit that evening at the theater, Alexandrine was making a bold polemical statement.

The couple's exit was no less noticed. They decided to leave in the midst of a scene, in order not to attract notice, but many on the parterre followed them out, virtually barring their passage as they tried to make their way to their carriage. Nor did attention to them abate in the following weeks. Each time they went to the theater, Lucien and Alexandrine found that all eyes were on them and that they made as powerful an impression as they had on that first evening.

Popular curiosity about the young, attractive, seemingly legitimate couple Napoleon loathed so much was extreme. One Sunday, Lucien and Alexandrine went for a walk with their three daughters (the baby boy stayed at home with a nanny) in the Prés-Saint-Gervais, a suburban park open to the general public and usually frequented by working-class families. The sight of the strikingly good-looking Alexandrine in the company of charming children and a man who resembled so closely the first consul aroused the curiosity of the walkers, who gathered around the attractive family. The couple overheard someone say: "Do you really believe that the brother of our First Consul would leave a woman like that? I dare you." "You're right, *commère* [busybody], where will he find a better one?" Similar comments followed; though all were well intentioned, Lucien and Alexandrine had to put an end to an outing that was no longer anonymous.

Lucien claimed that the stroll had been undertaken innocently. But it produced a detailed police report that Napoleon found thoroughly irritating: He told his mother to "warn Lucien that he was not allowed to make a bigger public impression than [Napoleon] himself." Napoleon had said something similar when Lucien, as interior minister, had held his crowded Wednesday audiences, regardless of the fact that the crowds were not the effect of popularity but of people's need for the ministry's services. (Joséphine also used to complain about these crowds to Lucien.) But the Prés-Saint-Gervais episode was much more worrisome for Napoleon, even more so than was the attention the couple attracted at the theater, since this time Lucien was just a private citizen who had caused a stir merely by taking a walk with his family. Although Letizia told Napoleon she refused to be the official bearer of his odious message, she did convey it to Lucien, telling him also that her response had been that Lucien was free to be seen in public with the woman he had chosen, since she was so perfectly suited to him, and much more to his taste than the woman the first consul had designated for him. Apparently even Joséphine repressed a giggle behind Napoleon's back when she heard Letizia's words.

It had been over four years since 18 Brumaire. The police reports and Napoleon's menacing messages were signs that no improvement was likely in his attitude toward Lucien and Alexandrine. Deciding it was time for a change of scene, they left for Italy, leaving their children behind.

FOUR

EXILE

1804–1807

Napoleon was a great discoverer of men, but he wanted these men's talent to be his alone, and desired always to be the spirit that stirred the masses. A midge flying from one brief love to the next without his permission was a rebellious midge.

—Alexandre Dumas, *Le Chevalier de Sainte-Hermine*

ITALIAN HOLIDAY

In early December 1803, Lucien and Alexandrine departed for Italy, leaving the children in Paris with their nannies.[1] They decided to make their way down incognito, just as Lucien had done when he had gone to Spain as the new ambassador three years before: He traveled as General Boyer, using his first wife's name. Arnault, Doctor Paroisse, and painters Lethière and Châtillon were members of the party. But the incognito proved hard to preserve once they arrived in Italy, and their passage through Turin, Milan, Bologna, and Florence excited some curiosity. A courier preceded them to Rome and alerted Lucien's uncle Fesch of their arrival. He had been made a cardinal a few months earlier and was the French ambassador at the court of Pope Pius VII, a gentle and humane pontiff—and powerless prey to Napoleon's will and whim. The ambassador's secretary was none other than Chateaubriand, who a few weeks earlier had made a joke at the expense of Fesch that had caused an uproar. He had quipped that it must be a curious sight indeed for the Romans to see a man who had arrived in town just a few years earlier as an army supplies officer now garbed in a cardinal's red robes—the pillager had turned into one of the church's sacred pillars. The joke was leaked immediately. Napoleon nearly recalled the impertinent writer, furious with him as he was with all disobedient men of letters. It took the intercession of Talleyrand and Fontanes to save Chateaubriand's neck. When the newlywed couple arrived in Rome, they hoped the writer would apprise them of the situation in the city.

Fesch welcomed Lucien and Alexandrine with great warmth, inviting them to stay with him in his palace, although they turned down his invitation. Lucien's sister Pauline, the Borghese princess, also lived in the Eternal

City and gave them an equally warm, joyous welcome. She had begun to host glamorous parties in her palace; and her renowned beauty would soon be immortalized by Antonio Canova in a sculpture of Venus, resplendent in her marble nakedness. But Lucien and Alexandrine did not stay in Rome long: The pope was indisposed and unable to receive them immediately, and, since they had been planning on taking a trip to Naples, they decided to leave. The pope transmitted his regrets over the delay in receiving them but expected to see them on their return.

The queen of Naples, Caroline, was the sister of Marie-Antoinette. The French ambassador there, Alquier, who had been Lucien's predecessor in Spain, told him that Caroline loathed the French, and Lucien avoided presenting himself at court. The cosmopolitan city held much stronger attractions in any case. The couple attended an opera at the impressive San Carlo theater—as in the Paris theater, all eyeglasses turned to their box. Over the next few days, the whole community of French residents in Naples wanted to call on Lucien, but he decided not to receive anyone—not even Chateaubriand, who was in town. Instead, the couple and their entourage went sightseeing. They took an archaeological tour of Pompeii and Herculaneum, went to the Posillipo Hill—which was undeveloped then—and to the Dog's Cave near Pozzuoli, long an obligatory stop on the Grand Tour. They ascended Mount Vesuvius, out of whose crater billowed a flute of smoke. It was an exhausting expedition, although they proceeded comfortably, in a palanquin carried by two alternating teams of four roughnecks. They visited a hermit who lived on the volcano and was an old acquaintance of Lethière, who accompanied them. The hermit provided the travelers with a frugal meal, partly composed of their own provisions. He was proud of the wine he kept for special occasions. Abstemious as ever, Lucien did not swallow a drop of it. Alexandrine usually drank only water but, curious about this special bottle, she tasted it, to Lucien's slight annoyance. Apparently it was excellent. The descent after lunch, on foot, was particularly difficult for tipsy and tired Alexandrine.

They stayed in Naples another few days, enjoying its beauty and awaiting in vain the volcano's expected eruption, then made their way back to Rome, where the pope welcomed them warmly. The Church's etiquette charmed Lucien, with its monsignori, the lace garments, and the elaborate, ancient choreography of it all. Soon after, Pauline's mother-in-law, the Borghese dowager princess Duchess Salviati of Florence, hosted a grand dinner, attended by Cardinal Consalvi, Roman prelates, and various elegant and vacuous characters. It was a full immersion into Roman society life. The couple went to the theater, visited the Pantheon and St. Peter's, seamlessly gliding from pagan to Christian Rome and back. It was a short stay, though they hoped to return soon and perhaps settle permanently, especially if Napoleon continued to treat them so nastily.

Pauline encouraged the plan. Lucien managed to get along with her husband, Camillo Borghese, a haughty nobleman who was indifferent to the outstanding collection of masterpieces that his father had amassed and enjoyed. Lucien and Alexandrine were wholeheartedly captivated by six-year-old Dermide, the son Pauline had had with her first husband, Général Leclerc. Camillo was not as affectionate to his stepson as Lucien was with his stepdaughter (Lucien also granted Anna a large income that she would receive when she came of age or got married), but Pauline and Alexandrine had in common the loss to yellow fever of their first husbands, the fathers of their first children. Lucien even thought of Dermide as a future spouse for his daughter Christine-Egypta. His affection for Pauline did not stop him, however, from reproaching her—to no avail—for having closed to the public the most beautiful parts of the villa Borghese park. She had become quite unpopular with the Roman citizenry; the dowager princess was much more appreciated.

The next stop for the couple was Venice. It was not a spectacular arrival. Their first glimpse of a gondola depressed them; it looked to them like a hearse. They learned that the bleak uniformity of gondolas' exterior was due to the sumptuary laws, rigidly applied since Napoleon had devolved the Venetian republic to the stiff Austrians. The rest of their stay did not improve much. The proverbial joie de vivre was gone from the Lagoon. They were bored, although they were ashamed to admit it, and the humid cold of a Venetian January got to them. The sea was choppy, so they were only able to get around on foot for the first three days, and walking around the damp city, battered by the northern winds, felt like a penance.

Almost three months had passed since they had left France. It was time to return and see their children. They took a different route this time, crossing the Alps at Mount Cenisio. It was February 1804, freezing and snowing, but a different kind of cold was awaiting them at home.

GOOD-BYE TO PARIS

As soon as the couple crossed the French border, the intrigues that they had left behind were upon them. In Auxerre, they met with Général Lacour, a relative of Alexandrine's who had served under Général Moreau, and who informed them that, to his shock, Moreau was being tried for having conspired to restore the monarchy in France. Hardly had Lucien had time to settle back into his family life in Paris than he was accused of being an accomplice in this presumed conspiracy. Fouché's spies, zealous as ever, were hard at work, not missing a chance to discredit Lucien. His indignation, shared by the outraged Joseph and their mother, found unexpected support in Napoleon, who dryly observed that "Lucien would not gain anything" from participating in the plot; clearly he considered his brother loyal only because he was powerless.[2] But by now the first consul was even more irritated about the unauthorized marriage than he had been before the couple's departure for Italy. He swore that he would never acknowledge as sister-in-law a woman who had entered the family without his consent.

The ill feeling toward Alexandrine constantly increased. Napoleon declared that Lucien's visits henceforth would be unwelcome. The court around Napoleon and Joséphine, especially those officials who were beginning their political careers, now carefully avoided Lucien and Alexandrine, and the family split into two parties—those who would and those who would not frequent the couple at the Hôtel de Brienne. Joséphine's twenty-year-old daughter Hortense called on them while the first consul was absent from town. She showed herself at her warmest and most amiable, while her husband, Louis Bonaparte, aged twenty-five, cowered in suppressed rage. Before deciding to marry her according to Napoleon's wishes, Louis had pressed his older brother Lucien for advice. Lucien had told him that if he accepted the marriage, he would be relinquishing his happiness, his freedom, and his authority as head of his own family. Louis swore that he would not marry, but in the end he did, and Lucien's words must have come back to haunt him.[3]

United by virtue of executive order, Louis and Hortense looked all the more mismatched when in the company of the enamored Lucien and Alexandrine. It was a glaring contrast. Displeased but not surprised by the clear disharmony in his younger brother's marriage, Lucien pretended to himself, and to them, that all was fine. He accompanied Hortense to her carriage and they hugged affectionately. "We will see each other often now, as I've hoped and desired for a long time," Hortense told her brother-in-law.[4] When Napoleon—who was both her stepfather and her brother-in-law—returned, he reprimanded her so vehemently, upon learning of her visit, for showing affection to Lucien and Alexandrine that she promised not to set foot in the happy household again. Louis did not dare interfere, but he returned to see the couple on his own, deploring the subjugation into which the first consul had cast him. Lucien refrained from reminding him that he had predicted this marriage to be ill fated. As for Hortense, he would not see her again for twenty years.

The only women in the clan—apart from Letizia—who stood unabashedly on the side of the outcasts were Joseph's wife, Julie Clary, who openly warned Joséphine that this rift was not only painful but also dangerous, and Julie's sister, Désirée, who had been Napoleon's lover for a short time and was now married to Général Bernadotte. Bernadotte himself was showing himself to be a true friend to Lucien, and Désirée sent their little son Oscar to play with Lucien's daughters. Elisa, who had brought up the girls after Christine's death, was now aggressively on the other side and at odds with her mother. Joséphine claimed to be obedient to her husband, although she gave as a "present" to Lolotte (Charlotte) and Lili (Christine-Egypta) a nine-year-old black servant from the Darfur, whom they nicknamed Othello. He fascinated the family with his tales from his country, which he still remembered even though he had been taken from his homeland at a young age. He did not stay long with them, because soon they would leave France for good.

Meanwhile, Napoleon was increasingly anxious about conspiracies surrounding him and menacing his hold on power. He became obsessed with them, to the point of paranoia. One Bourbon prince, the Duke d'Enghien, was stationed in Ettenheim, near Strasbourg, and Napoleon grew convinced, in great part thanks to twisted reports, that he was waiting there for the conspiracy to unfold in which Moreau was suspected.

At dawn on March 14, 1804, a company of dragoons awoke the duke and arrested him in the name of the republic. He was brought to Strasbourg and from there to the Château de Vincennes, just outside Paris, where he was court-martialed. By this point Napoleon had learned that his accusations were unfounded. Joséphine entreated him to change his mind and show some mercy. Instead, he had the charges against the prince commuted to more accurate ones: The Duke d'Enghien had been bearing arms against France, in alliance with England, Austria, and Russia, as he himself confessed at his trial. Although some of his judges initially recommended imprisonment, the death sentence was pronounced unanimously after a two-hour deliberation. The prince requested an audience with Bonaparte, which was denied. He was immediately brought to the place of execution, the Vincennes castle's moat. He took out from his vest a letter containing a curl of his hair and a golden ring and gave it to a lieutenant. The commander in charge of the execution demanded that he kneel. "What for?" asked the prince. "To receive death," he was told. He replied: "A Bourbon only kneels before God."[5] The soldiers fired on cue, then threw the duke's body into the freshly dug grave. It was 3:00 A.M., on March 21.

There was immediate European-wide outcry at the execution—notably by the Elector of Baden, since the duke had been on his territory, and by the Tsar of Russia, who demanded a period of mourning at court. Paris was shocked, but otherwise there was stunned acceptance of the event, mixed with fear at the increasingly bloody despotism it seemed to signal. Joséphine was deeply upset, and the parade of officials, consuls, ministers, and generals who visited Malmaison to congratulate Napoleon the next day only increased her dejection, however mixed were their own feelings. Louis and Hortense were present but silent. Cynical as ever, Fouché apparently remarked that this act was "worse than a crime: it was a blunder."

The execution also deeply shocked Lucien. As soon as he heard the news, he walked into his wife's room and said: "Alexandrine, let's get out of here! The tiger has tasted blood!"[6]

Napoleon did not regret what he had done, but it was a troubling time for him. He was consolidating his position, but there were costs. One of those was Lucien's decision to leave for good and to settle in Rome—a decision that the couple had been pondering for a while. Napoleon's words and actions toward them had only encouraged that decision, even rendered it inevitable; and the killing of the Duke d'Enghien made it all the more urgent. Madame Rémusat, who emphatically disapproved of the first consul's conduct over the affair, reported on his reaction to the irrevocable break with his talented brother that had occurred a short time before the duke's arrest:

> On this occasion I happened to see the First Consul give way to one of those rare bursts of emotion to which I have alluded. It was at Saint Cloud, late one evening. Madame Bonaparte was anxiously awaiting the result of the final conference between the two brothers; M de Rémusat and I were the only persons with her. She did not care for Lucien, but she disliked any family scandal. It was near midnight when Bonaparte came into the room; he was deeply dejected, and throwing himself into an armchair, he exclaimed, in a troubled voice, "It is all over! I have broken with Lucien, and ordered him from my presence."
>
> When Madame Bonaparte began to expostulate, he told her: "You are a good woman to plead for him." Then he rose from his chair, took his wife in his arms, and laid her head softly on his shoulder, and with his hand still resting on the beautiful bright head which contrasted with the sad face next to it, he told us that, even though he had resorted equally in vain to both threats and persuasion, Lucien had resisted all his entreaties. "It is hard," he added, "to find in one's own family such stubborn opposition interests of such magnitude. Must I then isolate myself from every one? Must I rely on myself alone? Well! I will suffice to myself, and you, Joséphine—you will be my comfort always."
>
> I retain a pleasurable recollection of this little scene. Tears were in Bonaparte's eyes as he spoke. I felt inclined to thank him when he betrayed feelings like those of other men.

As Mme Rémusat's firsthand account indicates (whether it is fully reliable or not), the first consul was deeply affected by Lucien's strong-headed, independent behavior.[7] He found it emotionally troubling as well as politically unacceptable, all the more so since he knew that Lucien could be of great help to him—precisely because of his uniquely fiery spirit and high intelligence. But there was no going back and no possibility for a reconciliation: Napoleon was certainly not going to accept Alexandrine, the woman who had led to his most valued brother being lost to the cause of expanding his reign and ensuring dynastic continuity within it. Everything had been argued and said, and no one had won the fight.

Letizia tried to plead for a truce, and encouraged Lucien to pursue it as well. Against all known protocol, Napoleon had always wanted his wife, not his mother, to head family reunions and decisions, but Joséphine maintained due deference to her mother-in-law. It was perhaps in that deferential spirit that Joséphine appealed to the ordinary human emotions that her husband was capable of evincing, by convincing him to write the letter of recommendation to the pope that Lucien had been requesting ever since that final break. This would make the rupture, and Lucien's impending departure from Paris, less unpleasant for everyone. Napoleon wrote the letter during the very short-lived truce that Letizia engineered. It was signed March 13, 1804, the day before the Duke d'Enghien was arrested, and read: "Very Holy Father, the senator Lucien, my brother, would like to sojourn in Rome to study antiquities and their history. I implore Your Holiness to welcome him with that goodness that is Yours, and to believe in my wish to be agreeable to You."

The letter was dry and brief, but it was better than nothing. Napoleon ominously told Letizia that Lucien should make use of that letter and that, if he stayed in France, he, Napoleon, could not answer for his actions, or indeed for those of Lucien: The quarrel might well end tragically. And no one wanted that.

Lucien and Alexandrine were as determined to leave for Rome as Napoleon was determined not to recognize their marriage and thereby initiate a reconciliation. The duke's assassination precipitated the couple's preparations for departure, which was fixed for the day before Easter 1804.[8] The servants worked hard to pack up the substantial Paris household. Tending to the logistics of the trip provided a distraction of sorts from the dark mood that reigned over the couple's last few days in Paris. The ever-faithful Doctor Paroisse was too ill to travel, adding to the sadness of the departure; Lucien was not looking forward to traveling without him.

Preparations were finished by the evening before departure. Crates and boxes filled with the family's belongings occupied four large carriages, which stood ready in the darkened courtyard. The post horses were expected at dawn. Joseph had been trying to talk Lucien out of the plan, but in vain. That night the brothers walked up and down Lucien's beloved gallery of paintings. The packing of the art—an enterprise in itself—was to begin the day after the family left. The empty areas of the palace resonated with countless moments that were about to become lost to the past. Alexandrine was seated by a fireplace in a corner. Fabrics of all sorts were strewn on the furniture and on the couches that had seated the guests of Lucien's great parties in earlier, lighter times, when he was a minister. These fabrics were gifts from his mother, wife, and sisters to Pauline, who was expecting them in Rome. Mademoiselle Sophie, Alexandrine's chambermaid, melancholy at this departure, which she did not believe would be short term, was busy packing up the fashionable objects, watched over by her sad mistress.

As Joseph left the palace, Lucien and Alexandrine exited the gallery and made their way to their bedroom, planning to get a few hours' rest before the departure. Suddenly a stranger appeared before them. Lucien felt Alexandrine's hand tremble briefly, and for a fraction of a second he found himself hoping that Napoleon had come to bid them to stay. But the man turned out to be Général Bernadotte, who exclaimed: "What, you force me to break in? You think you can escape without saying good-bye and without my coming to tempt you not to leave? Resist, resist, you must, who leaves the game loses. After all, what do you fear?"

"For myself, nothing; but it's much worse!"

"Oh, Fouché's little moves! As if they mattered! I wouldn't leave if I were you, my dear Lucien."

"Nor I, if I were the Général Bernadotte, for in that case I wouldn't be risking a fraternal war and everything that may follow it."

"Well! If you have that fear, leave, but remember, I repeat it—he who leaves his place loses it."

"No, my dear: there is nothing more for me to gain here, the stakes are too high. And . . ."

Alexandrine was exhausted: she chose that moment to retire, bidding a warm, emotional adieu to the general, who said as he watched her walk away: "At least one can't say that the First Consul didn't find a beautiful pretext to break with you." Lucien nodded pensively. He often considered that his wife's beauty had played a part in their troubles—that if she had been less striking, Joséphine might have taken more of a liking to her and tried harder to persuade Napoleon not to let them leave. In such a case, he and Alexandrine would have become Joséphine's allies in the divorce proceedings that the first consul was secretly starting to consider just then—Joséphine's inability to conceive was an increasingly serious problem for him. Inversely, Lucien's own divorce would have provided a perfect legal alibi for Napoleon's.

But all this was moot now. Lucien never went to bed: He and Bernadotte talked until dawn, when they heard the horses arrive in the courtyard. They warmly embraced in parting. It was the last time they would ever see each other.

At last the moment had come to leave Paris. The whole family embarked, Lucien and Alexandrine as somber as the girls were excited (their little brother was too young to realize what was happening). The train of carriages exited the palace's courtyard, made its way through the city that was just awakening to its early spring morning, and out through the Paris gates, due south.

"DOLCE FAR NIENTE"

This second voyage to Italy, like the first, was undertaken under an assumed name.[9] The convoy made its way though France as quickly as possible, and the first stop in Italy was Parma—the city where a future friend of the family and great writer, Stendhal (whose real name was Henri Beyle), would set his novel *The Charterhouse of Parma*. It was not a comfortable trip for

Alexandrine, whose new pregnancy was making her feel so ill and exhausted that they had to stop at a local hotel. Doctor De France, who had replaced Paroisse and was traveling with the family, advised her to take a bath to calm her nerves, but there was no bathtub to be found at the hotel. Inquiries were made in town, to no avail. The only tub seemed to be in the possession of a marquise or other who refused to either sell or lend it; nor would she consider offering a charitable hand, since these travelers were foreign to her. Had the incognito been abandoned, she probably would have behaved differently. But that was out of the question. Finally the hotel's owner suggested the use of a brand-new basin in his possession, large enough to bathe in, and Alexandrine was happy to accept. The bath helped enormously, and she was fit enough the next day to resume the journey.

Before leaving Paris, Lucien had met the Roman prince Vincenzo Giustiniani, scion of a proud dynasty claiming to descend directly from the Byzantine emperors. Despite his noble origins, the prince was in serious financial trouble, and when he heard that Lucien was leaving France, he offered to swap his estates with Lucien's in Le Plessis. Giustiniani's main palace was in Bassano Romano, only thirty-five miles (fifty kilometers) north of Rome: close enough to the city, but far enough from the heat that was sure to hit it in the approaching summer. A fresh and healthy climate was necessary for Lucien's pregnant wife, and for the children. The magnificent palace, decorated with frescoes by Albano and Domenichino, and surrounded by a lovely park, satisfied Lucien's demanding taste, and the family settled there.

It was a bucolic, picturesque part of the world. The park was rather neglected, since the absentee owners had not looked after it in years. But Bassano was rich with chestnut trees; woods alternated with meadows populated with grazing sheep that provided delicious milk, butter, and cheese. In the woods grew bounteous, fragrant wild strawberries that the girls enjoyed picking—there was an exceptionally sweet, white kind that they had never seen or tasted before. In the village the family met a young French priest named Don Joseph who had been deported there during the Terror and who warned them that the woods were full of grass snakes, usually harmless but one never knew. So the children's picking of strawberries—and wildflowers—came to an end. But there was plenty to entertain them, including village fairs, where the girls were allowed to dance with the colorfully clad peasants. Don Joseph joyfully adopted these compatriots before even knowing who they were, and soon became their generous factotum.

It was a heavenly place for the children, who frequently exclaimed "Ah! We have so much more fun here than in Paris"! There were no more lessons—except for music lessons given by a governess recommended by their friend Roederer, who had come with the family from Paris and who, while appearing naively charming and honorable, eventually revealed herself to be a perfidious hypocrite they would have to fire two years later.

Lucien and Alexandrine were comfortable in these luxuriant surroundings. When she was not with the children, Alexandrine started writing—and finished—the *Souvenirs* of her adolescence, tracing her young life until the age of twenty-five. Lucien made an attempt at writing his autobiography: Although he was only twenty-nine, he had already lived so much and so intensely that he was eager to set down his thoughts and memories on paper. He quickly realized, however, that he needed more time and perspective, so he did not pursue his project—not just yet. Instead, for the first time in his life, he tried to abandon himself to *dolce far niente,* that is, pleasant idleness, or contemplation Italian style (the phrase literally means "sweet doing nothing"). There was time to read, draw, take long walks, play the flute—which Lucien played badly but enjoyed. Letizia came to stay with them with a retinue of friends and servants, including faithful Saveria, while waiting for an apartment that Fesch was procuring for her in Rome to be ready. The very pleasant life of leisure they all led in Bassano could not have stood in starker contrast to Lucien's previous one—and especially with Napoleon's.

On May 18, 1804, in Paris, Napoleon proclaimed himself emperor. European monarchs were dismayed; French antimonarchists were shocked. The new emperor immediately denied succession rights to Lucien. Jérôme was excluded as well; like Lucien, the youngest of the Bonaparte siblings had married without Napoleon's consent, at the end of 1803. The bride was an attractive, well-born American woman from Philadelphia, Elizabeth Patterson, whom Jérôme had met in Maryland. Napoleon refused Jérôme's request to recognize the marriage. But unlike Lucien, Jérôme would give in to the political and emotional pressure. Napoleon barred Elizabeth's ship from docking at European coasts, and Jérôme divorced her while she was pregnant with their son (who was born in London in 1805, before Elizabeth returned to Baltimore with the baby). Eventually, in 1807, he married the German princess Napoleon had chosen for him, Catharina von Württemberg, and became prince of Westphalia.

Letizia was in Rome at the time of Napoleon's proclamation of himself as emperor. She said she refused to attend the grand ceremony in Paris, which would take place in December. (Upon Napoleon's strict orders, however, David included her in the gigantic canvas he painted of the event in 1806.) The denial of succession was a sharp slap in Lucien's face, and a "complete mistake," as Lucien told his mother in Rome one day, when he joined her there, "since the Empire, such as it is, is not the patrimony of our father."[10] "That is true," replied Letizia, "but this is no less of an atrocious injustice—to you, of all people, who stopped the Jacobins from outlawing him. Ah, ungrateful Jérôme! Poor child! Ah the nasty Napoleon. . . . Mister Emperor and Madame Empress won't ever see me again!"[11] "Calm down, Mother. On the contrary, you should go to Paris if he asks you to, and give him good advice." "Advice, sure—don't you see, Lucien, from what he has dared to do, the tyrant revealing himself to the world? No, I shall not go, unless it is to tell him that he is a tyrant." She started crying, despite herself, and became terribly upset. Lucien called Saveria, who wanted to alert the doctor, although that did not prove necessary. He asked Saveria not to tell anyone, especially Fesch, about the extreme effect the news had had on his mother.

Fesch, in fact, did not take the denial of succession as a particularly dramatic one: He told Lucien, taking his hand in a warm handshake, that it threw a shadow on the rise of the first consul to emperor and that he hoped it would all straighten out. Lucien thanked him for his kind words, adding "but I don't hope for anything, because I don't want anything—and dear uncle, you should do the same." Letizia, recovered from her initial reaction but still outraged, freely shared with her brother her thoughts about Napoleon's act: It was treason, injustice, ingratitude, malice on his part.

As for Alexandrine, she was riven with guilt: She felt she was the cause of this "exhérédation," as Letizia called it. Lucien quickly talked his wife out of this thought, by reminding her that she knew better than anyone that they both much preferred their honorable life as private citizens to one in which they would be courtiers of Napoleon and Joséphine. Moreover, the pope, a good soul, was on their side.

Cardinal Consalvi, Pius VII's able secretary of state, was surprised and saddened by the news of the denial of succession. After having seen the pope, the cardinal went to visit Lucien at the Palazzo Lancellotti in Rome, which the family, having left Bassano to be closer to Letizia, were renting for a few weeks while deciding where to settle down. Consalvi reported that his holiness was upset by what had happened and wanted to see Lucien as soon as possible. The cardinal added that surely the French nation would recall him—he had friends, and so on; but this was clearly consolatory talk.

At this point Lucien was learning the baroque ways of the Catholic Church. The prelates in the papal antechamber conveyed their condolences in an embarrassed fashion when Lucien arrived. But Pius VII greeted him warmly, literally with open arms, as Lucien kneeled at his feet. The pope told him that he thought this mark of ingratitude on Napoleon's part would blight his glory and that it diminished the pope's admiration for his great actions. The door was partially open, and the prelates witnessed the welcome and the words, to the satisfaction of Lucien's admittedly bruised ego. The entire diplomatic corps probably was informed of what had happened, since the next day Lucien received a large number of visits.

Everything in Rome pleased Lucien's vivid imagination and tickled his passion for antiquarianism. The Eternal City, capital of classical culture and of the Christian world, contained enough artistic treasures to make Lucien happy over many lifetimes. But all the art in the world could not compensate for the discomfort increasingly wrought by the summer heat, which was becoming oppressive. Lucien and Alexandrine, who was suffering all the more acutely for her advancing pregnancy, wanted to return to Bassano, but Letizia was opposed to the idea of having them live so far from the city. And so instead, they rented the Villa Taverna (now Parisi-Borghese) in hilly Frascati, only twelve miles (twenty kilometers) south of Rome. It too belonged to Camillo Borghese, who used it with Pauline as a summer residence, and was conveniently close to the Villa Mondragone, stately property of Prince Aldobrandini. He was a relative of Camillo, Aldobrandini, and was caring for Pauline's son, Dermide, since Camillo did not want the boy to accompany his parents on their trip to the medicinal spas at Lucca. Pauline needed to spend some time there because she was still suffering from bouts of the yellow fever she had caught in Saint-Domingue. Letizia, who wanted to relax at the spa, followed, leaving Lucien, Alexandrine, and the children to stay near their cousin Dermide.

The Villa Taverna was a nice enough place, spacious and set within an elegant park. But the whole area was rife with malaria—not the most pernicious version of the disease, but debilitating and recurrent. Quite a few of the French household staff feared it enough that they decided to leave. Lucien caught the fever, although Alexandrine and the three girls were spared. Little Charles, however, who was only a year old and still nursing, fell ill. Peruvian cinchona bark—from which quinine is derived—was the usual remedy, as it had been since the mid-seventeenth century. Lucien took it with some success, even though he would suffer from relapses for over two years. Charles's wet nurse had been given cinchona in order to prevent the baby from becoming ill, but the precaution had failed. The child's fevers were high and, given his young age, his life was in danger. A Prussian doctor named Kolrauch, who was vehemently opposed to the use of cinchona, decided to try instead some ammonium prepared in a novel manner. Charles was cured, though he remained somewhat sickly for the rest of his childhood. He had a good constitution, however, and, in time, recovered fully.

Aldobrandini often came to see Dermide, who was otherwise looked after by his governess.[12] Suddenly the child also fell ill with malaria. Sadly, the six-year-old boy was not as lucky as Charles. Already weakened by yellow fever, he died in mid-August. Camillo and Pauline were still in Lucca, where the news arrived quickly. Camillo and a friend of Pauline's who had accompanied them to the spa decided—with Letizia's approval—that Pauline was not well enough to be informed of the tragedy. Eventually, Dermide's tutor arrived from Frascati and told her that Dermide had fallen ill. He had been dead nearly two weeks before she finally guessed what had happened.

Pauline was devastated and blamed Camillo, telling her husband that, had it not been for him, she would not have been separated from Dermide, "and he would still be alive." She wanted to abandon Rome and Italy altogether and return to live in France. When Camillo told her that the emperor asked that she stay in Italy, she replied, sounding very much like Lucien: "What do his wishes matter? It's not Paris I wish to go to, it's Montgobert, where the general lies, and where my son will join him. Is my brother God? Does he have the right to decide my fate? I care no more for the trappings of his court than for his crown."[13]

For his part, Lucien was still worried about his son. He missed Doctor Paroisse and was impatient for him to arrive. As Bernadotte informed his friend in a long, affectionate letter, the doctor was still ailing but had decided to join Lucien, convinced that seeing him again would help restore his health. Bernadotte wrote that he was upset by "Napoleon's pusillanimity" and, reproaching Lucien for abandoning his duty as a republican, wished for him to be able to return to France and help him save the country from the self-declared emperor.[14] He closed his letter with a friendly good-bye, urging Lucien to take care of his own health in the fever-ridden climate he now inhabited. He also asked Lucien to give his warmest regards to Alexandrine and to tell her not to be distressed: "She is too beautiful and too good to excite the hatred of anyone, and mostly too intelligent not to realize that she is only a pretext for your exile, which Napoleon—if he dared—would thank her for giving him." Lucien was moved by his friend's generous concern, which was all the more acute since their political disappointments had grown so bitter. (Eventually, Bernadotte exiled himself and ended up becoming the king of Sweden; he contributed in no small part to Napoleon's later debacle in Russia.) Even Fontanes, Elisa's lover and a staunch supporter of Napoleon, wrote an epigram that acknowledged Lucien's past role in the country that he had been forced to leave: "Napoleon no doubt has saved the country / But Lucien has saved Napoleon!"[15]

Another epidemic—the Livorno yellow fever—struck Italy. There was a possibility that the contaminated areas, which included Tuscany, would be cordoned off from the Papal States to contain its spread, so Lucien moved his family to Milan. There, on December 1, 1804, Alexandrine gave birth to a girl they named Letizia; they asked Letizia *mère* to be her godmother. She had stopped in Milan on her way up from Rome to Paris, where the emperor had invited her to return—and she drove Alexandrine to tears by communicating her disappointment that this was a girl, provocatively asserting that Hortense would make a second boy. Lucien did his best to console his wife and told his mother that, like Joseph, he preferred girls to boys. Mme Mère responded: "You are right about that, if you want to lead a private life."[16]

Still hoping to reconcile the brothers and to breach some sort of "rapprochement," and worried about the possible consequences of Napoleon's becoming a tyrant, it was right for Letizia to move back to Paris.[17] She told Lucien that she would return to Rome if he decided to stay there, and in the meantime she bought from him the Hôtel de Brienne, so that he would have enough cash to live on. Pauline and Camillo, who returned to Paris as well, moved in with her.

In the spring, Lucien learned that Napoleon was planning to travel to Milan to be crowned king of Italy. Lucien left town, but not without writing to his brother that, as he had asked Joseph to inform his majesty earlier on, he had been in the city for a few months, to escape the epidemics. He explained that, just as he was about to return to Frascati with his family, he and one of the children had been struck with a fever again, so they had now decided to spend the summer on the northeastern coast, in Pesaro, where they were heading. And he added: "I hurry to inform Your Majesty of my departure for that city where I shall bring the same feelings of unalterable devotion, over and against the vexations that pursue me. Any sign of benevolence on your part, Sire, would be precious to me, for, although events have excluded me from the political family of French princes, I do not think I deserve your hate, and I implore you to spare me its manifestations."[18]

"PARIS IS WELL WORTH A MASS"[19]

For a little while in early spring 1805, Lucien thought he might be in a position to negotiate with the emperor. Joseph gave some encouraging signs, and

Letizia also wrote, urging Lucien to aim for a reconciliation and satisfy her wish to see her sons reunited. Believing that something might change, Lucien even prepared to return to Milan. Then he received another letter from Joseph, which reported that Napoleon would be delighted to see him in Milan and that he would do anything that was reconcilable with his "firm resolution never to recognize his wife as a sister-in-law," whom he did not wish to receive. It was now evident that no compromise was possible, although Joseph advised Lucien to do Napoleon's bidding and go to Milan—on his own—to see him.

Disheartened, Lucien wrote an amicable enough note to Talleyrand to inform him of his reaction to what he had learned and to state that he would be postponing his departure for Milan. Talleyrand responded by entreating Lucien to the "sacrifice" that the nation, his family, and his birth deserved. The next day, Lucien received a letter from his uncle Fesch containing a message similar to that which Joseph had delivered: The emperor wanted to do all he could "for Lucien," but nothing at all "for a married Lucien." Napoleon's intentions could not have been clearer.

And so, staying in Pesaro with his family, determined not to go to Milan, Lucien wrote a decisive letter to Napoleon, thanking him at first for his "benevolence" toward him, then conveying the disappointment he felt on reading in Joseph's letter about the emperor's "firm resolution" regarding his marriage. He was much aggrieved by it, since that meant that he would forever have to give up the public career he hoped his majesty would give him. He wrote: "a title that I were unable to share with the mother of my children would be a fatal gift that would poison my days." Lucien's tone was polite and respectful throughout, his words as dignified as those of a breakup letter could be: "I respect the veil that shields the actions of the emperor, and since reasons of State on one hand, and my honor on the other, unite to pull me away from any public function, I shall divest any last hope from my heart, and entirely embrace the private life that fate has reserved for me." There was one final request: "But for that private life to be happy, I need to believe that all my children, whom we bring up in admiration of Your Majesty, will find in you an uncle and protector, once they are grown; I hope they shall be able to live closer to Your Majesty than their mother and myself."

Lucien's steadfastness only increased the mounting pressure bearing down from on high: The emperor commanded, and it was outrageous that anyone should disobey him. The mere fact that he now wore a crown conferred on him an unquestionable authority that gave ammunition to Lucien's enemies, but also led to shifting allegiances among those who claimed his friendship and those who were bound to him by family ties. A string of letters followed Lucien's. Shortly after sending his missive to Napoleon, he received another one from his uncle Fesch. Tinged as it was with the intimacy that draws on claims of avuncular affection, it was blunt and sincere. Fesch did not shrink from citing what Napoleon had told him—that Lucien could live in Europe only if called to the throne after annulling his "illegal marriage." Failing that, Napoleon had sworn that Lucien would "bear for his whole life the marks of my curse," in the interest of protecting the throne against those who would want to rattle its foundations. Fesch pressured his nephew to listen to Napoleon and regain his "natural position" within the family fold, in everyone's interest.

That was not all. Enclosed with yet another letter from Fesch was a long letter from Talleyrand. The crafty diplomat had never claimed Lucien's friendship, but neither had he had occasion to act expressly against his interests. Now he developed in full the themes announced in his earlier appeal. He reminded Lucien of the emperor's desire to have all his family members gathered around him, for the sake of everyone's dignity—his, theirs, and the state's. The fate of Europe was connected to that of France, and the fate of France to that of the imperial family. The man who had destroyed anarchy and triumphed over two coalitions had no difficulty assigning a place and function to even those individuals who had disagreed with him, showing them "the necessity of not deviating from the road he was tracing for them." Even those who had conspired against him were now given the opportunity to serve him.

But amid all this "glory and happiness," the emperor's family alone seemed in an inadequate state, Talleyrand went on. While one brother who had been denied imperial inheritance—Jérôme—had finally accepted "due submission to the sovereign and head of the family," the other persisted in "preferring a woman over his honor, the interest of his country, everything he owes the emperor, his name, his own children." If only "Monsieur Lucien" realized that, by behaving in this way, he deprived his first two daughters of the recognition and privileges they were due by virtue of their name, confining them to a miserable existence; and made it impossible for the children he had with "Madame Jouberthon"—as Napoleon, and hence Talleyrand, persisted in calling Alexandrine—to ever live in France or its dependencies. By their very birth and blood, these children would be perceived by any successor to the throne as an "object of defiance," even as "enemies of their homeland," and this alone would condemn them to most unhappy lives.

As for Mme Jouberthon, once the passion she shared with Lucien was spent, as happened with all passions of the kind, she would wonder why she had "torn Monsieur Lucien away from the glorious destiny that awaited him." He would regret his actions, and she would find herself in the painful position of being condemned to live far from home and family with a man whose misfortunes she had created. Lucien had perceived he could no longer live in France; one day he would no longer be able to live in Europe. "All this for a love that soon will no longer exist, for a woman to whom he owes nothing but to whom he sacrifices his own happiness, that of the family he abandons, and that of his children whose sheer presence, by reminding him of having destroyed their lives, will become a burden once they have grown up." The emperor would never recognize this marriage to a woman who had entered the family without his permission or will, and against the interest of the family.

And so—the final point approached—there was only one solution, which both M. Lucien and Mme Jouberthon would accept if they really did love each other: Tear up the marriage contract that had been drawn against custom and established laws. In this way, Lucien would be able to return to Paris—with her if he so wished, and if he carried on with her within the bounds of decency that his rank demanded. He would be able to recognize their two children as his "natural children." The other two—those he had with Christine—would be given their inherited due. Mme Jouberthon would be relieved of the burden of having put a stop to a man's destiny. After all, a monarchy gave rise to duties that were all the more obligatory for those closest to the throne. Henri IV, for example, had converted to Catholicism, accepting that Paris was worth a Mass. What bound M. Lucien to the "world's first monarch" obligated him to attend in first place to what he owed the sovereign, the head of his family, the state.

A sinister tone pervaded the whole letter, in which menace and blackmail alternated with patronizing moralism and prophetic insight. The subtext was clear: If Lucien did not change his mind, he would be showing his inadequacy to regal calling. Not only that, but time was counted, wrote the diplomat, and if Lucien persisted in his resolve despite the emperor's serious warning, "one will have to consider him a dangerous man who, having received by virtue of birth eventual rights to the crown, would become a gathering point for all those who want to stir trouble; and he would thus inevitably be constituted an enemy of the state and of the emperor."

Lucien was digging his own grave, Talleyrand was implying, but in fact it was the emperor who would be wielding the shovel to bury his brother. The long dispatch closed with an attempt at softness and cajoling flattery: "Only one thing is missing for the emperor to be happy. One of his brothers still fails to recognize his duties toward him. And lives far from his homeland without the luster, the rank that the emperor would have liked to give him. Let him come retake the place that was destined for him, and enjoy the honors that await him by the emperor's side! Let him fulfill the hope that his talents and his character had led the whole of France to have for him!" Talleyrand himself would rejoice if his entreaty convinced Lucien to do the right thing.

The letter from Fesch which accompanied that from Talleyrand apparently had been composed in the presence of Napoleon, who had reprimanded the cardinal for having written so candidly to his nephew in the first instance. The emperor even claimed to have directed Fesch's hand on this one. The uncle expressed his deep fondness for Lucien in the same breath as he entreated him to make some "sacrifices," echoing Talleyrand's arguments in an emotional mode—without the diplomat's political finesse. He told his nephew that Napoleon did not want to break with him and that Lucien owed it to the emperor to return. He too bade him to hurry up: Now was the time for him to act in the right way, for very soon it would be too late.

Lucien was stunned even more than enraged by these menacing missives that mirrored each other in their appeal to family loyalty and patriotic duty, in their manipulative blend of emotional and political pressure. He found it humiliating that he might be convinced to be so cowardly as to grovel into the fold of imperial power and give up on the republican principles he believed in, let alone "sacrifice" the woman he loved and had married, and who was his legitimate wife—even though his own uncle, a cardinal, no less, had been convinced by the emperor that this was not the case. He did not believe that either Joseph or their mother approved of these goings-on, but he felt isolated and wounded.

Ever more convinced that he was making the only choice available to him, he penned a detailed reply to Talleyrand in which he patiently and courteously, indeed diplomatically, refuted point by point the latter's arguments. "Nobody on earth has more admiration for His Majesty than me," he began, then challenged the attempt to place him, an established politician, a man of consequence, a widower and father, on the same footing as Jérôme, so much younger and a minor still when he had married abroad. To the accusation that he chose a woman over his honor, he replied that honor and his wife were one and the same. He defended the legitimacy of his marriage, asserted that he much preferred his wife and children to that "fantasy of patriotism whose vague, uncertain contours, sometimes stained with blood and mud, disappear within the clouds of imagination." Since he had not had any duties toward the first consul, he had not neglected them either; but he recognized his duty before the emperor, which he fulfilled by disinheriting his first two daughters of any succession rights. Yet living as an ordinary individual was hardly a condemnation: In this case, Lucien wrote, he would communicate to his daughters "a part of my soul; born of me, they will live near me; brought up by me, they shall feel no envy and shall bless their lot; I can see that the fate of the world's top sovereign, with its genius and fortune, might be envied, but I am old enough to know that the lot of an ordinary lady is often preferable to the lot of the wife of Caesar or Charlemagne." As for his other children, they would live by the rights that Lucien alone transmitted to them. If Napoleon was prepared to behave like Nero, extending his arm over the Alps only to shed innocent blood, "if our sad country had to obey such a monster, of what matter would be the murder of my children?"

The other points were dismissed quickly. The quips about the durability of passion did not bear a response. He had not consulted his wife to make his decisions. He had no fear of being chased out of Europe. Behaving like a coward and a bad father and husband by deserting his children and dishonoring his wife would certainly not qualify him to sit on a throne. The example of Henri IV was fine, "but you, sir, do you believe that one mass is worth one wife and two children?" Finally, the menace of persecution was clearly from Talleyrand, not from his majesty, to whom he planned to write. "I am ready to make all sacrifices he believes will be useful to France, except for the sacrifice he demands; he is the one to choose my titles, and the place where I should retire; when he commands me to move, I shall obey without a murmur. If he orders me to leave Europe, I shall do so, but I can only leave my wife and children by ending my life."

Next Lucien wrote a brief note to the emperor alerting him to his response to Talleyrand, whose letter suggested persecution if he failed to do as told. "Since my departure from Paris, I was never put before such conditions as those advanced today. I ask His Majesty to excuse any inconvenience caused by my response to the minister, and to accept the tribute of my devoted and fraternal feelings."

Fesch informed Lucien that his note had no effect on the emperor.

Lucien could not help himself: He wrote again to Napoleon, in an excess of brotherly rage, and not without a remnant of tenderness, to which he appealed. If only Napoleon had children, he wrote, among a host of sincere exclamation marks and suspension marks, then he would understand. "Believe me, Sire, that my resisting you makes my lot as difficult as that of any living man; if it were only a matter of my happiness, I would sacrifice it to you; but, Sire, the honor and civil status of my children! death seems less horrid than that sacrifice!" If there was nothing left for him to hope for, then he begged to be ordered out of Europe; he was ready to go to America.

The reply was from Fesch again: The cardinal cited Napoleon's continuing refrain, which had become even harsher now: Lucien's marriage was an "*égarement*," a distraction, an erratic confusion; passions changed, cold reason did not; and so on. The emperor had said: "It isn't in my power to take away from him that name which he bore before I made it known to the world; but a child born long after that name has become my exclusive property shall never bear it in a country that is under my rule. Let him forget me as I shall forget him, let him stop writing to me, let him wait for the moment when the knife of some assassin shall have put an end to my life." Fesch himself wanted no part in this affair anymore. He had tried to act as a go-between for Lucien's own good. He now intended to come see him in Pesaro, and invited him to join him in Rimini, so they could speak. He also wanted Lucien to know that his wife should not be surprised that one would rather see Lucien happy without her than unhappy with her, or even happy with her, since that happiness caused the whole family's unhappiness.

Lucien was now convinced that Alexandrine was just a pretext for Napoleon to push him and his son away. There was absolutely nothing to be done. On May 26, 1805, the emperor was anointed king of Italy during a mass in Milan's cathedral, where he was also granted the Iron Crown of Lombardy (the same that had been laid on Emperor Charlemagne's head). Lucien and Alexandrine's firstborn, Charles, had just turned two.

ALL ROADS LEAD TO ROME

The brothers were equals in their hard-headedness—Lucien refusing to yield his honor before his brother's power, and Napoleon incensed at this affront. Neither one wavered in his respective position; and neither one wanted to give up trying to convince the other to change his mind. Napoleon's setting either-or conditions from imperial heights, without concession to ordinary diplomatic maneuvering or compromise, only perpetuated and accentuated Lucien's refusal. Repetition was the hallmark of the breakup. They were brothers, after all: It took them both a long while to accept that their split was final, that enmity would prevail over their fraternal bond.

Lucien was right to suspect that the condition of divorce for his return to the fold of power was a pretext Napoleon was using; it was a way for the emperor to test him. The marriage was the stated obstacle, but it was irrational to view it as such. Had Napoleon really wanted his brother back, he would have softened his stance and accepted Alexandrine. What was truly intolerable to the man who led the world and determined the course of Europe was Lucien's nerve to disobey him and to consider his private felicity more important than affairs of state. For there was the crucial fact of Lucien's republicanism: Everyone, except him, was now groveling before Napoleon because he was an emperor and a king, restoring monarchic culture within the polity, creating a court and playing the game of the ancien régime. Not only did this not make Lucien any more willing to obey; in Lucien's eyes it detracted from Napoleon's authority. The more Napoleon and those around him insisted on an objective link between his imperial glory and his right to demand a divorce, the more the fact of Lucien remaining married and pursuing a private life became a crucial political choice—all the more so for one whose public record as a young man had been so remarkable.

Lucien had always stood up to his older brothers when it came to matters of principle. He felt no need to make a secret of his opinions, now less than ever. In a letter to Joseph, whom he had always trusted, Lucien wrote that he refused to expose himself and his family upon the "golden mud" of France's new government.[20] The country was no longer a republic and had not even returned to being a monarchy; it had become a despotic empire, insofar as Napoleon had arrogated to himself the power to adopt any heir he wished (by virtue of a law passed by the Senate in May 1804).

But forthrightness was no longer innocuous; and it was uncouth for the younger brother of an emperor and king to disobey. Most of Lucien's relatives believed it was up to him to give in; since he did not, he was increasingly blamed for the split.

All this was putting a strain on Lucien's family ties. When his mother joined in the chorus of entreaties and warnings, he panicked a little. Letizia had long believed that a reconciliation might be possible, but Lucien's inflexibility now disappointed her. She began to blame Alexandrine, accusing her in a letter to Lucien of being a bad mother to her stepdaughters. Lucien wrote back, asking her, "How is it possible, my dear mother, that you should have forgotten all the care and maternal affection my wife has devoted to Lolotte and Lili? How can you suppose my wife is a bad mother and I a blind father?" Letizia also suspected her daughter-in-law of taking her son's money and investing it for herself in Paris. Lucien was incensed that his own mother could believe such rumors: "[A]bsence makes room for slander," he wrote, "and soon your affection or at least your esteem for us, which we value as much, will be taken away!" Lucien told Letizia how things in fact stood: He and Alexandrine had decided to take the education of their children into their own hands, without entrusting it to foreign tutors. Alexandrine was teaching them to read and write, a Mlle Adèle to dance, a M. Edouard to draw. Piano teachers were hired as well. Lucien often sat in on lessons, and it was all going as splendidly as could be. Alexandrine looked after her stepdaughters with extraordinary care, and they in turn looked to her as if she were their mother. As for Alexandrine taking Lucien's money, "Who is the despicable rascal who could have made you believe such things?"[21] He had simply allowed Alexandrine to sell her diamonds to pay off an 80,000 franc debt incurred by her first husband.

Now that parts of Italy, including Genoa and Lucca, had become Napoleon's fiefdoms, Lucien felt besieged by his family and increasingly in need to defend the moral rightness of his choice. In August 1805 he wrote to Elisa, whom Napoleon had made princess of Lucca, in response to a letter she sent Lucien in which she stated that, in her new position, one had to live only for glory and renounce affections. His reply read like a manifesto for the virtuous, private life he found himself leading:

This horrible maxim is perhaps admissible in the position of an Agrippina [Nero's mother] or a Catherine [de' Medici, queen of France] and, if it is true, it is enough to poison the great thrones of the earth and to make one pity those that fate placed upon them; but you, my sister, luckily you are in a different position: a princess of Lucca can live for herself and her affections—that even is her whole life; powerless in the pursuit of war, peace and glory, you do not need that awful reason of State that breaks natural ties, subdues the purest affections and leads bad princes from a worrisome and arduous youth to an old age filled with terrors and remorse; in a word, since you are happy in not needing to be feared, ensure that you are cherished.[22]

In early October 1805, it was Elisa's turn to give morally inflected advice to her brother. While a new war was breaking out on the continent and the emperor was at the head of an army, while all the brothers—including Jérôme, who had gone to Paris—and her own husband were doing all they could to be useful to France, brilliantly fulfilling the roles that Napoleon had given them, was it possible for Lucien alone to "remain idle in the most critical moment of the family's history? Must your gifts remain unused, and is there really no way to reconcile your affections with what you owe France as a brother of the reigning family, and as a Frenchman?" Could he not see that by serving his country now he would earn not only glory but also the favors and blessings of his family? "The sacrifice you would make would be great in this moment. . . . You would bring back happiness into your family. . . . I do not speak of my own satisfaction, which would be higher than anyone's—I have loved you ever since I've known you—I have spent by your side the sweetest years of my life, and if there have been clouds since our separation, believe me, my heart has forgotten everything."[23]

Tenderness and pressure continued to mingle in Elisa's clumsy attempts at recovering a relationship that had been deteriorating for years. She remained insensitive to the fact that the only way to do so would have been by embracing Alexandrine wholeheartedly. And that was something that she felt unable to do.

By late summer 1805, Lucien and Alexandrine were still uncertain about where they would settle. At some point, Lucien even considered purchasing the apostolic palace in Pesaro. Cardinal Consalvi politely wrote him from Rome that the bishop's residence was not for sale, but Lucien was always welcome to return to the Holy See, where the pope expected him with open arms.[24] In September, Joseph wrote to Lucien, reminding him that he was an enemy in the eyes of Napoleon, who was warning him to leave Italy because the country was soon to be the theater of an inevitable war. The best recourse, wrote Joseph— in the tone of the friend and confidant he had always remained—was for Lucien finally to return to France and do as he was told.[25] He also announced that Doctor Paroisse was finally well enough to travel to Italy to visit Lucien, who should attend to what his old friend had to tell him.

Far from changing his mind or leaving Italy, Lucien was about to move with his family to Rome: They had a strong desire to settle down, and they did so in the Palazzo Lancellotti, where Fesch lived. By the time Doctor Paroisse reached them—entrusted with the mission of persuading him to change his stance—they were already establishing themselves in the Eternal City. The two friends were delighted to see each other again at last; and of course, Paroisse failed in his mission.[26]

Napoleon was now busy with his campaigns and had eased his pressure on the rebel. After losing the Battle of Trafalgar in October 1805, the emperor gave up on trying to vanquish England and decided to focus exclusively on the rest of Europe. Success happened on land more readily than at sea: The French won the momentous Battle of Austerlitz against the Austrians and the Russians on December 2. As a result, on December 26, Napoleon was able to sign the Treaty of Pressburg with Austria, which marked the end of the Holy Roman Empire and was enormously advantageous to the emperor: Austria's possessions in Italy, Bavaria, and parts of Germany were ceded to France. It was a major achievement, and Napoleon thought it was time for him to become a living monument by engaging the sculptor Canova to finish the marble portrait the great artist had begun a couple of years earlier.

Lucien and Alexandrine were friendly with Canova—they had already become a well connected, fashionable couple in the Roman milieu. One day they went to visit his studio, where he was giving the last touches to the ten-foot-tall statue of Napoleon—only the head had been taken from life. He was explaining to the couple, as well as to other visitors, what he intended to do with the colossal piece, when a gentleman walked in. Canova welcomed him very politely; the man replied with a strong British accent. This was all the more surprising since English travelers were rare in Rome at the time.

Clearly well educated, the man loved the arts and immediately found common ground with Lucien. Alexandrine observed that he was unusually communicative for an Englishman. While his questions to Canova revealed an impressive erudition, at first he did not know who the artist's guests were. The couple was surprised to hear him ask the sculptor, in his heavily accented Italian: "But my dear Canova, tell me, *al fin del conto* [at the end of the day] why did you put this ball in the hand of your naked hero?" (Napoleon was represented holding a ball in his right hand.) The artist answered without missing a beat: "*Carissimo* my lord, it is strange that you should ask me this. *Perbacco* [for Bacchus's sake], this ball represents the world, the nations that are subjugated to Napoleon." "Ah! ah! I understand," replied the Englishman, "let's see then." He took his spectacles out of his pocket and started examining attentively not the statue but the ball. He finally stared at Canova and his visitors and stated, "Oh well! Surprisingly, I keep looking at your ball, my dear Canova, but I can't see England!" Canova replied: "True, my lord, it is not yet there: but as you can see there is plenty of space for the ball to be filled!"

Canova's wit was equal to that of the English visitor, but he did feel the need to apologize before his guests for having responded with a biting epigram to that respectable gentleman, who finally introduced himself as an Anglican bishop named Lord Bristol. Canova praised Lord Bristol's patriotism, and Lucien asked the sculptor how he could have accepted employing his great talent for the sake of immortalizing the conqueror of his own country. Alexandrine added: "Despite your genius, if I had been your hero's wife or mother, we would not be morally satisfied with his general expression: He looks more like an Attila or a Totila, those brutal types of heroes, than like those magnanimous men who rule fairly, such as Caesar or Charlemagne." Canova replied: "Your observation is correct. It has already been put to me, and I accept it without trying to justify myself, counting for that on posterity, and also on you, Madame, who clearly understands me better than anyone else!" With a complicitous smile to Lucien's wife, he said that his justification was in his signature, at the bottom of the sculpture, which read: "Canova of Venice." It was a subtle statement, since the ancient Venetian republic had fallen to Napoleon.[27]

Canova was devoted to his city and would have sacrificed anything for it, had doing so been of any use. That was a sentiment Lucien could easily understand. After all, he was sacrificing his political career to his convictions. But he had the means to do so, while still living as agreeably as he wished. He could easily support his family. He did not need to sacrifice material comfort or give up on a grand life. In early 1806, he acquired the seventeenth-century Palazzo Nuñez, or Bocca d'Oro, on the Via Bocca di Leone, not far from the Spanish Steps. (It is now the Palazzo Torlonia.) Not especially elegant, but comfortable, pleasant, and spacious, it was the perfect place for him and his family to settle in. The palace was rich in abundant, fresh water that flowed all the way from the Umbrian town of Trevi—the very source that feeds the famous Trevi Fountain. Lucien undertook extensive renovations and decided to construct a classical style "naumachia" basin—in effect an internal swimming pool—in which he could teach his wife and children how to swim. He had retained from his Corsican childhood his love of swimming, and this was a joyful project, for him as well as for them.

In his new home, Lucien could also indulge again his artistic passions: Finally he was able to re-create his gallery of art, now enriched with the prestigious collection of classical sculptures he had purchased from the Giustiniani family (owners of the Bassano palace where they had lived). His painting collection was outstanding. There were two major paintings by Bronzino (both in New York today—the *Portrait of a Young Man,* at the Metropolitan Museum, and *Ludovico Capponi,* in the Frick Collection), Velazquez's great *Lady with a Fan* (in London's Wallace Collection), Titian's celebrated *The Three Ages of Man,* Lorenzo Lotto's striking *Portrait of Giovanni della Volta with His Wife and Children,* the sensuous *Drunken Silenus Supported by Satyrs* by the Rubens studio (all in London's National Gallery), and the moving portrait by Rubens of his own wife, Hélène Fourment (at the Rijksmuseum in Amsterdam)—to name a few of the most notable works.[28]

PRIVACY ISSUES

Lucien merely wished to enjoy his comfortable private life, surrounded— and in a way protected—by artistic beauty and domestic peace. On February 15, 1806, Joseph entered Naples as king. By June, Louis would become king of Holland. Lucien wanted no part in the imperial family's expansion that followed the Treaty of Pressburg, and no confrontations. He was tired of defending himself and longed for an amiable status quo. But his family continued to perceive his material, and indeed spiritual, independence as provocative, and it put him at odds even with the only sister who had originally encouraged him to move to Rome, Pauline. She was in Paris, still recovering from the loss of her son as well as from her ill health. But in early March she found the time and energy to write a none-too-subtle letter to Lucien, in which she explained that it was crucial for him to understand how important a reunification was for both the Bonaparte family and for Lucien's own children.

She was clearly writing in the name of the whole Bonaparte clan, on whom the issue of succession was starting to weigh heavily: Napoleon's inability to produce an heir of his own by Joséphine was causing him, and the family, intense dynastic anxiety. Since his marrying into another royal European family might cause enmities and jealousies, it seemed most appropriate to plan on forging an internal alliance. The emperor had therefore adopted Joséphine's son, Eugène de Beauharnais, and would give him the kingdom of Italy; he had then adopted her daughter, Hortense de Beauharnais, now married to Louis. Pauline explained to Lucien that, had he been present, he could have preempted the worrisome rise of that "other," Beauharnais family, insofar as Napoleon could marry Charlotte (Lolotte), Lucien's eldest by Christine—who was then merely ten years old.

Pauline merely sketched the semi-incestuous possibility before moving on to emotional pleading. She told Lucien how much pain he was causing: Their mother was "still ailing," "aggrieved" at the rise of the Beauharnaises at the expense of the Bonapartes, "and she will die of pain if you consent to live apart from the whole family." Pauline understood that Alexandrine mattered, but then so did "a tender mother, a whole family made unhappy by you, and the good of your daughters." Any effort on his part to return to the family would be "recognized by the Emperor; he is fair, he is good, he will open his arms to you, and he will ensure a fate for your wife and your two children. As for the rank which is yours, the Emperor is ready to give it back to you." Lucien was "too clever" not to see that the Bonapartes could no longer behave like "simple individuals." If Lucien did not return to the fold, "we will be obliged to regard you as the main cause of our woes, and therefore forced to abandon all relations with you." She did not want that. "It would be very hard on my heart," Pauline wrote, "but inevitable if you do nothing for us. I hope you feel the importance of all this? It will be the only way of proving to us that you love us and wish our happiness."[29]

Pauline's attempt did not succeed with Lucien any more than had the blackmailing tone of Talleyrand or the guilt-inducing words of Fesch and Elisa. In fact, his response was positively angry:

> I am barely suppressing, my dear Paulette, the indignation that your letter of March 6th is causing me, in order to speak coldly of the proposition you dare make. So you believe that I should abandon my wife and children, rid them of their honor and civil status, that I must make this sacrifice to return to you and take up my rank in the political order; that if I fail to do this, I am the main cause of your troubles and that you will interrupt all relations with me. What are your troubles?

And he listed his siblings' various positions: "Duchess of Guastalla! Carolina of Clèves! Elisa of Lucca! Joseph, whose friendship with me is known, is King of Naples. You would need to be very unreasonable not to be content: what the Emperor does for his wife's family is due to his friendship for his wife and not to my love for my wife." He entreated his sister to "cultivate the Emperor's benevolence," to "think of what he does for you and not constantly of what he does for the others; do not think there is another family in your Emperor's family, and finally, in order to put an end to your troubles, stop hating the children of the good Louis and do not persecute those of Lucien with your revolting and silly proposals. . . . This advice is of more worth than that which you give me; as for your relations with me, this response is the last one."

Lucien did not stoop to mentioning the plan involving his Lolotte. But the comment about Pauline as Duchess of Guastalla was somewhat snide. Napoleon had just given her that title. Guastalla, however, was a mere village near

Parma, in the Emilia region of Italy—a small portion of the so-called Duchy of Parma, Piacenza, and Guastalla, which had belonged to the Bourbons until 1796, when Napoleon had first begun turning the area upside-down. Pauline was resentful of the modest size of the endowment she received, especially when compared to the rather more substantial holdings her siblings were granted. In order to pacify her, Napoleon devised the solution that she would be able to resell it to the kingdom of Italy, which was effectively a French annex, and included not only Emilia and Veneto but also Piedmont, Lombardy, and Tuscany. (Napoleon declared Tuscany a French department—even though it was under Bourbon rule as compensation to that dynasty for its loss of the same Duchy of Parma, Piacenza, and Guastalla.) Rome itself had become the French empire's "second city." Napoleon could play any card he wished. Pauline was all too happy to take up the invitation: She sold the duchy for the staggering sum of 6 million francs—an amount that, once invested, would give her a handsome annual income. She was able to keep her title—about which she had no complaint—along with the feudal lands that came with it. In short, she emerged from the arrangement in very good shape. As for the inhabitants of Guastalla, they felt cheapened by a transaction in which they played no part, simply being passed on like some bauble, *bijou de toilette,* as Lucien put it.[30]

The frequent accusations of greed spread by Napoleonic agents against Lucien conveniently omitted the fact that, had he divorced Alexandrine, he too would have been showered in gold by his brother the emperor. Instead, he soon found himself struggling. Letizia had bought from him the lavishly restored Hôtel de Brienne. By July 1806, the payment of the second half that was owed him—600,000 francs—had been delayed by several months: Napoleon refused to release his mother's funds precisely in order that she be unable to give them to Lucien, who in the meantime had decided to buy the Villa Rufinella in Frascati and was paying hefty interest (1 percent a month) on the money he had confidently borrowed.[31] Letizia apologized for the delay, about which she could do little. She was saddened by Lucien's resistance to his brothers, who, she wrote, all loved him and cared for his welfare, but she nevertheless urged her son to be extremely prudent when he spoke about the emperor. The overdue payment was made only in September.

In the meantime, however, Lucien was not to let these money issues—and his brother's control over them—ruin his summer. Life was full enough in any case. On June 14, Alexandrine gave birth to their second son, two months early. They named him Joseph Lucien. Lucien decided the new birth was an opportunity to write Napoleon with family news; the emperor did not reply, but Lucien was unaffected by the silence. There was the premature baby to think about. And the country villa was a great source of pleasure. The beautiful sixteenth-century residence, redesigned in the eighteenth century by the architect Luigi Vanvitelli, was supposedly built on the site where Cicero's villa had once stood: There the most public Roman intellectual had set his philosophical dialogues, the *Tusculan Disputations*. Lucien loved the idea of fashioning himself on the model of the Roman private citizen leading a life of cultivated, refined leisure in his country retreat, which included what he called "archaeology in action"[32]—physical excavations, as opposed to the mere study of antiquities and classics, which he had been pursuing all his life with great enthusiasm and keen erudition. He knew from the experiences of the previous owners—the Borghese family, and the Jesuits before then—that the area was rich in Roman and early Christian treasures. Soon he was unearthing some remarkable sculptures. One of them was a virile statue of an Apollo or, Canova argued when he came to see it, an Alexander the Great.

It was a happy, peaceful time, filled with intimate joys, with children, art, and antiquity—far from the violence, rumble, and bustle of contemporary wars and cares. Even the frightening earthquake that occurred in the region in late August became an opportunity for an adventure: No one was hurt, but some parts of the palace crumbled, and it seemed safer for the whole family to move out of the villa and into rustic cabins built on its grounds. Children and nurses were excited to camp out, as it felt to them; and Alexandrine, delighted with these unusual conditions, suggested they all stay in the cabins until the end of the summer. There were to be a few small aftershocks, so the decision turned out to be wise. Moreover, the cabins were closer to the excavation area than was the villa itself, so they could easily keep a close eye on the ongoing archaeological digs. An impressive number of objects emerged, although few were as valuable as the sculptures they had found at first. There were many anonymous tombs and modest coins, which seemed to indicate that the ground had served for the burial of slaves. There also emerged funerary lamps decorated with erotic themes and the grave of a mother and her children, which bore the name of Coruncanus, a character named in one of Cicero's own orations. This led to weeks of passionate research, speculation, and discussions with archaeologists and a new friend of theirs, the erudite Abbé Fea. Another grave was found soon after, which turned out to be that of the Rufini family—and this was deemed to be the origin of the villa's name.

The excitement of these endless discoveries was all-encompassing, and it continued after the family had moved back into the villa itself. A stream of Romans who were spending late summer in their country estates, away from the city's seasonal heat, came to visit, eager to see the archaeological sights, and Lucien was pleased to receive personally those who were artists, scholars, and amateurs. All this activity was distracting. Lucien was so entranced by his new occupation that he barely glanced at the correspondence that arrived from Paris, although he made an exception for his mother, who wrote that Fesch was about to return to the Eternal City after having spent a period of time in Paris with her.

When the time came for the family to move back to Rome, Lucien took with him the most beautiful of the statues that had been excavated, placing them carefully among the Giustiniani collection of sculptures in the Palazzo Nuñez. The start of autumn brought an end to the carefree atmosphere the family had enjoyed over that gorgeous, fertile summer of 1806. Almost immediately upon their return to town, the pressure resumed, this time in the shape of a new letter from Fesch. Its contents were nothing new: It urged divorce in exchange for a practical, comfortable arrangement for the children, and so on. Letizia contributed similar words. Joseph had done so a few weeks before, again pleading with Lucien to change his mind, and had reported to Napoleon Lucien's usual, negative response. But it was with his uncle that Lucien took issue—this time he hit him hard, gloves off:

Have you forgotten all honor, all religion? I wish you would at least have sufficient
common sense not to think I am like Jérôme [. . .] and to spare me the insult of your
cowardly advice. In a word, don't write me again until the religion and honor that
you are trampling under your foot have dissipated your blindness. At least hide your
base sentiments under your purple robes, and follow in silence your own path along the
highway of ambition.[33]

Lucien immediately wrote to Joseph, copying him his responses to their mother and to the cardinal, and telling him he hoped that they would leave him in peace at last.[34] A week later, in mid-October, Letizia wrote him: "Very beloved son, finally I have received the response that I was awaiting so eagerly, but how different it is from the one I would have been charmed to receive. God's will is that I am destined to live in sadness and misery."[35] She also reproached her son for having treated her half-brother Fesch too harshly.

Lucien wanted to hear no more. He was eager to avoid any further conflict, and the best course of action was to distract himself with other matters. Months went by uneventfully. While Napoleon's Great Army raced across Europe, dispensing death and reaping conquests, Lucien and Alexandrine pursued their peaceful life in the Palazzo Nuñez. Ever true to his passion for dramatics, Lucien had set up a little theater at home, where family productions could be staged just as they had been at Le Plessis. In April 1807, he wrote to Elisa about the *Mithridate*, by Racine, which the family and their friends had performed—in French—before a choice audience of two hundred, with much success. They would be performing *Zaïre* next, then *Alzire, Pygmalion*, the *Folies amoureuses, Cinna*, and closing with *Athalie* and the *Misanthrope*. It was a full season. Lucien explained to Elisa that he was in this way devoting himself to the "ideal world," disgusted more than ever as he was with the "political world." There was decidedly nothing to prefer to a private life: He wished for his sister "no greater principality than the one you possess." He closed with news about their children; the couple were expecting their seventh. It was an affectionate letter, devoid of the defensiveness and rage that had pervaded the correspondence in the previous year.[36]

Then came some good news from Paris, at long last: In late spring 1807, Lucien's old friend Lethière was appointed director of the Académie de France in Rome (the lovely Villa Medici, on the Pincio Hill, overlooking Piazza del Popolo).[37] Taking advantage of the painter's departure for Rome in July, Letizia sent Lucien some personal effects that she had found in the Hôtel de Brienne. She reminded him not to entrust the post with any confidential news and is likely to have given some confidential messages for her son to Lethière.[38]

The painter's promotion to the prestigious post had been Lucien's own doing in part; and it had not been smooth to obtain it for the half-black, fiery artist. Lethière's luck had turned one day, when he was sitting at the Café Militaire in Paris, and an officer had started making fun of his mustache and of the color of his skin. Enraged, Lethière had challenged the officer on the spot (as he had done with the Spanish count on Lucien's behalf)—and killed him. As a result, his studio had been shut down, and he had lost all his means of support. He had called on Lucien, his former patron, who, albeit disgraced, was still able to wield some influence. After the sudden death of the man who had been the director of the Villa Medici, Lucien had immediately begun lobbying on behalf of the painter and had written to the new queen of Naples, Joseph's wife, Julie Clary, his loyal friend, to help him nominate Lethière to the post.[39]

In the summer of 1807, birth and death succeeded each other rapidly in the household of Lucien and Alexandrine. In late July, Alexandrine gave birth to another child, Giovanna (named after the mother of Pope Pius VII). But baby Joseph Lucien, just over one year old, died on August 15, at the Villa Rufinella in Frascati—near where Dermide had seen his last days three years before.

The presence of their old friend Lethière was a great consolation to the family. His son was the godson of Lucien—after whom he was named. The painter went to see his friend and patron at Rufinella as soon as he could, on September 20. The two friends were thrilled to be reunited after some years of separation. Lethière's best student at the Académie was none other than the young Jean-Auguste-Dominique Ingres, who pursued Lucien's patronage and portrayed him amid Roman antiquities, with a charming smile and a book in his hand. The portrait depicted him leading the contemplative life he wanted from now on. But it was hardly the life that his brother wanted for him.

FIVE

EMPIRE

1808–1815

"But tell me, what is he like, eh?" said Prince Andrei again.

"He is a man in a gray overcoat, very anxious that I should call him 'Your Majesty,' but who, to his chagrin, got no title from me! That's the sort of man he is, and nothing more," replied Dolgorukov, looking round at Bilibin with a smile.

—Tolstoy, *War and Peace*

THE MANTUA MEETING

Joseph, king of Naples, was the only person in the family Lucien still trusted. Even Letizia had proved to be disappointingly receptive to the skilled slanderers working for Napoleon. In late 1807, Joseph left for Venice to meet Napoleon. On his way, he stopped to see Lucien in Velletri, not far from Villa Rufinella, then wrote to him from Venice on December 4.

The rather breathless, affectionate letter read like a last-ditch attempt at mollifying the rebel brother and making him understand, even empathize with Napoleon's point of view. The emperor loved Lucien in the end, Joseph wrote, insofar as he loved the family above all else. His one fault was to be "Emperor and powerful," otherwise he would do anything that Lucien wanted; it was just that, as emperor, he could not afford to be wrong. Lucien would find that Napoleon had become a "simpler, better" person, as if thriving within "the strange degree of power he has acquired." The emperor had even told Joseph a number of times that he had nothing for which to reproach Lucien, who had harmed only himself by marrying without Napoleon's approval; and he was upset that Lucien had not come to see him. The conditions for a meeting thus seemed propitious, according to Joseph. "[T]he rest depends perhaps upon a change of mind, a circumstance I can neither predict nor guess at, but I can tell you that the Emperor sees the future, that he wants to establish his dynasty before all else, that he loves his family, that nothing else has any bearing on his affections, but that he wants to remain the leader, and not to approve of anything he hasn't willed." Joseph found Napoleon fundamentally unchanged from the brother he had known from his childhood and discreetly encouraged Lucien to seek out a rapprochement.[1]

Because this was Joseph writing, because his tone was inoffensive and his words honest and humane, Lucien was persuaded to accept the overture, which he understood to be his very last chance at making up with Napoleon, his brother, emperor and king of Italy. He left Rome at once, on December 7, choosing as usual to travel incognito. He was in Modena three days later. Joseph had left Venice a couple of days before with the emperor, who was on his way to Mantua, and he arrived at Lucien's hotel just as he was about to go to the theater. Lucien and Joseph dined together and discussed the forthcoming meeting; and they met again the next day for lunch, after which their ways parted, Joseph taking the road back to Naples and Lucien going on to Mantua, where the meeting with Napoleon was to take place. Before leaving Modena, Joseph wrote the emperor that Lucien was eager to come see his majesty, given the goodwill Napoleon now had toward Lucien and his eldest daughter, but that he should be aware that Lucien had "sworn on his honor not to disown his wife and children."[2] Joseph had tried to talk Lucien out of his resolution, without success. He was sorry not to be able to report anything else to his majesty but entreated the emperor to act out of the goodness of his heart and the brilliance of his mind.

Napoleon was looking forward to the meeting, holding high hopes for a positive outcome regardless of Joseph's warning: He wrote to his mother that "Lucien has written to propose a meeting which I also desire strongly. Write to him on my behalf that his letter found an echo in my heart. I reserve to him the throne of Tuscany. He will reign in Florence and shall bring back to life the century of the Medici. Like them he loves and protects the arts. And like them he will give his name to the epoch of his reign."[3]

Lucien arrived in Mantua on the morning of December 13. He was shown to the guest room in the Palazzo Guerrieri—the Palace of Justice today—where he was to stay overnight, since the emperor was expected there only in the late evening. It was nighttime when Lucien was summoned to see him. Then he had to wait to be called into his brother's presence; exhausted by the long trip, he was half asleep when he heard a voice loudly whispering "Sire, your brother Lucien!"[4] while a door opened into a large, strongly lit room.

Lucien saw a seated figure, studying a map of Europe that entirely covered a round table. The man, his left cheek leaning on his left hand, was engrossed in placing colored pins onto the map. He did not respond to the announcement. Lucien stood there for some time in complete silence, unable to take in the shocking reality that this man was his brother, the emperor.

"Sire, it's me, Lucien," he finally said.

Napoleon looked up. He dismissed with a wave of his hands the mustached bodyguard who had introduced Lucien into the room, rose from his chair, and walked toward his brother. He had become rather corpulent since Lucien had last seen him, two and a half years before in 1804. The emperor took his hand, with a tender, nearly friendly expression on his face. Lucien made to embrace him, but instead Napoleon kept holding his hand, at arm's length, and said: "So it's you. . . . How are you? How is your family? When did you leave Rome? Have you had a nice trip? How about the pope? Does he like you, the pope?" The flood of questions bespoke embarrassment, and Lucien did not quite know what to answer. He simply said that he was well and was pleased to see that this was also the case with his majesty.

"Yes, I'm well," he replied, "but"—patting his belly—"I'm getting fat, and I'm afraid I'll put on more weight." He took some snuff, staring at Lucien. "But you! You're looking good you know. You were too thin. Now I find you almost handsome."

"Your Majesty likes to flatter me."

"No, it's true. But let's sit down and talk."

They sat near the large table. Napoleon moved around the colored pins. As Lucien opened his mouth to say something, anything, Napoleon asked him, point blank: "So, what do you have to say to me?"

"Sire, I await to hear what Your Majesty wants to tell me for himself. You were good enough to express the wish to see me; from what my mother writes, as well as Joseph, I can't conceal that I dare count on the return of Your Majesty's favor."

"And you can count on it all the more that this entirely depends on you."

"In that case, all my wishes will be fulfilled, for my greatest desire, my absolute will, is to please Your Majesty in all that can be reconciled with my honor."

"That is very well, but in what exactly do you reconcile your honor these days?"

"Well, Sire, these days, as usual, in the accomplishment of the duties set by nature and by religion."

"And politics! Sir, what about politics! Doesn't it mean anything to you?"

"Sire, politics, that art of governing well, which is the special virtue of kings, that of Your Majesty, I cannot participate in it, I am just an obscure individual, who has become, has had to become absolutely foreign to statesmanship."

"It was only up to you to be king like your brothers."

"Sire! The honor of my wife, the civil status of my children!"

"You always say your wife, you know full well that she isn't your wife, that she never has been and never will be, because I do not recognize her, I never have and never will."

"Ah! Sire!"

"No, I shall never change toward her, the heavens may fall on our heads, I shall never change. I may have forgiven you your faults, you are my brother, but her! . . . She will only have my curses, and those of our family."

Napoleon had been inquiring only after Lucien's daughters by Christine when he asked how his family was, and Lucien was getting irritated. Pretending to laugh, he said: "Sire, beware of curses, there's an Italian proverb, *la processione torna dove esce,* the procession returns to where it came from, and I wouldn't want that in this case."

Napoleon seemed insensitive to Italian superstitions. He merely repeated what he had said—adding that he had heard enough things about Alexandrine, then mitigating that statement: "I know that one tells me these things in order to please me. I know the world is full of calumny, but even then, heavens may fall, she shall never be my sister-in-law . . . in any case the law is clear. It is now a fundamental French law, like Salic law, that any marriage contracted by the imperial family without the consent of the Emperor is null. Do you understand that?"

"Sire, my marriage precedes that law."

"Yes, but it was made because of you."

Lucien smiled faintly at this.

"What are you laughing at? I don't find it funny. I know everything you, your wife, and my enemies who are your only friends say about this. . . .

No good Frenchman is on your side; the nation has passed its judgment on you. . . . Has anyone complained on your behalf about the sénatus-consulte [a law passed by the Senate] that excluded you and Jérôme? No, because everyone condemned your ridiculous marriages. Have no illusions about people's opinion, you can only regain your reputation by accepting my policy, which is what Jérôme has done."

Lucien began to grow angry: Napoleon was the one who had illusions about people's opinions, he said. "Courtiers who approve of your attitude toward me—my recompense for help I was happy to give you—are only doing their job. My servants tell me that I am right too!" The jibe began to ignite Napoleon's anger, but Lucien went on with increasing vehemence, standing up—as if performing an oration—and reminding his brother that the nation saw him, Lucien, as the "savior of the one who could save her" on 18 Brumaire, comparable not to Jérôme but to Napoleon.

Napoleon had regained his composure, sardonically describing Lucien's reaction to the whole affair as akin to the inflamed passions that ran in the Jacobin clubs. While Lucien had been "useful" to him on that day, said the emperor, it was not so clear that he had "saved" him. Not only that, but Lucien had had to be persuaded by Napoleon and Joseph, over a long discussion that lasted half the night, to promise he would not say a word to the Council about Napoleon's plan to "unify" power by concentrating it in his own hands. Lucien knew this was true, and he still regretted having made that promise; even at the time he had strongly felt that if Napoleon gained absolute power, he would be a dangerous man—capable of becoming a Genghis Khan or a Tamerlane. Napoleon argued that Lucien's opposition to his "personal rise" on 18 Brumaire canceled any debt he had toward this "bad citizen, denatured brother, blind to your own interests." He conveniently chose to ignore that Lucien had not merely assisted him but, once outside the Orangerie before the armed men, had indeed saved his political neck and perhaps even his life.

"EUROPE IS TOO SMALL FOR THE TWO OF US"
They continued to talk, in calmer tones now, about what had happened all those years before. It was nearly midnight by the time Napoleon ended that

discussion of "ancient history." He had not summoned Lucien for such "lecturing." Lucien was eager to leave. It crossed his mind—as it had earlier, on his way to Mantua—that Napoleon was perfectly capable of not letting him go home and of holding him captive. He knew he had to control his anger at all costs and avoid any further provocations. He still trusted his brother in some way—Napoleon was not exactly a tyrant, despite his tyrannical acts—but never before had he been in the presence of his brother as emperor. Power relations had changed radically, and it was a fearful moment when Napoleon said: "Listen to me, Lucien, weigh all my words. And let us not fight. I'm too powerful to want to expose myself to getting angry." But he quickly added, as if to reassure Lucien: "You came here in trust. Corsican hospitality cannot be betrayed by the emperor of France. . . . May that virtue of our ancestors and country guarantee the good faith of my words and your full security." That was more reassuring. Still, Lucien remained circumspect as Napoleon paced up and down the room, an expression at once dreamy and agitated on his face, until the emperor took his hand, squeezed it strongly, and said:

"We are alone here, aren't we? We are alone? . . . No one hears us. . . . About your marriage: I'm in the wrong. Yes, I've gone too far; knowing your stubbornness, your pride—for all this, you see, is only a matter of pride, which you call virtue, just as we sovereigns call politics everything that has to do with our passions—I shouldn't have interfered with your wife. I have felt this more than once. I repeat, I am certain that my confidants don't do her justice . . . many people have dared tell me good things about her, and maman tells me she loves her, because she makes you happy and is a good mother."

"Ah, Sire, that is so true."

"Good, good!"

Consul Lebrun, said Napoleon, was one of those who had spoken well of Alexandrine. (Joséphine was even convinced Lebrun was in love with her.) On one occasion Lebrun had said that he had reason to believe that the young lady's soul matched her beauty.

Those were pleasing and unexpected words for Lucien. But Napoleon went on: "I am far from despising your wife, but I don't like her, I even detest her because it is the passion that she inspires in you that has deprived me of the brother on whose talents I counted the most. What is certain, though, my dear Lucien, is that her beauty will fade, you will be disillusioned about love and you will turn against my policy, and I will be forced to persecute you whether I like it or not. For if you are not with me—let me tell you—Europe is too small for the two of us."

"Sire, Your Majesty is mocking me!"

"No, literally: either friend or foe."

"Sire, Your Majesty does not have a friend more devoted than myself."

"I won't see it in this way as long as you don't accept my policy. That's easier for you to do now than it has ever been. My family politics have changed . . . which means that your children, whom I have had to keep outside my dynastic plan, could be very useful to it: but they will have to be dynastically legitimized. You know full well that, since they were born of a marriage I haven't recognized, they cannot inherit rights to my crown. So what would you do in my place?"

"Sire, if Your Majesty wants my children to be included in his inheritance, it seems to me one would need a sénatus-consulte by which you'll simply declare that the children of your brother Lucien, although born of a marriage Your Majesty did not consent to, become able to succeed—"

Napoleon barely heard Lucien through, interrupting him to say: "I know I can do that, but I shouldn't; what about opinion? You'd be triumphant over me, fine; I understand that may suit you; but I can't give in to you without necessary compensation. What would the family say? What would my court say, and France, and the whole of Europe? Such a retraction on my part would harm me more than a lost battle."

"But, Sire, I am ready to compensate you in any way you wish for the sake of my children. Should I, and my wife, beg your forgiveness for having married without your permission?"

The emperor kept taking snuff between his fingers, without sniffing it. He seemed to hesitate, and Lucien tried again.

"Sire, surrender to my plea, you shall not have a more faithful servant than myself; I shall employ my whole life proving to you my gratitude."

"Good God, you press me hard, and I am weak! But I will not be so weak as to pass that resolution for your children: I can no more do that than recognize your wife! May the skies fall upon me, I repeat it, she will never be my sister-in-law!"

The unexpected return to the old refrain—after what had seemed like progress—made Lucien feel at once surprised, hurt, and furious. He tried to control his nerves, saying "Well, then, what do you want of me?"

"What do I want? A simple divorce."

"But you have always maintained that I was not married! If we aren't married in your eyes, how can we divorce? A divorce requires a broken marriage."

"Precisely. I told you, my family politics have changed. You see, by asking you to divorce, I am willing to recognize your marriage, but not your wife. And divorce won't harm your children, as would the annulment of the marriage, separation, and so forth."

"In my view, Sire, separation, divorce, annulment, anything to do with separation from my wife, is dishonorable for me and my children, and I assure you I shall never do anything of the sort."

"How can it be that despite your cleverness you don't understand the difference between what I propose today and my old request: Your annulled marriage rendered your children bastards, both in civil and dynastic terms, and so did your separation, since it followed on my not consenting to your marriage, thereby annulling it."

"Annulled in your eyes, Sire. All this may be the case as far as inheriting your crown is concerned. But believe me, the civil status of my children is recognized throughout Europe. You are free to do as you wish with a throne you've conquered with your sword, but not with the patrimony of our father Charles Bonaparte, which no one would think of denying to my children. They are all legitimate before God and religion—when the pope gave one of our daughters the name of his mother, he did not view her as illegitimate, even though he is perfectly aware of your opposition to this marriage."

Napoleon proceeded to explain again to Lucien that he wanted a divorce in order to legitimate the children dynastically—since ordering a divorce implied his recognizing the marriage. Lucien would not even need to separate from his wife; she would be "honored" as suitable if she accepted gracefully this "oblation" to his politics and to France's future. "If she refuses, she will stand accused, along with you, of having sacrificed your children's true interest to a matter of self-esteem. Your children will remain lowly individuals by your fault and will have all the right to curse you and your memory. Give it a thought."

"Sire, I hope my children will always be worthy of myself and their mother. History will teach them ours, and if they are capable of the feelings you menace me with, I disown them already for being of my blood."

"Now, now, you are incorrigible, always taking everything so tragically. I don't want any tragedies, you hear? Just think about it."

"I already have: I shall never deviate from what I believe to be the honorable path. If that is what one calls incorrigible, then, yes, that is what I am."

"It's not my fault, you don't want to give in, you prefer a woman—"

"My wife, Sire!"

Lucien had been trying to leave for a while. Every now and then Napoleon seemed to want to end the conversation—but then started talking again. This time it was about their relatives, and Joséphine's. If he had given the Cisalpine Republic to her son, Eugène, he said, that was only because he needed someone trustworthy there. In fact, he would rather give it to Lucien. He was not too happy with Joséphine's daughter, Hortense, even less with her husband, their brother Louis; and their own mother, Letizia, was apparently jealous of Elisa's being Princess of Lucca. No one was ever happy. Pauline was the only reasonable one, at least in terms of ambition, because she was "the queen of trinkets"; and her beauty increased with age. Joséphine was getting old, and since she could no longer have children, she was sad and boring, living in fear of divorce, or worse. She cried each time she had indigestion, believing someone was trying to poison her so that Napoleon would be free to marry someone else; that was "detestable."

But in fact a divorce would be necessary soon enough. Had Napoleon divorced earlier, he would have older children by now—"you should know, I am not impotent as you all used to say." "I, Sire," replied Lucien, "have never said that, for the good reason that I believe quite the opposite is true." Napoleon revealed to his brother that he had a few children now, two of whom he was certain were his, one by a young companion of Hortense he had met with her friend Madame Campan, the other by a gorgeous Polish woman

married to an old man—"oh I know he is impotent"—and that one was
an angel, of whom one could indeed say that her soul matched her beauty.
To Lucien's smile, he replied, "You laugh at seeing me in love; yes, I am in
love, but that is always subservient to my politics, according to which I must
marry a princess, even though I would rather crown my mistress. That is how
I would like you to behave with your wife."

"Sire," Lucien replied, "I would agree if my wife were merely my mistress."

Napoleon did not react, musing about his own choices with regard to
a new wife. He would always regret not having "taken" Princess Augusta,
daughter of his best friend, the king of Bavaria—how stupid to have "given"
her to Eugène, who was unable to appreciate her and was unfaithful to her
even though she was the most beautiful and best of women. He then asked
Lucien how old was his eldest daughter, Charlotte. "Almost fourteen," responded Lucien. "If you had accepted my policy," said Napoleon, "I would
already have betrothed her to the prince of Asturias or to some other great
prince, perhaps even to a great emperor."

Then he returned to the matter of divorce. The main point was that
Napoleon's divorce from Joséphine would not be noticed too much if Lucien's divorce from Alexandrine took place at the same time, or a little earlier,
since Lucien's would attract all the attention. "Yes, really you ought to do
it," Napoleon stated, and in response to Lucien's silent, astonished gaze, he
added "Why not?" For a second the emperor looked embarrassed: He was so
used to everyone doing his bidding, on command, that, for a moment, he
forgot that he was talking to the hard-headed Lucien. But he repeated, "Yes,
you ought to do that for me—but, my dear President"—as if Lucien were
still president of the Council of the Five-Hundred—"this would be favor for
favor, and this time I would not be ungrateful."

≈∂ ∂≈

Lucien, resolved as ever never to separate his political and private position
from that of his wife, felt gratifyingly superior to his brother at this moment
and sank into a sort of reverie. Barely listening to Napoleon's words, he observed this man who would not have become first consul without his own

actions on 18 Brumaire—he liked to remind himself of that—and who, despite his now-tremendous power, continued to cultivate his irritation against
a woman whose only fault was that she was Lucien's wife, and this at the expense of natural, fraternal love, even gratitude. There was no more doubt in
Lucien's mind that Alexandrine was just a very convenient pretext for keeping him away from power: Napoleon was intent on proving to himself again
and again that his decisions alone mattered in the world. Now, as Lucien's
attention returned to Napoleon, his brother talked about his dynastic plans,
reiterating that Lucien's divorce would minimize the public ill effects of his
own, increasingly necessary divorce from Joséphine, who, at forty-four, was
past childbearing age.

But Lucien was convinced that Napoleon had enough nephews already
to ensure adequate succession. Broaching as delicately as possible the matter
of Alexandrine's contrasting youth and fertility, he told his brother there was
no parity in this necessity to divorce for the sake of children. Surprisingly,
Napoleon was not offended at this unpleasant reminder: "Your wife . . . well,
your wife! . . . haven't I had you informed of this? . . . she'll become Duchess of Parma, and your eldest son will inherit her title without having to
lay claim to your French princedom, the first title I'll give you while awaiting a better one, that is, an independent sovereignty." Lucien smiled at the
word "independent," because he knew how little independence his siblings
enjoyed in Napoleon's empire. "Well yes, independent," said the emperor,
"because you'd know how to govern, whereas the others. . . ." There followed a string of complaints regarding those "others," especially Louis, king
of Holland.

Then, with a devilish glint in the eye and whacking his hand onto the
map of Europe, Napoleon said with increasing feverishness: "As for you—
choose. You see, I am not fibbing: All this is mine, or will soon be; I can
already do what I please with it. Would you like to have Naples? . . . I'll take
it away from Joseph, anyhow he doesn't care much for it, he prefers Morfontaine. . . . Italy, the most beautiful jewel in my imperial crown? Eugène
is only its viceroy, and far from despising it, he hopes I'll give it to him, or
that he'll inherit it if he outlives me. He'd better not count on this, I will live
until I'm ninety, I need to in order to consolidate my empire completely. . . .

In any case, Eugène will no longer suit me in Italy once his mother is re-pudiated. . . . Spain? Don't you see her fall into my hands, thanks to the blunders of your dear Bourbons, and the ineptitude of your friend the Prince of Peace? . . . Wouldn't you thoroughly enjoy reigning where you were once only ambassador? . . . But so, what do you want? . . . Tell: Everything you could ever want is yours, if you divorce your wife before I divorce mine.

"Oh! Sire, I would not even be tempted by your beautiful kingdom of France for the price of my divorce, and—"

Then the emperor's tone changed from vehemence to complete dryness. Taking a new, imperious air, he interrupted, saying: "Do you by any chance believe you are on more solid ground in your private life, of which, by the way, I could easily deprive you, than I am on my thrones? Do you believe that your friend the pope is powerful enough to protect you against me, if I want to seriously torment you?"

Napoleon's pride had been struck, all the more so since he knew that Lucien benefited from the pope's friendship and did indeed have reason to believe he was on solid ground in his Italian exile. But having closed the door to Lucien's political life, the emperor was perfectly capable of tormenting him, as he put it, in his private life. Remembering Napoleon's benevolent warning that he was too powerful to want to be angered, Lucien chose not to say anything except that he hoped the pope would never need to protect him. He made sure his tone was humble and moderate, without being ab-ject: That was the only way to demonstrate to the emperor how unwavering were the principles by which he lived. Lucien proposed again and again the sénatus-consulte that would recognize his children; again and again Napo-leon repeated "everything for Lucien divorced, nothing for Lucien without divorce."

Realizing the conversation would lead nowhere, irritated but eager for the meeting not to turn nasty before it ended, Lucien made a gesture to depart—discreetly enough, given that etiquette required it be the sovereign who dismissed him. Instead, Napoleon took his hand again and said, in a strangely confidential tone: "If I divorced, you would not be alone in doing so with me; for Joseph awaits my divorce to declare his." Julie Clary was "only good at producing girls" rather than the boys that were needed—girls were merely of use for political alliances, and these daughters, Zénaïde and Charlotte, were still too small even for that. "But didn't you say that your eldest is fourteen? Well, that is the age; would you not be willing to send her off to maman, for example?" Lucien replied that he would be happy to do anything for the emperor that would not contradict his own principles. "Good, good," answered Napoleon, rather brusquely, "in this case, I'll have maman ask you to send her." Although Letizia and Elisa had been thinking of marrying Charlotte—Lolotte—off to Napoleon, the emperor's plan was to marry her to a prince. Then, referring to the old days when he used to pull children's ears, he added: "Don't you fear for your spoiled child. Tell her we'll be good friends, I won't pull her ears."

Napoleon continued talking. He seemed obsessed with the need for nephews: They would be buffers between the children of Louis and Hortense and those he himself hoped to have, "because, once Empress Joséphine is repudiated, their grandmother and her son Eugène, whom I should never have made so powerful, will always be the enemies of my legitimate and even adopted sons. No, there's only one way for me to neutralize the power of Louis's children, and he only ever loved the first one, who died in Holland." Napoleon might well legitimize or adopt the natural children he had mentioned earlier, he mused. After all, Louis XIV had legitimized his bastard sons. (Lucien refrained from reminding Napoleon that the Sun King's dispositions had been annulled after his death.)

The emperor then breezily returned to the theme of Joseph's divorce: He was sure that it would occur. Lucien said that he would believe it when he saw it. Napoleon, now good-humored, said jovially: "Oh yes he will! Joseph will do it, and you too; the three of us will do it together, and we'll remarry the same day." Lucien had become rather serious, he added; he seemed an ancient sage. "You should stay with me for these three days; I'll have a bed prepared for you near my bedroom." Lucien, more wary of his brother's charm than of his threats, refused the offer politely, on the pretext that he would need the leisure to meditate on everything Napoleon had told him. The offer was reiterated. Lucien resorted to the excuse that one of his children was ill, and he needed to get back. "You're going to discuss things with your wife; well, good-bye to our plans for a rapprochement," Napoleon retorted.

"Sire, I daresay you are mistaken; Your Majesty's projects don't have a better ally than my wife, and if her children were to benefit from them, then she would be all too happy to change her position. It is a great source of grief for her to be the object of Your Majesty's personal hatred. I sometimes worry that she may collapse from anxiety over this."

"Really! I'm sorry about that. Take care that she does not die before you get your divorce, for then I would no longer be able to legitimize your children."

This was meant as a joke, although Lucien did not find it funny. Finally Napoleon dismissed him: "Well, leave then, since you want to—and keep your word." The brothers had had enough of each other. Napoleon extended his hand and presented his cheek, which Lucien kissed in a respectful rather than fraternal manner before rushing out of the room. As he heard the emperor calling out to Méneval, his private secretary, he accelerated his pace, eager to get back to his carriage. It had been waiting since midnight, which had struck long ago.

THE CITIZEN OF FLORENCE

A few days later, Napoleon reported to Joseph on his meeting with Lucien. His "thoughts and language are so different from mine," he wrote, "that I had trouble understanding what he wanted." What Napoleon did understand was that Lucien would consider sending his eldest daughter to Paris, to stay with her grandmother:

If he still wishes this, I would like to be apprised of it immediately; this young person will have to be in Paris in January, and escorted on her way to Madame either by Lucien or by a governess. Lucien seemed to me torn between various feelings, and not strong enough to decide which one prevailed. I have exhausted all the means in my power to induce Lucien, young as he is, to devote his talents to my service and to that of the country. If he wants to send off his daughter, she will have to leave without delay, and he will need to send me a declaration by which he puts her entirely at my disposal; for there is not a moment to lose, events are pressing, and my destiny must be accomplished. If he has changed his mind, I also need to be apprised of this immediately; for I shall find an alternative.

Tell Lucien that I was touched by his pain and by some of the feelings he expressed
toward me; and that I regret all the more that he does not wish to be reasonable, nor
ensure his peace of mind, as well as mine.[5]

Joseph chose not to disturb Letizia's peace of mind; she wrote to Lucien in late December 1807 that Joseph had found the emperor in "the best of dispositions" toward him, which enhanced her hope and happiness.[6] She did not know the whole truth. With Lucien, Joseph could afford to be much more candid. On the first day of 1808, he wrote to him an affectionate letter in which he explained the importance of sending Lolotte to Paris with the aim of marrying her off advantageously: Lucien had erred in not giving Napoleon an immediate, straightforward answer regarding this arrangement, which would ensure "the well-being of the family and especially that of your daughter."[7] Napoleon was perfectly capable of replacing her with someone else, wrote Joseph, and if this happened, everyone would suffer—not only Lolotte but also the other children, his wife, and himself. It was all up to Lucien; and if he refused to do this, then "I don't know you anymore—how, with the mind that you have, can you believe one may fool a man such as the emperor, how can you not feel that not to send your daughter is akin to having him buy her." Joseph cared deeply for the welfare of Lucien and his family. But he was also intent on maintaining a good relationship with the emperor, and he took his duties toward him seriously. He ended his letter by telling Lucien he would gladly come embrace the children, whom he loved, but he had learned not to sacrifice the future to a moment of satisfaction.

Lucien decided not to send Lolotte to Paris immediately—she was not quite fourteen yet, and he was in no rush to part with her. He also utterly disliked the husband Napoleon had proposed for her—the prince of the Asturias, estranged son of the king and queen of Spain, whom he had met in Madrid.

In the meantime, a dramatic development ensued: French troops occupied Rome on February 2. Lucien was unabashed about taking sides with the pope, who, just a few weeks later, gave him the fiefdom of Canino, a small town north of Rome, in exchange for much-needed financial support to the papacy. Given that Napoleon sought to break with the pope, the emperor did not appreciate this alliance and decided to put pressure on Lucien for him to leave the Papal States. He wrote to Joseph on March 11:

> *My brother, Lucien is misbehaving in Rome, even insulting Roman officers who are on my side, and he is showing himself to be more Roman than the Pope. I would like you to write him to leave Rome and to retire to Florence or Pisa. I don't want him to stay in Rome, and if he refuses to leave, I only await your reply to have him taken away. His behavior has been scandalous; he says he is my enemy and that of France. If he persists in these feelings, the only refuge for him is America. I thought him bright, but I see that he is just a fool. How could he stay in Rome when the French troops arrived? Wasn't he supposed to retire to the countryside? Worse, he stands against me. There is no word for this, I shall not suffer that a Frenchman, and one of my brothers, should be the first to conspire and act against me along with the scum of the clergy.*[8]

In late March, Letizia wrote to Lucien confirming that he must leave Rome at once, so as not to lend substance to the rumor that his hatred for the emperor was turning into antipatriotism. The letter's tone was dry; Letizia told her son he should move to Tuscany in order not to worsen his situation any further, and signed herself "your most distressed mother." The pressure was on again—not surprisingly, for there is no doubt that Lucien was behaving provocatively. He also knew that he had no choice other than to leave Rome.

On April 17, 1808, he and his family arrived in Florence, staying the first night in the hotel Aquila Nera, where he registered under the name of General Boyer, his usual incognito. He was recognized all the same and treated with deference. The next day the family moved into temporary lodgings at the elegant Palazzo Ximenès, lent to them by a Corsican cousin of the Bonaparte, General Pascal-Antoine Fiorella, while they searched for a villa in the countryside. There were offers of such a villa from, among others, Tassoni, the resident minister of the kingdom of Italy, who immediately started writing confidential reports about Lucien for the benefit of the French court.

Florence welcomed Lucien and his family warmly. When they appeared at the theater, the public spontaneously offered them a standing ovation and escorted them to their carriage at play's end, just as had happened in Paris a few years before. The rumor was spreading that Lucien would be the next king of Etruria. As the Duchesse d'Albany, who had been the mistress of the poet Vittorio Alfieri and then of the painter François Gérard, wrote from Florence: "We are a bit sorry not to be a capital anymore, and if we could have had Lucien as sovereign, everyone would have been happy. Yet Lucien does not want to be anything but a citizen, and one of foremost standing at that: As king he would only be playing second fiddle. He busies himself with the arts, buys a lot of paintings and does a lot of charity work. He has a beautiful wife who is a little over the hill, and a slew of children." In another perceptive letter, she wrote: "It is said that Lucien has a lot of wit and character. One wishes him to be king of this country, but it is said he does not want a throne. His wife is still quite good-looking; although she is said to be still young, she is corpulent, not much of a quality in this country, where one likes women to be thin and slender. They live in a very retired fashion. I would admire his resolve to remain a private citizen if I did not believe that, given how very rich he is, he would be happier as a sovereign."[9]

While Lucien managed to keep up at least the appearance of a happy life, he was increasingly anxious about his precarious position and worried that Napoleon might act against him in a brutal way. In a letter she wrote him in May, Letizia entreated him to "stop complaining about whoever it may be and realize that your unpleasant position might prevent you from seeing things the way they are and make you unfair toward your brothers, who are all sincerely attached to you."[10] Their attachment would soon be proven by their actions: Jérôme and Louis—who was acquiring the property of Frascati—pitched in to help him out of ongoing financial troubles, by contributing 200,000 francs. Joseph took care of this family loan, which involved complex pan-European transactions, with the assistance of Roederer, his minister of finance, and a few other trusted friends. Even then, Lucien felt he had good reason to fret, and was preparing himself for the eventuality of a speedy departure to America.

In the midst of all this, in April, Napoleon had named Joseph king of Spain. As soon as he received Joseph's acceptance of this powerful position, the emperor ordered that they meet in Bayonne, which was on the overland route from Naples to Madrid. He also asked Joseph to stop on the way to see Lucien and gauge whether he might have thought things over and changed his mind. And so, on May 27, 1808, a few days after he had left Naples, Joseph met with Lucien in Bologna.[11] He had more offers from Napoleon, all contingent on Lucien's divorcing Alexandrine, of course: The throne of Portugal could be Lucien's, or indeed the throne of Naples, or, finally, the title of viceroy of Spain. As ever, Lucien showed no interest, adding that the latter offer was unlikely to be of any substance, since Napoleon was against the division of kingdoms between brothers. He also warned Joseph that Spain would be a thorny place to rule—as he himself had seen firsthand during the year he had spent there negotiating a difficult peace treaty. They discussed at length matters of government and heredity, agreeing to eventually marry Lucien's daughter Lolotte to Joseph's son, in order to counter the rules that prevailed in Spain, according to which heredity was passed on through daughters: Such a marriage would prevent a daughter of Joseph from ruling over a non-French population. For Lucien, the plan was acceptable, on the condition that he was able to move to America immediately.

The prospect of leaving Europe for America was becoming more real every day. Lucien had written to his mother at the end of April about the hypothetical plan. Letizia was desperate at the very thought of his moving overseas; by June, she wrote a frantic letter to Joseph, in the hope that he ensure never to put such a plan into action: "[Y]ou are a brother just as I am a mother, I just beseech you not to leave me in this state of uncertainty, or I would not have long to live."[12]

There was nothing certain in Lucien's life, but, however temporary the arrangement, he settled as comfortably as he could in Florence, setting up most of his three or four hundred paintings and hundreds of antique sculptures, art objects, and some precious furniture from the Roman palazzo in the rented villa.[13] He still kept over forty masterpieces in Rome, where the collection was known as galerie Bonaparte, an extraordinary, not-to-be-missed marvel, according to most visitors. He commissioned portraits of himself and his family from the best artists living in Florence, including Gérard, and from his friend Fabre, who a few years before had painted him, Alexandrine,

the children, Letizia, and Elisa. The Florentine artist Giovanni Antonio San-
tarelli portrayed the whole family in his lovely cameos.

Lucien's good manners and generosity made him popular with the Flo-
rentines. The Italian states under Napoleonic control had been ravaged by
war and welcomed a peace-loving, enlightened patron of commerce and the
arts such as Lucien, who was opposed to the heavy taxations imposed by
local administrators. His private actions bespoke his virtues: For instance,
he tried to buy and restore Michelangelo's house. He provided dowries for
the two daughters of a poor peasant whom he had met during a walk in the
countryside. But despite such displays of optimism and grandeur, and despite his evident potential as an able citizen-prince, Lucien was not about to
reenter the fray of public life. In his mind, there remained only one possible
course of action: sailing to America. He made plans to sell a part of his collection to Joseph or to Napoleon for two million or at least one million and
a half francs—a fair sum, which would have allowed him to leave soon and
live well overseas.[14] Joseph could not afford to buy it, but in the meantime,
the 200,000 francs he helped provide for Lucien were a temporary help.

Elisa helped as well. She had fully reconciled with Lucien and wrote
him affectionate letters. The Princess of Lucca was jealous of the favor
granted by Napoleon to her younger sister, Caroline, who suddenly became queen of Naples when her husband, Joachim Murat, was called to
replace Joseph on the throne. In what she perceived as her downgraded position, Elisa could not resist the temptation of visiting—in incognito—her
rebel brother with whom she now felt a renewed bond. Eager to smooth
over the recent frictions with Lucien, she made affectionate overtures to
Alexandrine, who was pregnant again, and even paid for some of Lucien's
expensive art commissions.[15]

By October 1808, family matters were far from Napoleon's mind: He was
busy negotiating a European truce at Erfurt, in Germany, with Tsar Alexander and the German princes (a peace that would soon be followed by more
wars). During his absence from Italy, Lucien and his family were able to en-

joy some respite from imperial pressure. Madame Mère, who thought of the emperor as the father of the whole family and still wished that Lucien eventually would obey his will, had advised her son in late September to forget once and for all about America—after he had urged her to request passports for him and his family from the emperor.[16] "If your stay in Florence becomes too unbearable," she wrote, "then rent or buy a little country villa."[17] Pisa would be a good place, she thought.

But there was no need for a house in Pisa. Letizia was unaware that Lucien had already, and discreetly, acquired a sizable property in Canino, where the pope had given him his fiefdom; and this was no mere country villa. Still, her intervention seems to have lifted the imperial ban on Lucien's leaving Tuscany—it was always she who exerted the greatest emotional and moral authority on Napoleon. In mid-November, Lucien and his family moved to the Canino property, north of Rome, very near the Tuscan border but back inside the Papal States. Lucien wrote to his mother that he was living in great tranquility in the little village of Canino, where he was busying himself with his lands, turning an old Templars' convent named Musignano into a farm, building barns, and restoring the main property, while the family stayed in the village houses.[18] On rainy evenings, he worked on an epic poem on Charlemagne. The collecting continued; artists and engravers visited. Alexandrine was due to deliver their fourth child in two months (counting the daughters they each had before meeting, this was to be the household's eighth child).

Their son Paul was born full term in February 1809. Spring was as peaceful and uneventful as the autumn and winter had been. The family stayed put in their new property until June, when they went for the summer to the spa town of Bagni di Lucca, staying near Elisa, who had her summer residence there and warmly welcomed them. By then she had become grand duchess of Tuscany, compensation enough for Caroline's crown and motive enough for her to regain her loftiness. She had insisted on exerting some control over her brother's life by forbidding, for no clear or explicit reason, her friend Madame d'Abrantès from having any contact with him.

Still, the chatty Mme d'Abrantès went to see the Tusculum villa in its inhabitants' absence. She was intrigued by the situation this "elder of a family of kings" had put himself in, willfully remaining a "simple citizen under his brother's despotic rule," and seeking consolation as a disillusioned republican in Tusculum—on the very land where Cicero had spoken freely, spiting the tyranny exercised by his erstwhile ally, the future emperor Octavian.[19] In Rome, Mme d'Abrantès frequented some of Lucien's friends; she noted how appreciated he was there and learned how active he was as a patron of the arts. She was told that he cultivated his gardens for the pleasure and well-being of guests and visitors rather than for his own. She had never much liked him in Paris, but now she began to see his virtues and to regret that she was not able to visit with him. The man was infamously controversial; but from what she saw and heard, his private life was much more virtuous than passing acquaintance or public rumors suggested.

LOLOTTE IN PARIS

When Napoleon had told Lucien that Europe would be too small for the two of them, he was not speaking lightly: The emperor wanted to rule over the whole continent, and dissidents, even potential ones, could not be allowed anywhere. His thirst for domination never seemed to be quenched. In Spain, Joseph played king puppet while the unspeakable horrors of war, eerily depicted by Goya, ravaged the country: Cruelties were perpetrated by the French army against a civilian population that reacted with equal violence.[20] Meanwhile, Napoleon was engaged in Austria. He occupied Vienna in May 1809; after a setback at Essling, he crossed the Danube on July 4 and defeated the Austrians at Wagram two days later. Frantic diplomatic negotiations ensued, and by October, with the Treaty of Schönbrunn, Austria ceded Istria and Carinthia to France and Salzburg to Bavaria. One secret clause in the treaty was that Napoleon was to marry a young Austrian princess, Marie-Louise, daughter of the Holy Roman Emperor Francis II. In planning this new alliance, Napoleon disregarded how unlucky had been the previous marriage of a French monarch (Louis XVI) to a princess from Vienna—and the notable fact that Marie-Louise was the great-niece of the hapless Marie-Antoinette.

Napoleon divorced Joséphine on December 15, 1809. The divorce was a painful experience—especially for Joséphine, who soon afterward left for Malmaison, but also for Napoleon, who knew that he was to "marry a womb." But that was the point: He had divorced for the sake of heredity and would remarry for the same reason. This was no passion but an alliance made for the national good. That Napoleon had not been able to persuade Lucien to do the same—to submit to the ordeal that the emperor himself had subjected himself to, sacrificing the love marriage contracted in his passionate youth for a larger purpose—continued to be intolerable to him.

It had always been crucial for Napoleon's strategy, and especially his vanity, to discount from imperial eligibility the many children Alexandrine was bearing Lucien: Her impressive fertility was a maddening reality he did not want to contend with, for in no way could he suffer Lucien to be superior to him in that regard—or any other. In recalling the meeting in Mantua to his minister Roederer over a year after it occurred, the emperor raised his voice in a fit of extreme rage: "My whole family must be French. When Lucien, in Mantua last winter, dared to speak to me as if I were a foreigner, I told him, 'Leave, poor wretch, get out of my presence; no more relations between us'! I have conquered Spain; I have conquered it so that it be French!"[21] The unexpected fury with which he uttered those words seemed the expression of deep, personal rather than political frustration.

The news of Joséphine's "sacrifice" was accompanied by rumors that Louis and Hortense were divorcing. On December 25—ten days after the Senate declared Napoleon's marriage void and before the identity of the emperor's new bride was announced—Elisa wrote to Lucien about this other separation as probable rather than certain. Lucien's prophecy that the unions imposed by Napoleon would fall apart seemed to be coming true; it was a vindication, but hardly a consolation for him. And in the face of overwhelming family pressure, he himself was relenting to a degree, making plans to send his daughter Lolotte to Paris, two years after the emperor's request. In the same letter, Elisa alluded to her wish, shared by Mme Mère, that Lolotte marry Napoleon (neither Elisa nor Letizia knew yet whom Napoleon had picked as his new bride) to avoid any risk of dispersing power outside of the family, as had happened with the Beauharnais clan.[22]

On New Year's Day 1810, Lucien announced to Joseph that Napoleon requested Lolotte's presence in Paris. She should be sent to Letizia.[23] The timing seemed right to him. Now that Napoleon was finally acting on his legitimate need to bear some heirs, Lucien's stubbornness regarding his own marriage might perhaps matter less to him; some accommodation might be found. But Lucien had no more notion than Letizia of the extent of Napoleon's fury. On February 3, the emperor summoned Andrea Campi, Lucien's factotum, who was serving as a messenger between Paris and Canino, and exploded:

> When I made him minister, [Lucien] embezzled funds and accepted bribes of which I have recently had proof. [Whether some zealous agent had fabricated this ten-year-old evidence, we do not know.] I should have had Mme Jouberthon arrested. Their first son is a bastard. . . . You say he's my friend! Did I see him in Austerlitz or at Eylau? When I was on the battlefield, he was sleeping with his wife! I loved the empress: It is because of him that I had to divorce her, because I had to think of the future. If he doesn't leave his wife, let him leave for America. . . . If he stays, I will have him arrested with his wife and children, and he will die in prison. I claim to have a right of life and death over my family. They will say this is despotism, but Europe will applaud. Who are his friends? The Faubourg Saint-Germain, the Bourbon partisans! How shameful! And he calls himself my brother![24]

By late February 1810, all plans regarding Lolotte were finalized: Lucien and his family made ready to dispatch the fifteen-year-old to France. Campi would accompany her. After meeting with him, Alexandrine wrote an effusive letter to Napoleon, in reaction to the offer she received of the Duchy of Parma, in exchange for her divorce:

> *Ah! Sire, what can be, or perhaps cannot be my response to His Majesty? May I be able to tell him the truth without displeasing and offending him? . . . Only slander could have damaged me in Your Majesty's eyes. . . . If I had one day the strength to believe, as Your Majesty does, that the duties and virtues of private life, even in a woman's heart, should yield to the duties and virtues of one's country's politics, I would not want to partake of such duties and virtues. . . . And if I could decide to sacrifice the happiness and honor of being the cherished companion of a man such as your brother Lucien, only God in heaven might compensate me for it; down here such compensation is not even in*

the power of the all-powerful Emperor to whom I have the honor of addressing myself
at this moment.

No, Sire, the duchy of Parma, any other sovereignty . . . could not be any kind of
compensation for me . . .

Sire, I throw myself at your feet. It is as impossible for me to secretly part from
Lucien as it is for him to leave me publicly. We belong to each other in life and in death.
It only befalls me to implore of you, for the first time, the one favor Lucien ever solicited
from Your Majesty. Sire, allow us to live peacefully in some corner of your Empire.

Alexandrine signed "very humble, very obedient servant and subject"—but
Alexandrine Bonaparte nevertheless.[25] That name in itself signaled everything but submission to the emperor's will. And the tone of her entreaty was
far too heady to move Napoleon, as Christine's letter had managed to do
many years earlier.

❧ ❧

Whatever hope remained for a positive solution to the long-term feud between the emperor and his headstrong brother and undesired sister-in-law
thus rested on the frail shoulders of Lolotte. Her arrival in Paris on March 8,
1810, did not seem to change the situation. Two days later, Letizia wrote a
harshly worded letter to Alexandrine about the unhappiness that their marriage had brought to the family, urging her to accept to divorce. "The Emperor wants your divorce: It depends on you to persuade Lucien to effect it,
if he refuses to ask you for it. . . . Do not hesitate between a life filled with
bitterness and grief, which you must expect if you go on being stubborn, and
the perspective of a happy future."[26] She assured Alexandrine that their children would be recognized by the emperor and become kings and queens, and
that the dissolution of their marriage would not put an end to the friendship
and affection Letizia felt for her. Needless to say, the letter did not persuade
either Alexandrine or Lucien to change their minds.

Lolotte was blissfully ignorant of the battle that was raging behind her
back and unaware that she was being used as a pawn in it. From the moment
she set out for the French capital, she wrote nearly daily letters to her parents,

reporting to them upon her arrival how she was shown into her room and how, after speaking with her aunt Pauline (Letizia was out at the theater) and then resting for a while, she awoke in tears at the thought of being so far away from her family.[27]

She had never left home before, and she would remain inconsolable, though she tried her best to control herself, as her father urged her to do. The emperor welcomed her a few days after her arrival, embracing her quietly. Slowly she settled in. A dancing teacher was found for her, as well as a piano teacher and a singing teacher. Soon enough she found she was too busy with lessons to write her letters home as often as she wanted to—and as Lucien and Alexandrine wanted her to do, since they had asked her to write about all of her experiences and thoughts, as long as she entrusted her letters to a friend and sent them with the proper precautions. But she was miserable, lost her appetite, and barely went out. Only religion kept her afloat, though she did see her uncle Jérôme, who gave her two cashmere shawls, and the emperor just once more. At the end of March, Paris celebrated the upcoming marriage of Napoleon and Marie-Louise. Lolotte did not participate. She barely saw a few fireworks over the city.

Soon enough, though, she did begin to live a little. She wrote to her parents that she began to gain a little weight again though she continued to cry whenever she thought of Canino. Despite her extreme immaturity and extraordinary naiveté, so apparent in her letters, Paris had some effect on her, and she acquired a measure of sophistication. She proved a keen observer of her surroundings and family and an attentive recipient of whatever gossip reached her young ears, describing new outfits, outings, activities, likes and dislikes, and people with verve as well as candor. She heard enough to be a useful informant for her family in Canino, for instance writing that Cardinal Consalvi, the pope's right arm, would not be coming back to Paris because he had refused to attend the divorced emperor's wedding. There was also the news that Pauline was unwell and wanted to take to the waters, but was desperate because the emperor wanted her to throw a party before leaving that would cost her 120,000 francs, and she did not have that money. The new empress, meanwhile, had told Pauline that she was pregnant; indeed, she was vomiting all the time and visibly putting on weight at an alarming rate. When Lolotte's aunts came to visit with Letizia, they spoke ill of the emperor and entreated Mme Mère not to go see him more than once a month. Letizia followed the advice. Lolotte could have reported this to the emperor when she saw him, she wrote, if she had followed her aunts' example and been a bad girl—but she did not have it in her. Meanwhile, everyone in Paris was talking about her potential marriage, some guessing to the prince of the Asturias, others to an archduke, others to the grand-duke of Luxembourg.

When Lolotte lunched with Cardinal Fesch and Jérôme and his wife, Catherine—king and queen of Westphalia—she reported that the latter was "ugly beyond belief." On another occasion, there was a lunch at Letizia's home with Pauline (who was very affectionate with Lolotte), the king and queen of Westphalia, and Fesch, where both Pauline and Jérôme advised her not to marry an old man. There was more: After lunch, Pauline told her confidentially that Caroline Murat, queen of Naples, had suggested to the emperor that Lolotte should marry the grand-duke of Würzburg, and that she, Pauline, had persuaded the emperor not to take up this idea: The man was ugly and in ill health, had bad teeth, and was an admirer, not to say companion, of the queen of Naples herself.

It was the first time talk of Lolotte's marriage had been so concrete. Of all the family, Elisa (who had taken care of her when she was a child) was the one who had the least to do with her; she was heavily pregnant and feared to miscarry. As for Jérôme, she wrote, he was upset about being already married because he seemed to have wanted to marry her, Lolotte, even though he had declared a short while earlier, at another family meal, that she was not pretty; to which Pauline had responded that she found Lolotte good-looking because she resembled her. Lolotte had gone on to eat quietly while they spoke. That same evening, at the theater, she had overheard Jérôme discreetly telling Letizia that it would be good to marry her to the prince of the Asturias. Lolotte promised her father that she would refuse such a party if it were ever proposed in earnest; and whatever happened, she would never respond to any proposal without consulting him. Letizia had told her what the emperor had decided: If Lucien came to Paris (and thus divorced, although Lolotte did not know this), then Napoleon would marry her well. But otherwise the emperor would adopt her—at this thought, she wrote in parentheses, "think, dear father, what a torment it would be for me to be adopted by a bad man who would deprive me of my father"—and marry her off as disadvantageously as he could.

Lolotte had sharp comments for the whole family: The queen of Naples, Caroline, was behaving oddly and was constantly in the company of a young ambassador, a certain Meternik (this was Metternich, the future Austrian minister, who was rumored to have had a liaison with Pauline as well). Everyone was noticing it. Later, in mid-May, Lolotte wrote to Alexandrine what she thought of the looks of the family that surrounded her. The painter Jean-Baptiste Wicar had begun a portrait of her, depicting a tall, slender girl with fine features, dressed in the colorful garb of a Canino peasant. If it resembled her at all, the portrait would have stood in sharp contrast with the women Lolotte described: Pauline—who sang badly, in French and Italian—was attractive enough, but not charming, and she, Lolotte, did not like her looks. The queen of Naples was supposed to be a beauty, but in fact she was short and very fat. Grand Duchess Elisa was not pretty, and as for Jerôme's wife, Catherine the queen of Westphalia, and Julie Clary the queen of Spain (she was married to Joseph), they were both "extremely ugly, and not at all, but not at all pretty." Catherine had no children yet, and Elisa's daughter Napoleona had no grace in her gestures or speech—"I think that when she grows up she will lose much more because her eyes are extremely small, her nose is pretty but won't stay that way." As for Zénaïde, Joseph's daughter, she seemed a nice, fat girl, and Charlotte, her sister, seemed ugly; neither of them wore a corset yet, though the elder was eighteen. What a difference there was, she wrote, between these cousins and her own siblings, Lili (Christine-Egypta), Anna, Charles, Letizia, Jeanne, and Paul (who was teething at that time).

Lolotte desperately wanted to go back home. She wrote one lachrymose letter after another begging her father to arrange her return. Her brutally sincere letters certainly emphasized the contrast between the affectionate atmosphere of Lucien's family and the hypocritical, ambitious nature of the imperial court. Caroline Murat complained of the bad education Lolotte had received at the hands of the detestable Alexandrine; and she had some reason to protest, since Lolotte was used to expressing all of her emotions.[28] Her French, moreover, was less than perfect.

All of these confidential letters were expedited to Italy via the family friend, as had been planned; and the precaution used for them to go unnoticed was a double-sealed envelope. As it happened, this was no challenge for Napoleon's secret police. The letters were duly intercepted, and all of Lolotte's cutting remarks were read to the emperor. At first he might have found them amusing—he knew his sisters and was not one to balk at criticizing family. But when he himself began to be the target of her criticism, he had enough. (The letters containing the most egregious remarks about him probably have not survived.) On May 22, Napoleon wrote an angry letter to Letizia, telling her that he had never wanted Lolotte to come to Paris and that she, his mother, was to blame for this disaster. When he had welcomed the girl with open arms, he did not know that she was already ruined by Letizia and corrupted by Lucien's morals—that she was so bad-tempered, ill educated and heartless. Lucien wanted her back? He could have her back at once. He no longer considered Lucien's family part of his own and wanted to have nothing ever more to do with any of them.[29]

The words of an immature but self-confident teenager had wounded the all-powerful emperor's vanity; they were as unpardonable as the passionate and determined actions of her father.

THE AMERICAN DREAM

In the meantime, alarmed by his elder daughter's distress, Lucien had been doing all he could to retrieve her. He sent worried letters to her and increasingly frantic ones to Napoleon: He was both disappointed and angry, having sent Lolotte to Paris, as he wrote the emperor, in the belief that her presence would suffice for a reconciliation without requiring Lucien's divorce. If things went well, he would also have sent his second daughter, Lili. But the plan had not worked, so the emperor should order Letizia to send the girl back to her family. Given the emperor's renewed ultimatum—"divorce or America"—Lucien had started organizing the family's departure for the New World, which he planned for May, and informed Napoleon that he had written to the minister of police in order to obtain passports; he hoped to find an American ship bound for Philadelphia. Lolotte was to be returned immediately—if she were kept in Paris and unable to accompany the family on their crossing, Lucien wrote the emperor, "a scandal would be unavoidable, and despite the proscription, I will come looking for her even inside the Tuileries."[30]

For once, the brothers were in perfect agreement: Napoleon had no intention of keeping Lolotte in Paris; he could not possibly tolerate the insolent creature any longer. Mme Mère did not understand why the girl should leave—no reasons were given in the letter Napoleon sent her from Dunkirk asking her to send Lolotte away—but when the emperor, upon returning to Paris, showed the girl's letters to the whole family, Letizia conceded, subsequently falling ill out of despair. Her plan had failed, just as had failed the plan of swapping the Duchy of Parma for Alexandrine's divorce; and now no reconciliation between her sons was even thinkable. But for Lolotte, the sun shone. She told her parents' friend Mme de Laborde in Paris before her departure, "Well, I'll still have been a princess for three months!"[31]

Lolotte was back in Canino in the early days of June. After a nerve-wracking wait and a long delay, the French passports had arrived almost at the same time, on June 1. With a touch of bureaucratic sarcasm, Alexandrine's papers were issued under the name of "Madame Jouberthon, widow." Lucien entrusted Campi with the management of his properties and prepared himself and his family for the momentous crossing of the Atlantic. Organizing it for the major household was a complicated affair; the logistics were redoubtable and the politics thorny, since wars were raging, and the seas were populated with the British fleet.

Nor was this large family to be alone on the ship: Among those who were to undertake the crossing as well were Father Maurizio, a longtime family friend, chaplain, polymath priest, and astronomer, who acted as a tutor and music teacher to the children; André Boyer, Christine's brother and so Lucien's brother-in-law; the painter Châtillon, who faithfully accompanied Lucien in all his exiles; the vaudeville writer Joseph Servières, who had married Lethière's natural daughter (a portrait painter herself); the family doctor Henri De France; and numerous servants and chambermaids, including the washerwoman. It was an expensive undertaking, which required Lucien to borrow some money, pawn his property and diamonds, and sell some of his paintings as well as some of his horses and carriages. It was mid-June by now.

Lucien asked his brother-in-law Murat for help. The king of Naples managed to make available an American ship named the *Hercules,* a handsome three-master that had been kept in Naples. Murat had it armed and sent it to the port of Civitavecchia.

Finally the time of departure had come. It was none too early. Napoleon's imperial sights were causing more family drama elsewhere. On July 1, 1810, Napoleon forced Louis to abdicate the throne of the Netherlands, annexing the country to his growing empire. No crowns were safe, no European countries untouched by Napoleon's warmongering.

Lucien's family made their good-byes to Tusculum, where they had been for the early summer, and were onboard the *Hercules* a few days later. The ship left Civitavecchia on August 5. The first day of navigation was very pleasant, but on the second, a violent summer storm rocked the vessel and its terrorized passengers, with the children becoming seasick. The ship stopped outside the port of Cagliari, in Sardinia. The captain requested the permission to dock and disembark, but permission was withheld, and the ship was kept off the coast. Lucien learned that the British Royal Navy might well seize the *Hercules.* He wrote dispatches to anyone who might help; there was nothing to be done. A messy few days followed. The English ambassador to Constantinople, Sir Robert Adair, arrived on another ship, the *Pomona;* he met with Lucien at length and even gave him a lavish party onboard the *Pomona,* but still no valid passports for Philadelphia were forthcoming. It seemed that the English feared he might provoke a diplomatic mess, while the Sardinians continued to deny the *Hercules* permission to dock, because the neighboring Corsicans were also wary of Lucien. After a few days of negotiations, the captain of the *Hercules* and all of its passengers were transferred to the *Pomona* and taken as prisoners by the English. By August 24, Lucien and his family were transported to British-run Malta, where they were lodged in Fort Ricasoli, a military fortress and a rather uncomfortable place, although Alexandrine confessed to enjoying the "burning atmosphere of this truly African island"; she was even "enchanted to be there."[32]

Seen from the depressing prison that was the fort, however, the island's burning atmosphere quickly lost its charm. Lucien transmitted a letter to Letizia via Queen Caroline, informing her of what had happened. To his

Corsican friend Antoine-Jean Piétri, he wrote: "Exile and death are preferable to dishonor, and the Emperor, who no longer respects anything, wanted to force me into dishonor. . . . I think that the abdication of Louis, my banishment, the banishment of the Pope and the Spanish war have opened everyone's eyes."[33] Shortly after, the English government allowed the family to be transferred to the much more suitable residence of Sant'Antonio, the summer house of the leaders of Malta. It was a beautiful place, which Lucien and Alexandrine made even more agreeable by purchasing a substantial amount of furniture—trying to provide the impression of normalcy for the children. There they stayed until December—under the guard of some fifty men. Meanwhile, on the suggestion of Cambacérès, at the end of September Napoleon wrote to the president of the Senate to strike Lucien's name off the list of senators (until then Lucien had retained the title nominally), at once humbling his brother and taking away from him the annual salary of 80,000 francs that went along with the senatorship.[34] Napoleon used a diplomatically neutral reason to justify this act: Lucien, having been "absent from the French territory for five years and without authorization," had "thereby revoked his senatorial rights." Although Lucien would soon stop receiving his salary, he did not learn that he had been struck off the list of senators until 1814.

Throughout these tough months, Lucien and Alexandrine hoped they would be freed and allowed to go on to America. But their artistic production continued. Lucien worked on his long poem *Charlemagne* and started to write a short one, "L'Amérique," which included two dozen stanzas celebrating American independence from the "tyrant of the sea," achieved by the great George Washington, who "governs without pride, frees his country,/ with wisdom carries the scepter and with wisdom puts it down."[35] While celebrating the victorious rebel against English oppression, he also aimed at his tyrannical and unwise brother—trying to kill two big birds with one poetic stone. Liberation remained a sheer fantasy, though. The response to Lucien's request for passports for Philadelphia finally arrived from London in November: His majesty George III could neither authorize the trip to America nor prolong the residence in Malta but had arranged for asylum in England, "in a tranquil and healthy place," where, it was promised, Lucien would be able to reside with his family and travel companions. A war vessel was being prepared for their journey.

The prisoners left aboard an English frigate that had been captured from the French off the coast of Algiers and that, ironically enough, still carried its proud original name, *Président*. In mid-December, Châtillon executed a drawing representing the whole family gathered around Lucien playing backgammon with the ship's captain. It was a rough, three-week voyage over choppy seas, and the ship arrived at Plymouth harbor on December 17.

An extraordinary sight awaited the family: Crowds gleefully cheered them, welcoming them to England. Lucien's mistreatment at the hands of archenemy Napoleon was infamous, and the British perceived the newly arrived Bonaparte as a hero and ally for standing up to him. A satirical color print was published a week after the family's arrival, entitled "Universal Murderer of Domestic Happiness, or the Fraternal Tyrant." It depicted the couple and their seven children before a servile-looking messenger of Napoleon who, stating "Votre Serviteur Mr Lucien!!—your imperial Brother is determined to make you great and happy,—here are the terms," presented them with a document on which was written "Lucien, Kick your wife and Children out of doors, I shall marry you to a Princess and make you King of Rome, comply immediately or dread the vengeance of your Brother, Napoleon." Lucien's response: "He seems determined to make me a Villain! But I am determined there shall be one honest man in the family, and will fly to that Country, where character is respected." Alexandrine: "Oh my dear Lucien! here is an end to our domestic peace and happiness." Christine: "Sister is that a friend of my Uncle's?" Lolotte: "Then let's go to England, Father, for that is the only place where Honor and Virtue find partizans."[36]

Lucien was separated from his family for a few days to deal with the authorities alone. (The moment of their separation, which caused much anxiety, was captured in a melodramatic sketch by the artist Jean-Baptiste-François Bosio.) But everyone was reunited swiftly enough, and from Plymouth, the colorful pageant proceeded on to Wales, where they were to rent the country seat of Lord Powis, near Ludlow. Their stay proved pleasant enough, until, in June 1811, Lucien and his landlord quarreled over lease matters. Soon after, Lucien was able to buy a castle not far from there that had belonged to a French émigré: Thorngrove, near Worcester. The castle effectively became the family's new home, their new exile from exile.

They adapted to this new situation as best they could; and England did prove a haven of peace. They were effectively prisoners, in the custody of officials, but they were treated with respect, courtesy, warmth, and kindness. At Thorngrove, Lucien was able to re-create the household they had left behind, including part of his art collection—paintings, drawings, engravings, sculptures, gems, antiquities. Letizia sent money (unbeknownst to Napoleon, of course) to help with expenses, now that Lucien was deprived of his senatorship salary. Life was comfortable, and suitably luxurious.

For a whole year, though, no news arrived from Italy, as Lucien wrote to Campi in December 1811; he suffered from this enforced isolation and, especially, from not being able to communicate with his mother.[37] The family was well liked in Worcestershire, but the inability to leave England weighed on Lucien and Alexandrine. Any restriction on the freedom of movement is an imposition that can make the most lavish abode feel like a claustrophobic cage, however gilded its bars.

Lucien grew impatient. Refusing to admit defeat and still hoping he would have his way, he wrote a letter to the Prince of Wales requesting permission to go to America; the letter was returned to the sender some weeks later, unopened, with the intimation that Lucien must never presume to write directly to the prince again. To Lucien, this was a personal bluff: Outraged, he wrote to his warden an indignant, albeit dignified letter: "Accustomed to write directly to His Holiness the reigning Pope and several sovereigns in Europe (without counting the Princes of my family) I would have believed that there was something sacred attached to the name I have the honor of bearing, that would allow me to be exempted from the official rules. Better instructed, I will conform myself to the general custom."[38] Lucien might have refused power; but, bearing as he did the full consequences of what, after all, was his freely chosen path, he was not beyond referring to his name as reason enough for respect as an equal from royal households, given that all his siblings wore crowns. Perhaps, as Chateaubriand would put it, Napoleon had "rammed these crowns onto new kings' heads, and off they went like a couple of conscripts who had exchanged caps by order of the commander"—but members of the Bonaparte family, including Lucien, were not to be messed with, even in England.[39]

With the prospect of a long-term residence in Thorngrove, there was no alternative but to spend the time as pleasantly and productively as possible. The children thrived, exceptionally well tutored by English teachers, and enjoying their lives in green Worcestershire. Lucien resumed work on his *Charlemagne;* Châtillon illustrated it, and Father Maurizio translated the first cantos into Italian. Samuel Butler, a classicist and bibliophile who was at the time headmaster of Shrewsbury School, translated it into English, committing himself to long negotiations to ensure its publication. When Madame de Staël was traveling in England, she wrote to Lucien about his composition: "I have read a canto of your poem, which I found charming, though you have left in a few careless touches in it, and for Paris one must be exact—here, the charm of its overall conception and of its images will delight—there are also verses of the greatest beauty—where does your talent come from?"[40]

Butler introduced Lucien and Alexandrine to Lord Byron, who was "electrified" by *Charlemagne:* "M. Lucien," he wrote to Butler, "will occupy the same space in the annals of poetry which his imperial brother has secured in those of history—except that with posterity the verdict must be in his favor."[41] Byron's admiration for the artist and the man—"I never knew a being more warm in heart, more amiable and inoffensive yet independent in spirit"—was remarkable, although his generous prediction regarding Lucien's place in the history of poetry was off the mark. In 1814, there appeared in the literary magazine *The Champion* a critical review of the poem: "The brother of Buonaparte [*sic*] may be allowed to take his rank among poets, as Buonaparte himself had done among kings. But the historian of Charlemagne does not appear to us to present quite the same formidable front to the established possessors of the seats of the muses, as the imitator of Charlemagne did to the hereditary occupiers of thrones." It continued:

"Our poet is not the same monster of genius that his brother was in power. In the career of fame, he does not risk the success of his reputation by the unlimited extravagance of his pretensions. . . . *Charlemagne* is the work of a very clever man, rather than of a great poet. It displays more talent than genius, more ingenuity than invention. . . . But the whole wants more character: it does not bear the stamp of the same presiding mind: no new world of imagination is opened to the view: we do not feel the presence of a power which we have never felt before, and which we can never forget."[42]

Butler also grew to be an intimate family friend, describing on one occasion a family scene that evoked quiet domestic happiness, despite the limited liberty Lucien and his family enjoyed in their movements. Showing Butler his medals with great affability, he knelt down at a cabinet on one knee and, supporting a large heavy drawer on the other, selected the best and rarest for his inspection. While the drawer was being returned into its place, Butler observed it was full of small pieces of paper. Lucien explained: "C'est pour les enfans."[43] Puzzled at this, Butler could not understand how this might amuse them, but he realized that each piece was a wrapped sugar plum. Lucien appeared to dote on his children without spoiling them.

Alexandrine gave birth to another son, Louis-Lucien, on January 4, 1813, three days before Lucien's saint's birthday, on whose occasion she wrote a little poem dedicated to her husband. Châtillon illustrated it with a beautiful drawing representing the Muses going to Thorngrove. And in many ways, Muses did indeed inhabit the place. Toward the end of their stay, in 1814, Lucien also began to develop a passion for astronomy, after having met John Herschel—the astronomer, mathematician, chemist, and pioneering photographer, whose celebrated father, William Herschel, had discovered Uranus. He purchased in London three telescopes made by the elder Herschel himself and began to study the heavens, assisted by Father Maurizio.[44]

But the Muses alone did not suffice to nourish a large family. Throughout the four years they spent in England, Lucien's financial situation deteriorated, and soon it became clear that the only solution was to sell more pieces from his beloved art collection. Already in 1812, he had published a catalogue, illustrated with engravings of his paintings and sculptures. On February 6, 1815, the whole collection was auctioned off in London, and ever since it has remained dispersed in the best museums and private collections around the globe.

THE FALL

While Lucien wrote his imperial poem and started gazing at the stars, Napoleon kept his sights fixed on his last, and fatal, earthly obsession: Russia. The great strategist had programmed this war to last three years: Poland would be conquered in 1812, Moscow in 1813, and Petersburg in 1814. The first part of the program was achieved as Napoleon had wished, but once the French army reached the second objective, the wildly unexpected auto-da-fé of Moscow upset the emperor's ambitious plans.

The Russian campaign was a long, bloody, horrendous debacle. It was a tragedy of epic proportions that only the pen of Tolstoy could manage to capture in its layered complexity.[45] One of the many causes of this disaster, however, was Napoleon's propensity to surround himself with mediocre men who did not dare contradict him: He had eliminated those endowed with qualities he lacked but sorely needed. The absence of independent judgment would prove lethal to him.

It is hard to know how closely Lucien was able to monitor his brother's downfall. In his comfortable English exile he must have heard some muffled or selectively amplified echoes of Napoleon's victories and defeats. In September 1812, the emperor's longtime enemy, Mme de Staël, had gone to Stockholm for nine months. Jean-Baptiste Bernadotte, Lucien's old friend who had mourned his exile, had been made king of Sweden by the Swedish parliament two years before. So when the talkative writer visited Lucien in 1814, she must have reported many intimate details and given him a sense of the crucial role Bernadotte had played in Napoleon's troubles. The spectacular and painful erosion of the Grande Armée in Russia was helped in no small part by Napoleon's dismissal, in the midst of the Battle of Wagram in 1809, of this distinguished man whose brilliant military mind had earned him the title of marshal of France.

In May 1814, Napoleon was forced to abdicate. He agreed to leave Paris and exile himself to the island of Elba. Now that his brother had lost his fearsome power, the British finally allowed Lucien to leave England and return to Italy. Yet he worried about the fall of Napoleon: It signified the beginning of the dissolution of the family he never had wanted to disown, and his joy at being freed was mitigated by the fact that his liberation was caused by his brother's downfall. He had only ever hoped to be reconciled with Napoleon, not for Napoleon to be defeated. In spite of the long-term feud, in spite of his intense political disagreements with the imperial rule that had grown out of his own postrevolutionary republican ideals, and in spite of all the difficulties the first consul and emperor had inflicted on him, Lucien did not delight in his brother's misfortune.

His request to pass through France on his way back to Italy was denied by the new government. Châtillon presented letters to Talleyrand, who remained indifferent and did nothing to help. Lucien therefore had to take a detour through Germany and Switzerland. He traveled without his family, who had stayed behind in England: He preferred to ensure first that the pope would welcome him. The trip lasted about a month, and, on the very evening of his arrival in Rome—May 27, 1814—he was received with great warmth by Pius VII, who had regained the Holy See he had temporarily lost under Napoleon. The pope immediately conferred on Lucien the title of Prince of Canino, and Lucien dedicated his lofty *Charlemagne* to him.

Lucien was returning from his second place of exile just as Napoleon was settling into what would turn out to be his first one. Canino is only a few miles from the Tyrrhenian Sea, almost straight across from Elba, so that, after a long decade, the two estranged brothers now ended up in geographical vicinity, separated by a distance of barely 150 miles. Lucien decided to make an effort to reestablish a rapport with Napoleon. Mme Mère, meanwhile, had joined Napoleon in his exile. So had Pauline: As soon as Napoleon had fallen from power, Camillo had divorced her, humiliating her by showing off his new mistress.

Letizia wrote to Lucien that she was upset to hear that Alexandrine and the children had still not arrived, adding that the emperor received his letters with great pleasure.[46] It was true that now Napoleon saw no point in continuing to bear a grudge against his disobedient brother. However, he was reported to have said, "Of all my siblings, he is indisputably the most gifted one, but he has hurt me the most. His marriage has been a terrible thing. Marrying a bourgeoise, a beautiful Parisian woman, right at the moment when I wanted to found a dynasty! I did everything in my power to prevent him, but unfortunately he has always had a soft spot for women."[47]

Lucien did not know of that double-edged remark. He was happy to be back in Rome and to see his old friends again, Lethière especially, who was still the director of the Academy of France in the Villa Medici. The fiery painter had found a way discreetly to show his support for his former patron during his English captivity, by sending his large canvas of Brutus condemning his sons to death to the 1812 Salon in Paris—the art exhibition of the official Académie des Beaux-Arts, which took place every year or two. The picture was a thinly disguised allusion to the Duke d'Enghien's death, where the man at the center of the picture, passionately pleading for clemency, was done in the likeness of Lucien, while a figure wrapped in a toga, standing stone-faced behind Brutus, starkly resembles Napoleon.[48] The pictorial reenactment of the violent episode that had driven Lucien out of France was a courageous act of loyalty on Lethière's part.

Napoleon never accepted his exile and kept plotting to return to France, where his supporters were still the majority of the country—despite the attempt by the Bourbons to regain clout and the restoration of their rule in May 1814, when Louis XVIII became king, helped by the maneuvers of Talleyrand, who never worried about loyalty or allegiance. Meanwhile, Rome celebrated the return of Lucien and Alexandrine, whose fashionable and comfortable social life soon resumed. The couple also made some new friends, notably Caroline of Brunswick, Princess of Wales and future wife of King George IV. When she left Rome to visit Greek ruins, Lucien wrote to her in something of a neoclassical rapture: "Leave, Madam, this enslaved, disfigured, mutilated Greece. Greece is not in Greece anymore: it is in Rome."[49]

Lucien was not only contemplating the past, however: He paid close attention to Napoleon's movements and reportedly told the princess that he knew of the emperor's planned escape from Elba, barely ten months after his arrival there, and of the itinerary he would take to get back to France. Napoleon knew that the time was strategically right for him to return, given the weakness of the Bourbons and the chaotic situation in Europe, with the main Congress of Vienna powers—England, Austria, Prussia, and Russia—in a state of tension that threatened to escalate into further war. On February 26, 1815, at 9 o'clock in the morning, exploiting the temporary absence of the English fleet, Napoleon sailed from Portoferraio, on Elba, to the south of France. Three days after his landing, on March 5, Letizia proudly wrote to Lucien: "I have the pleasure of giving you the news of our dear emperor's departure from this city [Portoferraio] and of his arrival in the Gulf Juan near Antibes. . . . The emperor said that evening that he had enjoyed the day as much as that which won him the battle of Austerlitz . . . vive l'empereur."[50]

The Congress of Vienna had made Napoleon an outlaw just a week before; troops were being gathered, and war would come. But as he had foreseen, Napoleon was welcomed like a savior in France and marched triumphantly all the way to Paris, while Louis XVIII, the Bourbons, and the turncoat Talleyrand fled the scene. Joachim Murat, king of Naples, was now in a position to threaten the pope with an invasion of the Papal States, on his way north with Napoleon's troops to push the Austrians back across the border. Lucien was against the plan and tried to dissuade his brother-in-law from undertaking it or, at least, to persuade him to minimize the damage such an invasion might cause. Pius VII asked Lucien to convince the emperor himself to stop Murat in his tracks. Murat, in fact, would end up bypassing Rome and failing in his plan, but in the meantime, the pope had decided to leave the capital for Genoa, via Florence, along with the College of Cardinals. Lucien left two days later, on March 24, "to avoid any appearance of connivance with Joachim.[51] Alexandrine, once again pregnant, stayed behind with the family at Villa Rufinella, under the protection, requested by Lucien, of the influential Cardinal Giulio Maria della Somaglia.

At the moment of his departure from Rome, accompanied only by Father Maurizio, Lucien did not know whether he should join the pope in Genoa or Napoleon in Paris.[52] Quickly, however, he opted to go to Paris and join his outlawed brother. He planned to travel via Switzerland and from there perhaps to England, where his daughter Christine (Lili) had remained. Lucien and Father Maurizio crossed the Alps and reached Geneva by early April. They traveled until reaching Charenton, just outside Paris, where Lucien decided to stay for a while. News soon arrived that the emperor wanted to see Father Maurizio, so Lucien, entrusting him with a letter for Joseph, who was already in Paris, sent him on to the capital.

Before seeing him off, Lucien advised Father Maurizio, in case he had to mention his name in the presence of the emperor, not to refer to him as "Prince of Canino" but as "Prince Lucien." The precaution would soon reveal itself to be moot: When Napoleon, after making Father Maurizio wait at the Tuileries for some hours, finally received him in the company of Joseph, he did not pronounce a single word about Lucien. Instead he immediately launched into a lengthy panegyric of the pope, whom he called a "man of conscience": Napoleon had thought him weak because of his passive resistance to imperial power and tried to isolate him, but when he saw the pope also resist the Bourbons, he realized that this man in fact had the strength to stick to his principles. Now that Napoleon had finally recognized the pope's true nature, he wanted to do everything for him, recognize his rights and guarantee his states. This was the message that Father Maurizio should take to the pope, via Lucien—as a way of neutralizing Murat and showing the pope that Napoleon did not approve of the actions of the king of Naples against his holiness. But there was another message here: Given the excellent terms that prevailed between the pope and Lucien, Napoleon was also tangentially acknowledging that he had misjudged his brother in trying to impose his will on him, that he in fact respected him for having obeyed the voice of his conscience, and that the time had come for them finally to work together.

The next step was to deliver Napoleon's message to the pope in Genoa, demanding of him in exchange for the emperor's protection that he would put pressure on the new international alliance not to wage war on France.

Lucien and Father Maurizio left Charenton and made their way to Genoa, via Switzerland again. They were stopped in Versoix, on Lake Geneva, but thanks to a letter of recommendation from Cardinal della Somaglia, the two men managed to negotiate their stay without being arrested, as had been threatened. Versoix is near Coppet, where Mme de Staël had her famed property, and they spent some time in her company. For over a decade, visits to her there—after Napoleon had exiled her from Paris—had been obligatory for Europe's greatest minds, from artists, writers, and poets to philosophers and diplomats. Mme de Staël had wielded considerable political influence and infuriated Napoleon, who could not abide such an intelligent, powerful woman who was not even physically attractive. She and Alexandrine were the two women Napoleon hated most. But now Lucien found himself pleading with her to support the emperor and French honor.

After a few days in Versoix, spent trying to decide which route to take to Rome, Lucien received a letter from Joseph in Paris, requesting his presence there. Lucien therefore turned back, reaching the capital on May 7. The emperor welcomed him with extraordinary warmth, as Lucien described the meeting at the Tuileries in a letter to Alexandrine. It was entirely different from their last meeting in Mantua: The emperor handed him the grand cordon of the Legion of Honor, with which he had traveled from Elba to Paris, and he said, "It is too shameful for me that you don't have it," adding some kind words about his pregnant sister-in-law. Lucien, unable to mask his surprise, laughed and responded: "Is it for her?" "No, but for your son." "What if it is a daughter?" "It's the same, she will wear it." Lucien signed off his letter by saying "Let God protect one who is not only a great man, but a great heart."[53] Lucien was now to be a prince of the empire.

In the late spring of 1815, Lucien and Napoleon took leisurely walks in the gardens of the Elysée. A friendly atmosphere prevailed, and the two brothers seemed to be reconciled. Yet after eleven years of exile, Lucien felt some understandably contradictory emotions regarding the newfound intimacy with a brother who had so harshly persecuted him. The old Jacobin, the one-time man of Brumaire, the former minister of the interior and ambassador in Spain, the rejected senator who had renounced his public life to protect his private life—this multifaceted character did not have any coherent plan when he arrived in Paris. He knew that he wanted to support his brother but also that he should use this opportunity to revive the republican cause he had never given up on—just as he had never accepted giving up his marriage. In effect, the return to Paris awoke in him his passion for politics.

The brothers exchanged "very confidential views" on Napoleon's first and second wives, Joséphine and Marie-Louise,[54] and on their common feminine acquaintances such as Mmes Tallien, Récamier, and de Staël, about whom Napoleon even ended up admitting: "I was wrong: Madame de Staël made more enemies for me in exile than she would have in France."[55] Lucien knew this was true and that the emperor had harmed himself by turning so many women against him. Napoleon seemed newly sheepish in this respect: He spoke of his behavior toward Alexandrine with a measure of regret he did not attempt to conceal. It is not clear whether the emperor was sincere or whether Lucien wanted to believe his brother was regretful. At any rate, Napoleon did not spare any efforts to show benevolence toward his brother. Offering him the prestigious residence at the Palais Royal was one manifestation of extreme goodwill, although Lucien took care not to make himself entirely at home, just keeping the servants who were already there and were willing to stay on.

Those were the last days of imperial glory, but Napoleon did not know that. At a family banquet, he said, "There are only elder and younger siblings in the imperial family, each to his own rank. And so, let's have Joseph to my right, Lucien to my left, and Jérôme after me." The holy trinity of the brothers was finally reunited, although Napoleon showed unusual signs of sleepiness: He seemed generally weakened and hardly ready to battle the powerful Holy Alliance.

The Bonaparte siblings plunged into feverish preparations for the Champ de Mai—the assembly planned at the Champ de Mars in Paris, in the tradition of the medieval assemblies of warriors in March or May. It was to be their first public appearance. Lucien advised Napoleon to abdicate there in favor of his only legitimate son, born of Marie-Louise—

the four-year-old king of Rome, also called Napoleon. When Napoleon had been exiled in Elba, his fleeing mother had taken little Napoleon to Vienna. (After Napoleon's downfall, the Congress of Vienna eventually conferred on Marie-Louise the title of duchess of Parma, Piacenza, and Guastalla—which Alexandrine had once turned down.) But it was not too late for Napoleon to abdicate. The emperor knew that this gesture might be his only means to keep the succession alive even if he lost the impending war. Yet a few days later, instead of announcing his abdication, he changed his mind. Lucien criticized him for this, as he had often dared to do in the past; and Napoleon got angry with him, just as he had often done in the past, accusing him of talking nonsense.

"What has become of your firmness?" Lucien asked his brother. "Leave these doubts behind. You know very well how costly it is not to dare."

"I have dared too much already," replied Napoleon.

"Too much and too little. Dare one last time."

"An Eighteen Brumaire!"

"Not at all. A very constitutional decree. The constitution gives you this right."

"They won't respect this constitution and will oppose this decree."

"That will give the rebels all the more reason to dissolve the Chambers."

"The National Guard will come to their rescue."

"The National Guard only has one arm. When they need to act, the shopkeepers only think of their wives and shops."

"A missed Eighteen Brumaire can lead to a Thirteen Vendémiaire, a military coup."

"Here you are discussing when you need to act. They act, and don't discuss."

"What can they do? They are all talk."

"Public opinion is in their favor. They will pronounce you deposed."

"Deposed! . . . They'll dare!"

"They will dare everything if you dare nothing."

Lucien, deeply aware of how different the situation was now from what it had been in 1799, was disappointed at how little Napoleon had changed. The old enmity was rekindled; soon the emperor declared that he did not want Lucien to have a seat in the legislative assembly. Clearly fearful of a new 18 Brumaire in which he would lose, he aired offensive suspicions about Lucien's hidden ambition to become its president. Lucien wanted to leave Paris and quit everything, but Joseph stopped him. The three met, just as they had done after Brumaire and during the consulate, to discuss the Champ de Mai project. Costumes were to be chosen. Lucien did not wish to appear in white but in his National Guard uniform. Napoleon laughed bitterly at this, looking him in the eye: "Yes, so that you [vous] make more of an effect in your National Guard uniform than me as emperor, isn't that right?" Lucien admitted that this was in fact true: His vanity had gotten the better of him. He decided to put on the white suit (the color of truce), even if it did not particularly flatter him.

In the end, he looked good enough. The event was a great mise-en-scène—the family's last. The public enthusiasm at the first appearance of the emperor at the Champ de Mai (on June 1, 1815) was palpable. It would have been a perfect moment for Napoleon to abdicate. As one contemporary witness said, doing so in the midst of such a national triumph would have been a most glorious way for Napoleon to end his career: It would have been perceived as noble.[56] Yet Napoleon did not seize the moment. Convinced that, if he abdicated, Lucien would want to be regent instead of Joseph, he tried to start a feud between the two. But Joseph was eager to reconcile yet again the incompatible Lucien and Napoleon; and he succeeded in doing so, at least in appearance.

By the time the emperor finally left Paris to join the army on the battle-field, Lucien had a bad premonition about the outcome of the war. Early news arrived from Waterloo on June 18, announcing victory. The cannon was fired to signal the news, even though Lucien, skeptical, had advised Joseph not to allow it and to await confirmation.

He was right. The terrible truth about the debacle was out twenty hours later. Paris was in uproar. The emperor's enemies regrouped, and the Royalists began political machinations. Joseph was not in a position to repress any party. The allies' defensive diplomacy triumphed over Napoleon, who returned to Paris to face an outraged state council.

At the meeting of the Chambers on June 22, the abdication of the emperor in favor of the king of Rome was back on the table. Napoleon said to Lucien: "In Brumaire, we drew the sword for the good of France. Today we must throw that sword away. Try to win back the Chambers. United with them I can do everything. Without them, I might be able to do much for myself, but I could not save the country. Go, and I forbid you when you go out to harangue those people, who are crying out for arms."[57]

Lucien went to the Chambers, where deliberations were long. In the end he failed to sway the floor. Lafayette asked Lucien to talk his brother into abdicating, but Lucien did not intend to give up yet. He argued that the legislature should be dissolved, just had happened on 18 Brumaire. The emperor turned to his brother and gently responded: "My dear Lucien, it is true that on the 18 Brumaire we could only plead the welfare of the people, and all the same when we asked for a bill of indemnity a general acclamation was our answer. Today we have every right on our side, but we ought not to take advantage of this."

There was a pause and then, using an imperious tone that Lucien had heard many times, Napoleon continued: "Prince Lucien, write at my dictation." First he turned to Fouché—who was back on the political stage and nonchalantly playing both sides, just as he had always done—and said: "Write to those good people to be quiet. They will soon be satisfied." Lucien waited for Napoleon to begin his dictation. From the quiet room, the assembled men could hear crowds outside intoning "Vive l'Empereur! Aux armes!" Lucien had barely written a few lines when, understanding what was happening, he refused to go on and rose, making for the door. But Napoleon ordered him back; the message had to be completed:

When I began the war to uphold the national independence, I counted on the union of the efforts and the wills of all, and on the support of all the national authorities. I had reason to hope for success. Circumstances seem to me to have changed. I offer myself as a sacrifice to the hatred of the enemies of France. It is to be hoped that they will prove to be sincere in their declarations, and hostile only to me personally. Unite yourselves to secure the welfare of the people and its continuance as an independent nation.[58]

Lucien, along with Carnot, Napoleon's first minister of war, who was also present in the room and under whom Lucien had once served as a lowly soldier, argued that the message should be more precise: Dynastic continuity was constitutional, and the emperor should be explicit about naming Napoleon II to the succession to avoid a return of the Bourbons. Napoleon said, "The Bourbons! Well, at least they are French and will not be under the rod of Austria." For Lucien, this was wrong—his brother's son was thoroughly French—and he cajoled Napoleon into adding to his message: "I proclaim my son, under the name of Napoleon II, Emperor of the French. The Princes Joseph and Lucien and the Ministers now in office will form a Provisional Government Council. On account of my interest in my son I feel I must ask the Chambers to lose no time in passing a law to create a Regency." An objection arose to the presence in the declaration of the names of Joseph and Lucien; they were promptly erased. The finished document was then communicated to the Chamber of Peers and the Chamber of Deputies.

Lucien then went off to the Chamber of Peers, joining Joseph and Fesch. There, as soon as he could, he walked to the tribune and spoke vehemently: "The Emperor is dead! Long live the Emperor! The Emperor has abdicated! Long live the Emperor! There can be no interval between the Emperor who dies or abdicates and his successor. I demand that in virtue of the continuous force of the Act of the Constitution the Chamber of Peers shall, without debate and by a spontaneous and unanimous vote, declare that it recognizes Napoleon II as Emperor of the French. I give the first example, and I swear fidelity to him."

A few people echoed his "Vive l'Empereur!" but dissent could be heard as well. The senator Louis-Gustave Doulcet de Pontécoulant, who had served Napoleon from 1805 but had also been made Peer of France by Louis XVIII, disagreed with Lucien's declaration and even went so far as to question his legitimacy as a speaker in the Chamber: "By what right does the Prince of Canino propose a sovereign to the French people? Who has declared him French? His only title is that of Roman prince." Lucien tried to interrupt Pontécoulant, who did not let him speak: "I am sorry, Prince: Respect that equality of which you have yourself given an example, and to which the Chamber has been responsive." He went on: "I declare that I will never recognize as my sovereign a child, an individual who does not reside in France. To take such a resolution would be to close the door on any useful negotiations." Lucien finally was able to reply, "I am told I am not French! Well! At least I feel French. We are all here thanks to the Constitution of the empire; and so our oath to Napoleon II should not even be a decision we make, but a declaration that cannot come too early if we are to avoid a civil war."

Lucien's speech met with little enthusiasm. This was not going to be another Brumaire. Only eighteen members of the Chamber, against fifty-two, voted to make him a member. The question of Napoleon II was dropped, and the debate now centered on the representatives to the next government commission. Fouché was chosen as its president. As one of the first acts of his presidency, Fouché wrote a letter to Lucien ordering him on behalf of the provisional government to leave France for good. The man who had provoked Lucien's first exile from Paris now notified him of his last.

EPILOGUE
1815–1840

Yes, if I plunge into myself, I feel that my strong irascibility as a young statesman, offended in his pride as an administrator, wounded in his political convictions, and much more and above all, the sensitivity of a husband and father, banished and persecuted for so many years—all these feelings today are replaced by compassion at the sight of the painful image of this brother, novel Prometheus, chained, moribund and finally dying on his rock, his chest devoured, without a doubt, not by the cruel symbolic bird of the fable, but by the weight of the memory of his glory, and the regrets of his abuse of power.

—Lucien Bonaparte, *Plan to publish my* Mémoires secrets

THE RESTORATION

The announcement of Napoleon's abdication caused a predictable stir throughout Europe. In Paris, crowds of the emperor's fans, outraged and angered, gathered in the streets, from the Place Vendôme—where Napoleon had erected a column to celebrate his victory at Austerlitz—to the Elysée, calling for him to stay on. As for Lucien, he was regarded by many people in France as a friend of liberty who had left the country to avoid conniving with his brother and had not partaken of the imperial success but had come back at a time of uncertainty and danger.

Those were days of high tension for the opposition politicians. On the very day he became president of the executive commission in charge of government, Fouché instigated a debate in the Chamber of Deputies to recognize Napoleon II. But the popular agitation did not die down. The next day, June 24, Fouché asked Napoleon to withdraw from the capital. The ex-emperor immediately fled to Malmaison with Joseph. Soon Jérôme and then Lucien were told to follow their brother's example and leave Paris, "in the interest of the tranquility of the state and of his own."[1] The brothers were in Malmaison by June 25. Fouché and his party regarded Napoleon as their prisoner, a prized warranty for their own political survival in the coming days of the Restoration. It was an anxious time for the Bonaparte brothers. Joseph had decided to go to America, and he told Lucien that, as soon as he was safely on his way, Lucien should follow him there. For now, Lucien expected to return to Rome, where he could be of use to the rest of the family, while Joseph occupied himself with arranging an alternative means for Napoleon's planned escape across the Atlantic, in case the provisional government should block the frigates or behave treacherously in any way. Napoleon considered an escape to America but in the end demanded political asylum in Britain. Instead, he was made a prisoner and sent under British custody to the remote South Atlantic island of St. Helena. Lucien was insolvent, having spent more than 200,000 francs on furnishing the Palais Royal. Napoleon had given him almost 2 million francs in bonds, saying with little conviction "It will be worth what it will be worth."[2] Those bonds were soon to be voided by the returning Bourbons. Lucien bade farewell to his brother and left with Châtillon disguised as his secretary, without yet knowing exactly how and when he would manage to get back to Italy and his family. He had double passports—one under his name and one under his customary incognito Boyer. Over several days, he went back and forth to Le Havre and Dunkirk with the idea of crossing into England, but there were simply too many obstacles. He then headed back south toward Orléans. His situation became embarrassingly confused. The Austro-Prussian-Russian-English allies had begun occupying all of France. He avoided them as much as he could while observing the reactions of the population still loyal to Napoleon during the bloodless invasion of France.

On his way to Grenoble, in Bourgoin, he ran into the Austrian army. He pretended to be a Roman citizen, one Cavalier Casali, but his French accent betrayed him. He was brought to Turin, first to the Hôtel de l'Univers and then—to his dismay—inside the walls of the citadel.[3] He protested his arrest and wrote a bold letter to Metternich (who had been the lover of Lucien's sister, Caroline Murat), now prime minister of Austria: "I cannot be considered but a Roman prince because I am nothing else. Despite the intention by Emperor Napoleon of making me part of his dynasty by law, that law was never passed."[4] Lucien used the argument that had been used against him in the Chambers to free himself. Formally, he was right—although he adopted it with disturbing rhetorical nonchalance. Metternich, perhaps amused by Lucien's shamelessness, replied elegantly that he was "very charmed" to inform him that he was not to be detained by the Austrian authorities.[5] Talleyrand then tried to prevent Lucien from returning to Rome because he "had plotted in the latest conspiracy," but the evidence was thin at best and all Talleyrand did was delay Lucien's release.[6]

Lucien finally arrived in Rome in September. Just a few days before, his wife had given birth to their seventh child (the tenth in their household), a boy they named Pierre. At the end of that eventful year 1815, Charlotte married Prince Mario Gabrielli, the wealthy nephew of a cardinal. The beautiful and good-natured girl who at fifteen had nearly become queen of Spain was now, at twenty, to settle into a cozy Italian family. Lucien and his family were thus able to get on with their lives. All the Bonapartes except Napoleon and Joseph—Letizia, Pauline, Louis, Jérôme, and Fesch—were forced to reside in Rome. It was admittedly an infinitely softer exile than that imposed on Napoleon, but the city was becoming less and less hospitable to them. Lucien was placed under heavy surveillance. And when Lethière was abruptly recalled to France in 1816—thus ending his tenure at Villa Medici—Lucien lost one of his oldest and most loyal friends. At that time, he also frequented Manuel Godoy, the former Spanish "Prince of Peace," who had also been exiled to Rome.[7] But besides reminiscing about the good old times of their reckless youth, they did not have much to rejoice in together. Lucien and his family, despite being under surveillance, were free to travel within the Papal States, returned to La Rufinella for long periods, seeking "domestic tranquility and felicity," but even there, peace was hard to find.[8]

Life resumed, however, and at La Rufinella Lucien started enjoying again his artistic and archaeological activities. On one lovely autumn day in early November 1817, he got up as usual at dawn, as did Châtillon, the painter who had never abandoned him and who, over the years, had even begun to look like him.[9] A new program of excavations was on their minds, and they explored the terrain to ascertain the best areas to start digging. As they returned to the palace, they met Alexandrine, on a walk with her three daughters. (Her first, Anna de Bleschamp, had just married Prince Alfonso Hercolani of Bologna.) Lucien noted that his wife seemed sad; to his worried inquiry as to what might be the matter, she responded, smiling: "It's nothing—but you know, sometimes the most ordinary event can arouse sad premonitions. Well yes, I won't deny it, I'm sad despite myself—I just witnessed a scene that had a distressing effect on me." She then told him how, as she was walking by a laurel arbor, she had heard birds crying and then seen a sparrow hawk fly off as she approached the trees. Staring closely, she saw a nest covered in blood.

Lucien made light of her emotion and ordered that lunch be served at the huts by the dig. The afternoon passed normally. Just before dinner, a bell called the household to the living room. One of the guests, a Monsignor Cuneo, was absent, but it was decided to start the meal without him; the prelate might have been delayed on a walk. But time ticked on, and there was no sign of him. By dessert he still had not appeared. They began to worry: Perhaps he had been kidnapped by Barbone, a famous bandit who sometimes roamed the ruins of the Tusculum hills. Lucien decided to send out a search party made up of country guards and servants, which set out immediately. Just then, a light murmur was heard in the corridor of the ground floor. The dining room was on the first floor, and the servants who remained in the palace were busy there. Eager to give Lucien and Alexandrine news of a person whom they cared for, and believing that Monsignor was back, Châtillon left the table and hurried downstairs. He was followed by Charles, the eldest son, and by Cesare, son of Prince Hercolani. As Châtillon reached the mezzanine, he stopped and asked loudly if Monsignor had returned. A few low voices responded "Yes, yes!" just as a thud resounded in the corridor, near another staircase also leading to the first floor. A coarse man suddenly appeared before Châtillon, seizing him and screaming: "Here's the prince!"

The quartermaster in Lucien's employ was just entering the palace as the men were dragging Châtillon out, but it was too dark for him to see much: He took them for soldiers who might be after Lucien. He hurried to the living room, where Lucien was alone with Father Maurizio, and alerted him to what he thought he had seen. Lucien immediately ordered the bells rung and asked Brunot to discreetly head for Frascati and notify the governor. Shortly after, André Boyer learned that brigands had kidnapped Châtillon, mistaking him for Lucien, and thereupon distributed weapons to the servants. The terrified Alexandrine and the children hid in a remote apartment of the palace, not realizing that the bandits had long left the premises.

Châtillon barely spoke Italian, yet he convinced the kidnappers that he was not Lucien but a painter, "pitto-re," by drawing a portrait of the bandit De Cesaris despite suffering from a wound to his head, inflicted by the butt of a gun. The ruthless De Cesaris was impressed with his talent, as were his acolytes, and demanded that Châtillon send the portrait to the governor of Rome and write to him on the back. They also demanded 15,000 francs from Lucien for his freedom. Châtillon explained that he was just a friend, not a relation, and that this was a sum the prince could not afford. But they insisted, and while they awaited his response, he was made to tell stories about Napoleon's exploits. Lucien decided to send 1,500 francs instead, which the bandits accepted. Before releasing the painter, they gave him a beautiful dagger as a souvenir. De Cesaris said: "My compliments to the prince. I would not have accepted this reduced sum—it ruins the job. But you are French, and he is the brother of a great, unhappy warrior."

Although the situation ended well, Lucien and his family no longer felt safe in their beloved Tusculum. Their decision to leave was a sad one, deplored by their friends and acquaintances. Cardinal Della Somaglia, the secretary of state in Rome—whom Lucien described as cultured, clever, and generous, a sincere friend to whom Alexandrine dedicated one of her poems—deplored that "these beautiful grounds should be deprived of our modern arts patron, of the man who had the wisdom to pursue domestic happiness, keeping at bay social unhappiness. Tusculum shall become a desert, a sad solitude."

The family returned to Rome. Pius VII remained welcoming and friendly to them, but Cardinal Consalvi had grown rather cold: He feared the new French ambassador in Rome, the Comte de Blacas, who was a zealous hater of the Bonaparte. One day, as Blacas rode in his carriage, he ran into Lucien, Alexandrine, and the smaller children taking a walk on the Pincio hill, at Trinità dei Monti, and exclaimed: "[T]he Roman government should spare me the presence of the abhorred blood of the usurper."[10] Châtillon, who was there, tried to challenge him to a duel, but the ambassador hid behind his diplomat's status—and the painter was menaced with expulsion. The pope was upset about the nasty remark, which made the rounds of Rome. Constant police surveillance continued, and the once-fresh air of the Eternal City began to grow stale for Lucien.

Joseph had been able to escape France on July 25, 1815, by sailing to America under the name of Mr. Surviglieri, aboard an American ship called *Commerce*. A British warship had intercepted her but let her through, never suspecting that Mr. Surviglieri, whose papers seemed perfectly in order, was a fleeing Bonaparte. Joseph was traveling with an interpreter, a cook, and his secretary; but his wife, Julie Clary, along with their daughters, Zénaïde and Charlotte, had reached Brussels (from Paris) by the time he arrived in America.[11]

From New York, Joseph wrote to Lucien that he had just learned from Julie of his detention in Turin and of his forthcoming release. He was eager to be reunited with his family and asked for news from everyone—Lucien's family, their mother and siblings—but would not be sailing back in the spring. He praised the country he had arrived in as beautiful; its climate was temperate, its people welcoming, and "one lives here more freely and pleasantly than one could possibly imagine."[12] Joseph knew that his correspondence would be intercepted by the papal police, and perhaps this upbeat tone was meant to tease them, although he added some caveats: The big cities in the New World were a third more expensive to live in than Paris, and if one wanted to live in the countryside, one would have to gather a large number of people in order to create a proper society.

Later, in a letter he wrote Lucien in early 1816, his characterization of the host country was more precise: "The last one to arrive here is as well regarded as the man who was born here—if he arrives with some money; one lives here as one pleases, receiving no favors but not owing them to anyone either; one is not under the scrutinizing eye of an anxious police, or of the itchingly curious."[13] He went on to tell Lucien that he had taken a little house eight miles away from New York; people urged him not to leave town, but he wanted to see no one. With the winter snows, however, he had just returned to New York. People here were "reasonable," and a foreigner who refused to mix into local politics was well respected by both parties—for there were two parties here, just as in England, he explained. He hoped that his wife and daughters would come; he planned on spending only the three winter months in town, so they could set up house in the country and live off whatever was left of their fortune. The climate, he said, was not much more harsh than in Europe, and one could choose between the heat of Charleston and the cold of Boston, and everything in between. But American cities could not compare with those in Europe. He wrote again of how expensive life was, especially luxury goods, while also observing that no one in America spent more than 100,000 or less than 30,000 francs a year: A moderate fortune enabled one to live like everyone else. There were theaters in the big cities, but the arts were still generally "foreign plants"—one could find a few amateurs, and very few artists. Many houses were devoid of even a small library, poets and painters were nowhere to be seen, although important houses had their musicians and the daughters of rich families knew some music, just as all children knew how to read and count by the time they were sixteen.

Joseph seemed comfortable in his exile, though he felt he was too far away from his family. In the summer of 1817, he settled in the estate of Point Breeze, in Bordentown, New Jersey—near the Delaware River, and some thirty miles (fifty km) from Philadelphia. Here he installed his collection of paintings, objets d'art, rugs, and furniture. In the spring of 1818, he wrote to his wife: "If you were here I don't think you would regret Morfontaine, the place where I am now is more beautiful, and every day it becomes more so."[14] That summer, however, he met Anna Savage, who would become his new companion. At this point, he was expecting only either Zénaïde or Charlotte to sail over. In March 1819, Lucien wrote about his desire to follow Joseph to America with his family: As a Bonaparte, he was being harassed to no end in Italy. In response, Joseph offered another long description of life in America—of social, economic, and work conditions there, of the state of culture, of general customs. His assessment was still positive (the poverty of cultural offerings being one exception): "[T]he government, the country, the climate, and the inhabitants please me equally—I am not exacting and they are not. Tranquility, justice, calm, one finds all that. People are often crowded in the cities, at the balls, in traveling, on the steamboats, but they are never rude or offended. Each respects his neighbor and is respected in return."[15]

Napoleon himself thought of America as the best destination for the whole family. As he said to a general guarding him in Saint Helena: "Joseph will build a great establishment in America. It will be the refuge of all my relatives."[16] Lucien held on to his old dream of sailing to the New World— and to freedom. But his plans had to wait. There were growing family concerns, and mourning: Elisa died in Trieste on August 7, 1820, aged 43. And Napoleon, perhaps poisoned by arsenic, certainly devoured by a stomach cancer that had also killed their father, Charles, died in his remote exile at 51, on May 5, 1821.

WEDDINGS, FUNERALS, AND EXCAVATIONS

It took six weeks for the news of Napoleon's death to reach Rome. The pain was acute for the whole Bonaparte clan, especially for Letizia—now 65—who fell seriously ill. Political considerations about the perpetuation of the dynastic line were also at the forefront of the family's preoccupations, however; now seemed the right time to plan the marriage of the two cousins, Charles and Zénaïde, promised by their respective fathers, Lucien and Joseph, so many years before. Napoleon would have agreed to the match, having said before dying that Joseph's daughters should only be married to Roman princes. The dowry for Zénaïde was set at a hefty 700,000 francs, which would also relieve Lucien's financial situation for a while.

The cousins actually had never set eyes upon each other. A portrait by Jacques-Louis David of Zénaïde and her sister, Charlotte, was sent to Charles in Rome, so that the introduction could at least be made in style. While Charlotte had joined her father in America in December 1821, Zénaïde had remained with her mother in Brussels, the city where David too had found political asylum; and it was here that the marriage would be celebrated, on June 29, 1822—over a year after Napoleon's death, as Joseph had specified would be the correct delay to observe. Joseph had long been expecting Lucien in America: As early as February 1822 he had not only rented a house for him in Philadelphia but also prepared a country residence.[17] But the months were passing. It proved a challenge for Lucien and Charles even to

get to Brussels; they obtained the required passports only after the intervention of Cardinal Consalvi, whom Alexandrine had written to on behalf of a
rheumatism-ridden Lucien. Father and son were then blocked at the border
of the Papal States. Again it took Consalvi's word for them to receive authorization to move on—via Austria and Germany, since they were not allowed
into France and had been asked to avoid Piedmont and Switzerland. They
finally arrived in Brussels in mid-March.

For Lucien, traveling to Belgium would have been a first step in his plan
to sail to America; he counted on embarking from Ostende. But the plan
was again shelved. He ended up leaving Brussels before his son's wedding,
returning to Italy in late April. Alexandrine had written again to Consalvi:
She explained why Lucien was changing his itinerary and needed to return
to Italy, and specifically to the Papal States, where the family wanted to continue living. One of the reasons she gave for this change was that Charles
and Zénaïde were to stay in Europe rather than join Joseph in America as
initially intended. There was also Lucien's ill health. He had been suffering
from a chest inflammation for a while, aside from rheumatism. In truth, he
still wanted to cross the ocean, but not in this state, as he wrote to his mother
from Livorno, where he stopped—incognito—on his way back to Bologna
(in the Papal States) to join Alexandrine, who had been living close to her
daughter Anna, Princess Hercolani. Lucien was also suffering from a bout of
melancholy at this point. By his own judgment, it was no time to undertake
a lengthy voyage to the New World.

Life in Bologna with Alexandrine and his family proved restorative. Here the
couple were far from the papal police, and they bought a beautiful villa just
outside of the city, in the parish of Croce del Biacco.[18] In the meantime, the
newlywed Charles and Zénaïde traveled at a leisurely pace across Europe for
a few months, on the way to Bologna. Charles was beginning his career as an
ornithologist and naturalist and stopped in Germany to visit a few scientists.
Once the young couple arrived in Bologna, in August 1822, the reception
Lucien and Alexandrine gave them was extraordinarily cool, so they only

stayed three days and went on to Rome—a city that Charles was eager to show Zénaïde, and where they would stay until May 1823.

Charles was furious with his parents, but especially with Lucien, for the poor welcome they had given their niece and new daughter-in-law. Granted, Zénaïde had not kissed Alexandrine's hand when she arrived in Bologna, but it was odd for Lucien, of all people, to stand on such formalities. Alexandrine in fact wrote a very nice letter to Charles, describing the pleasant setting at Croce del Biacco and trying to lure the couple back to patch up the situation, but when no response came, Lucien lashed out against what he perceived as his son's disobedience and disrespect. One of the many reasons for his anger was Charles's using for himself and his bride the titles prince and princess of Musignano: He was a count, but Zénaïde, as the daughter of the erstwhile king of Naples and Spain, effectively was a princess, and Charles preferred not to "demote" her. Lucien accused him of "cowardice," but Charles defended himself for calling himself a prince. Had his father not rejected titles all his life? There was also the fact of their trip through Europe: In Lucien's view, it had taken them far too long to get to Italy. Charles, after all, was only nineteen years old; Lucien was not used to granting him so much freedom, and he blamed Zénaïde for Charles's deviation from filial duty. But the son reacted to the father with the same hard-headedness and righteousness that Lucien had displayed at his age, replying to his father's missive with a long and dignified letter: "Ah, my dear Papa, you know I have always been a submissive son, and you always have been for me the best of fathers, why save me all your anger when I most need your love, since I must share it with the best part of myself? Why, if you wish to persecute me, did you defend me from the ambitious tiger who overshadowed my childhood? Why did you leave me to be suffocated by his hirelings? If my wife was to be a victim, why did I marry her?"[19]

Two days after writing this to his father, he also addressed a short letter to his mother, asking her to stand in his defense: "I will do anything to please him as long as it does not hurt Zénaïde. The happiness of my wife is my first duty." These were almost the same exact words that Lucien had used with Napoleon in Mantua as well as on countless other occasions. But the circumstances differed vastly, as Lucien reminded Charles: Surely titles would impinge little on the young couple's "happiness," as Charles was claiming. Lucien wrote him appositely: "[H]ave I asked you to divorce?" The point was simple: It was paramount for him that Charles use the title of prince, to which he eventually would have a right, only once his father had authorized him to do so. The epistolary exchanges were intense and heartfelt, but in the end the skirmish did not last; and the couple had a wonderful time in Rome, staying at the family house on Via Bocca di Leone.[20]

In January 1823, Alexandrine gave birth to her last child, Constance. And by late May, when her son and daughter-in-law left for America—from Antwerp—to join Joseph as they had planned to do a year earlier, Zénaïde herself had just become pregnant with her first of what would be twelve children. The couple were thankful when the seventy-five-day crossing came to an end.[21] The ship moored in New York in mid-September; Joseph and his daughter Charlotte traveled there to welcome the couple. Their arrival at Point Breeze was extremely pleasant: Joseph gave the couple the private residence he had built for Lucien. It was on the shore of an artificial lake, complete with an underground passage connected to the main villa that was of great use when it rained or snowed. There was an immense park, and the hunting was excellent. All this was a source of great joy for Charles, since one of his main ambitions was to study the flora and fauna of America, and he could start his research right on the property.

In a letter to his mother, he described how happy was their life with Joseph and Charlotte, and how they liked America, which Charles said he found "an admirable country," endowed with "the most perfect government that has ever existed, including those of Athens, Sparta and Rome." Elections were coming up, and he admired how citizens could not sell their votes as they did in England. Of course one had either to work hard here or be "immensely rich," he observed, and he too noted, as had his uncle, that any nonbasic goods, such as service, staff, or clothing, were three times as expensive as in Europe. He also wrote his father that paintings were not worth anything in America and that Joseph was sending to Europe all those he no longer wanted—he did not think Lucien should send any of his paintings over, given how high customs taxes were.

They retained the habits and pleasures of the Old World. The family often read plays by Racine, Corneille, and Voltaire after dinner, each taking on a role. Charlotte was very good, although Charles missed Lucien's acting talents. He asked to have sent over one of Lucien's tragedies—of which Charles could recite a few verses—as well as a few of his mother's romances. Just a few days before, in late October, he had read to guests, in French, "L'Amérique," the poem Lucien had started writing in 1810 in Malta, and which he had later dedicated to Joseph. The audience was very special: It included Madame Adams, wife of the minister of foreign affairs John Quincy Adams, son of the second president—and himself the successful candidate in the next year's presidential elections. She and the other guests were all "enchanted." Mrs. Adams had heard Lucien's name among those of "the heroes of independence." Charles commented of the United States: "Oh, happy country, which possesses that which Italy is so far from possessing."[22]

Charles expressed to his father his concern about his brothers being educated by the Jesuits (he had been home-schooled by the brilliant Father Maurizio) as well as his strong antimilitary convictions: "Only civil courage is true courage," he wrote, going on to flatter his father: "It is that of Cato, Cicero and . . . yours, my dear Father."[23] From such a distance, he was a good son, not only admiring of his father but also studious and committed, citing the republican classics even though his passion for natural history, rather than the humanities, was growing every day.

Across the ocean, Lucien was also developing his scientific interests, growing ever more fascinated with astronomy, which he had begun studying nearly a decade before in England. In 1825, Alexandrine found a small house in Umbria, at the foot of the Apennines, by a lake of extraordinarily pure water, where Lucien and Father Maurizio spent some time gazing at the stars. In 1828, with the help of Father Maurizio, Lucien set up in Senigallia—on the Adriatic coast in the Marche region—the telescopes by Herschel senior, which he had bought from Herschel junior. Eventually he boasted to have discovered 20,000 stars—and he planned to catalogue them, though that project never came to fruition.[24]

In the meantime, however, the financial situation of Lucien's household had become quite worrisome. As he wrote to Joseph from Rome in late August 1826, income from the Canino property was halved, and he could no longer pay the interest on his debts.[25] He even had had to face courts. Uncle Fesch agreed to buy the Canino debts, easing Lucien's position to no end. The point was, though, that Lucien was no longer interested in Canino, in fact he was "disgusted" by the problems it was causing, and he was willing to take as revenue from it whatever Joseph and Fesch thought appropriate. He was already selling his livestock for his daughters' dowries. Fesch became the estate's administrator. Lucien and Alexandrine had been spending their time in Bologna and later in Senigallia. As far as he, Lucien, was concerned, his only wish was to stay in his "retreat" or to go back to England and make a living from his pen.

Those were difficult years. Pauline died in 1825, aged forty-five; the beautiful body that had been so famously sculpted by Canova was ravaged by disease. And new tragedies soon struck the family. Paul, the restless, third-born son of Lucien and Alexandrine, had been living in Bologna with his half sister Anna Hercolani. In late 1827, when he was eighteen years old, he had left town without his father's permission to sail to Greece and fight for its independence from the Turks. He obtained a position as a low-ranking officer on the English frigate *Hellas,* commanded by Lord Cochrane, who had known Lucien in England. The day before the key Battle of Navarino— which would give Greece its independence—Paul accidentally shot himself; he did not survive his wound. But that was not all. Shortly after, in February 1828, Lucien and Alexandrine's secondborn daughter, Jeanne, who had been living in the Marche town of Jesi and had married a local nobleman, died of an illness she caught after a carnival ball; she was only twenty-one years old.

Despite these terrible blows, Alexandrine managed to remain much more grounded than her husband, whose increasingly dreamy attraction to poetry and to the skies was a comforting, albeit creative means to escape the hard realities the couple had to face. It was she who eventually managed to force him to return to earth—quite literally, by drawing on an old passion and embarking on an occupation that would soon prove highly fruitful: excavations.

Tusculum had sat on a mine of Roman antiquities. Not Canino. It lay at the heart of ancient Etruria, and in early 1828, an incident happened that revealed the treasures under the property. Farmers were plowing one day, in the plain of Cavalupo, when the ground suddenly collapsed under the weight of the oxen, revealing an underground grotto that contained two broken Etruscan vases. The farmers did not directly alert their employers, the prince and princess of Canino, who were in Senigallia in any case. Instead, they spoke of their discovery to two agents on the staff—who kept the find secret, proceeded to look for other, similar treasures, and sold whatever bounty they came across to a M. Dorow, who bought them in the belief that the rightful owners had been informed of the proceedings. It was not until the end of September, when Alexandrine returned to Canino from Senigallia—Lucien remained on the Adriatic coast for a while, immersed in his astronomical explorations—that she discovered what the two men had been up to and promptly fired them. She then inaugurated official excavations in a field near the grotto, by the Ponte dell'Abbazia. Initially, only a few vases emerged from the ground, but the fragments were of good enough quality that Alexandrine decided to press on with the search. Mount Cucumella, an artificial hill nearby, became the center of operations; digging took place around its periphery, under her guidance.

Letizia wrote to Lucien from Rome, expressing her disapproval of this new activity of Alexandrine's: Excavations were not a lady's business, especially since she needed to be assisted by servants while on her own; moreover, her presence there would surely attract beggars, and so, between one thing and another, a good four or five thousand francs were sure to be dissipated.[26] Regardless of his mother's concern, Lucien was so preoccupied with the heavens—just as his wife was sifting through the earth—that he did not return to Canino until December. But when he arrived, he found already assembled an impressive collection of antiquities. His enthusiasm lit up immediately. He gathered a team of a hundred workers to enlarge the excavation. Within three or four months and within the confines of a few hundred square meters, over two thousand objects were recovered from their ancient resting place. For each, Lucien had their location and date of discovery recorded as they were cleaned, and the finds—which comprised a large variety of objects, including painted and inscribed vases—were minutely catalogued. The resulting *Catalogo di scelte antichità etrusche trovate negli Scavi del Principe di Canino* was published in the nearby city of Viterbo in 1829. Lucien, whose love of antiquity and mythology was by now thoroughly revived, concluded from the richness of the quarry that it must have signaled the location of the Etruscan town of Vetulonia—Vulci in Italian.

This was no mere amateur venture, as the Tusculum excavations had been; the finds were important enough to be made public rather than added to a private gallery, as Lucien had done earlier. And so the couple created the world's first-ever Etruscan Museum, in Vulci. From then on, most of the family income would derive from the sale of these archaeological objects. Today, the objects they dug up and collected are to be found not only in the museum at Vulci, which still stands, but also in the Vatican Museum, the Louvre, and the British Museum; and they have contributed immensely to our understanding of Etruscan civilization—although some were in fact revealed to be Greek.

Thanks to the antiquities, the family's finances improved significantly. The couple resumed the rural pleasures and scholarly, artistic, and scientific activities they had cultivated for all those years. Lucien had the leisure to settle down again. In 1830, he acquired yet another villa, in Florence this time, but spent most of his time between Canino and Senigallia, busy with archaeology in the one and astronomy in the other. Both he and Alexandrine continued writing poetry. Alexandrine's literary output increased, and she dedicated a long poem she wrote about Queen Bathilde (seventh-century queen of the Franks) to Cardinal della Somaglia, who had protected the family from the worst of the various threats that had darkened their days in recent times.

LAST YEARS AND LEGACY

But politics soon infringed on quietude again. Post-Napoleonic Europe was a cauldron of agitation, of general dissatisfaction with a newly returned conservatism, with unstable economies and high unemployment. A strong wind of liberal thought and ambition flowed over the old continent, along with a newly vigorous current of Bonapartism, which united all sorts, from the unemployed to intellectuals, impoverished students to idle soldiers. A large number of secret societies sprang up; in Italy, one of those was the Carbonari, a gathering of anticlerical liberals who eventually would play an important role in the establishment of Italian national unity, and many of whose members were also Masons. Lucien, who had been a Mason for a while, was one of those who developed relations with the Carbonari. So did his son Charles upon returning from America in 1829.

An unpopular Bourbon king was ruling France. Charles X, the brother of Louis XVI, seemed to have learned little from the Revolution. In late July 1830, he ordered the dissolution of the Chamber of Deputies. In response, on July 28, an insurrection broke out in Paris. The people erected six thousand barricades, crying "A bas les Bourbons! Vive la République! Vive l'empereur!" The insurrection succeeded. Charles X eventually left France and was replaced by Louis-Philippe, who would be the last king of the French. For the Bonapartes, this unrest seemed a golden opportunity to regain power. Hortense's sons, twenty-six-year-old Napoleon-Louis and his twenty-two-year-old younger brother Louis-Napoleon (who would become Napoleon III) convened in the region of Romagna in northern Italy and plotted with the Carbonari to bring back the king of Rome, Napoleon's half-Austrian son, whom the erstwhile emperor had designated his successor and who was now the nineteen-year-old Duke of Reichstadt. But the plot, which effectively aimed at supplanting the pope's authority, was uncovered and bloodily repressed: Napoleon-Louis was killed, and Louis-Napoleon was exiled in Greece.

Lucien did not choose to participate in the bustling activities surrounding this plan, however strong his views. But his sons and nephews eagerly entered the fray of political action. The sixteen-year-old Pierre, the most restless and hotheaded of his sons, took part in the plot, disregarding the fact that he resided in the Papal States; he too was caught and ended up spending six months jailed in Livorno. After his release, he was forced to leave Italy, so he joined his uncle in America.

In the meantime, Joseph had already begun to think of returning to Europe. He followed the news there closely by corresponding with central actors of the time, including Prince Metternich. In July 1831, he wrote to his mother that France would do justice to Napoleon by restoring his son to govern the country.[27] By March 1832, Joseph subscribed to the new Bonapartist slogan, *Napoléon, liberté, égalité,* and admitted that "America isolates us too much."[28] He entreated Lucien to go to London—the best place from which to observe and organize events, as he put it. Lucien would finally be able to realize all his ideals there, or come to America from there if need be. Joseph would gladly join him in London if Lucien wanted him to. If Lucien indeed did leave Italy, he should make sure that Charles and Zénaïde, who had been back in Rome for a while, with their children, remained on good terms with the pope.

Pierre had just arrived in Philadelphia at that point, and Joseph also informed Lucien that the "ardent" boy's intention seemed to be that of starting a military career, although it was difficult to do so in America, where the military status was not highly regarded and there were only six thousand conscripts throughout the nation. A few months later, in November 1832, Pierre was in Colombia: Lucien wrote encouraging him to continue his military career there.[29] As for himself, Lucien told him, he had decided to meet Joseph in London, where the latter had arrived in late July 1832, in time to learn that there was no longer any reason to have left the United States because Napoleon's son Napoleon II had just died prematurely in Vienna, aged twenty-one. But Lucien had set his mind on going to London, and he would not stay put.

❦

Lucien left Canino on March 27, 1833, leaving Alexandrine behind to take care of the family, and arrived in London on April 23.[30] He met there Joseph and Charlotte, who was eager to return to Italy. One week later, the two brothers—accompanied by Lord Dudley Stuart, who had married Lucien's daughter Christine-Egypta—went to see the Duke of Wellington. The man who had defeated the French emperor at Waterloo had paid Joseph the honor of a visit a few days before, and protocol demanded that Joseph return the call. Upon arriving at the duke's grand residence, Apsley House, they saw the huge statue Canova had done of the naked Napoleon—which Lucien and Alexandrine had seen nearly thirty years earlier, not quite finished in the artist's studio.[31] The joke Lord Bristol had made about the little marble globe not containing England was now fully on them.

On May 15, Lucien's son Pierre arrived in London from America, after having proudly served in the Colombian civil war. Against his father's hopes, he had not been able to stay very long in Colombia because, as a nonnative, he could never aspire to become an officer in the army created by Simon Bolivar. Pierre soon had to make his way back to Italy, so in early June, Lucien entrusted into his hands a letter for Father Maurizio, in which he complained that "in the truly threatening crisis of this country art objects have no value" and so it was not worth sending anything there. Moreover, the "celebrated collection" of William Hamilton, housed at the British Museum, was "pitiful"; the English simply did not want "to spend a penny to buy a good artwork." In closing, Lucien expressed his hope that Pierre, who seemed to be increasingly agitated, would "behave well: in any case I shall consider what I must do, but I believe in his change: he has a good heart and his head, if he calms down a bit, will become a man's head."[32]

Lucien led a dazzlingly fashionable life in London. It could not have been a more different stay from the last one, when he was not a free man. He frequented high society, and, through his son-in-law Dudley Stuart, he forged new, influential friendships with the aristocracy—he dined with the Duke and Duchess of Bedford, the Duke of Buckingham, the Duke and Duchess of Hamilton, and so on. Many were members of the House of Lords—and his newly found closeness to parliamentary politics inspired him to devise a plan to destabilize the Bourbon rule. On July 7, 1833, Lucien published in the Parisian paper *La Tribune* a long polemical pamphlet entitled *De la République Consulaire ou Impériale*.[33] Since Brumaire he had not much practiced his rhetorical skills, but they had not deserted him.

Napoleon, Lucien wrote in his somewhat self-serving narrative, had contained the "revolutionary torrent" with the "consular dyke." Then, tired of being the "messiah of the people," he had downgraded himself to the "rank of kings," and, set against the mounting pressure of England, he had failed to pursue peace and progress for the whole world. Now it was impossible for anyone else to achieve the labor of the "modern Hercules." And so it was time to renounce the equally old traditions of Louis XIV's monarchy and Napoleon's empire and to pursue a new kind of republic based on these premises: unlimited freedom of the press, universal right to vote in popular elections, limitation of taxes, military devoted to the defense of the borders, and a national guard exclusively employed as local police. All of these goals required a strong executive power, whose structure should be determined through a general plebiscite. Lucien's preference was for a consular republic, although if people wanted the chief of the executive to be called an emperor, he would not have the right to command an army. He would receive a fair but not excessive salary (100,000 francs a year) and would enforce all the stated policies and agreed-on goals.

Lucien was aiming to go back to France, but Joseph disagreed with his activism. Joseph's secretary Mailliard wrote in his journals in August that his employer was unhappy about Lucien, and he described him as "a man who speaks well but doesn't feel anything."[34] Lucien kept insisting on his position and tried to persuade his prudent and skeptical elder sibling that he, Lucien, was right. He felt he was fighting a personal battle no less than a family war, noting that he might have to make of his cause "an individual affair if the others do not reenter" France.[35] Lucien's proposal took a long time to reach the French Chamber of Deputies, where it was eventually discussed on January 22, 1834; it was quickly dismissed, just as was rejected the petition offered by one deputy to reopen French territory to all members of the Bonaparte family. Lucien kept demanding justice in eloquent appeals to the French people and to the Chamber of Deputies, trying to pave the way for his family's return to France—to no avail.

In the meantime, Joseph, who took on his customary role of negotiating messy family business, attempted to reconcile Lucien and Jérôme, who had arrived in London in early May and with whom, Mailliard reported, Lucien was not getting along. Maillard's dislike of Lucien grew by the day: He found him changeable and devoid of firmness in his principles, despite his evident intelligence. Joseph, in his view, was far the superior of the brothers.

Months went by fairly uneventfully, until the next spring. Lucien had started writing his memoirs as well as a pamphlet on the One-Hundred Days (Napoleon's swan song to power, named for the duration of his return as emperor after Elba until his final demise): He was trying to accomplish through his private writing what he had failed to achieve through his public speaking.[36] The forced inactivity was weighing on the Bonaparte brothers, who felt increasingly powerless and nervous. A woman provoked even more tension between them: Madame Sari, an attractive though manipulative Creole woman, was rumored to be having an affair with Lucien. Her husband, a Corsican man named Mathieu Sari, who was in Joseph's service, challenged Lucien to a duel. The business was settled, yet again, by Joseph's intervention. After the Saris' departure from London on May 1, 1835, Lucien announced his intention to leave for Italy, where Alexandrine was ill.[37] He complained about the gossip that was spreading in his regard. Mailliard was glad to see him go: He could no longer stand this "homme de *plaisir* et du *moment*," guilty, in his eyes, of an epicurean and money-wasting lifestyle that contrasted so unfavorably with his employer's dutiful morality.[38]

In the end Lucien did not actually leave, because he was taken up with writing his memoirs and having them simultaneously translated into English by a lady named Anna Maria Gordon, who for many years had been the nanny of his two youngest daughters. At this point, after three years of supporting her husband's attempts to reenter France and regain his lost status, Alexandrine began complaining of Lucien's prolonged absence. In early 1836, she wrote him a reproachful letter in response to his argument that she was glad to know he was "forced to write in order not to starve": In her house, it was "not for lack of food that his wife is dying." She was happy that Anna Maria was doing a good job translating his writing: "I am too sincere not to admit that Lucien has near him an affectionate person whom I know; but with the same sincerity I confess that this prolonged position is an unfortunate incident in the life of two married people, or at least of one of them."[39] What sort of affection had grown between Lucien and Anna Maria is not known, but it was evidently not hard for Alexandrine to imagine it being of an intimate enough nature that he would not be in a hurry to return to Canino.

In the same letter, Alexandrine informed Lucien of other family events. Pierre was in Canino and expecting his father's reply to his latest news: His planned marriage to a Laetitia Besson, known as the daughter of an admiral but in fact an illegitimate daughter of Lucien's uncle Cardinal Fesch, had failed, because money was not available. In his reply, Lucien admitted to Pierre that he had financial troubles and entreated his son to "wake up, young Bonaparte, and live up to your name! Promise your beloved that you will marry her in a year, and start your career, find your path as did your uncle and your father, and return to our embrace as a man."[40]

What Alexandrine had not mentioned in her letter was how difficult it was to deal with Pierre and with Antoine, their two youngest sons, respectively aged nineteen and eighteen. Their formidable grandmother Letizia died in Rome on February 2, 1836, aged eighty-five. Lucien did not return even then. Now that she was gone, and in the absence of their father, the youngsters were misbehaving. Together with other truants, they dressed up like bandits and, armed with shotguns and pistols and accompanied by Corsican attack dogs, looked for trouble on their territory, causing fear and disturbance, and spent time with women of ill repute. Out of regard for their respectable older brother Charles, papal authorities chose not to interfere. But things all came to a head when the brothers shot dead a gamekeeper on their estate whom they had fired and who, in revenge, had wounded his substitute. The new cardinal in charge, known for loathing the Bonaparte family, seized the occasion to arrest the brothers, who in the meantime had requested passports to go to England. On May 2, 1836, as Pierre entered a café in Canino (Antoine had gone home), a patrol of carabinieri surrounded him and shouted that he was arrested in the name of the law. But Pierre— the headstrong son of the prince of Canino, the proud nephew of Napoleon—refused to acknowledge the police's authority and reacted violently: He stabbed the arresting officer in the heart, killing him on the spot. After a further scuffle with the other carabinieri, Pierre was restrained by a blow to the head.[41]

He was interned in the nearby fortress of Viterbo before being taken to Castle Sant'Angelo, the infamous papal prison in Rome, where he was to be tried. Alexandrine started pleading with the pope and the cardinals. Lucien, reportedly "overcome" by the events, could not or would not return to Italy, making the ordeal even harder on her.[42] After seven agonizing months in jail, Pierre was condemned to death; but the pope immediately commuted his sentence to perennial exile from the Papal States. In early 1837, Pierre sailed back to America. In New York, he spent some time with his cousin Louis-Napoleon, Hortense's son. He had become another family renegade who, a few months earlier, had attempted a coup d'etat that failed pitifully in Strasburg, at the French–Swiss border. King Louis-Philippe, instead of pressing charges, which would have made him seem a victim, had ordered Louis-Napoleon's deportation to the United States.[43]

Pierre still wanted to pursue a military career but was rejected from the American army. Feeling dejected and isolated in New York, he sailed back to London on a ship called *Wellington*, accompanied by Louis-Napoleon, and hoping that his father might help him sort out his life. But Lucien, too angry or perhaps too ashamed of his son's behavior, refused to see him, as did Joseph.[44] It was thanks to his half-sister Christine-Egypta Dudley Stuart that Pierre got hold of enough money to travel to the Greek island of Corfu with his mistress and illegitimate son and continue his reckless adventures as a mercenary.

A keen observer of Pierre's dissolute life was the Italophile writer Stendhal: As French consul in Civitavecchia from 1831, he often visited Alexandrine in nearby Canino. He was an admirer of Lucien who also developed romantic feelings for Marie, the gracious young daughter of the prince and princess of Canino, who had, he said, a "noble soul."[45] Pierre's explosive combination of romantic ideals, hot temper, and rebelliousness went into the character of Fabrizio Del Dongo, the hero of Stendhal's great novel *The Charterhouse of Parma*—in which Father Maurizio also served as a model for the wise, absentminded astronomer Abbé Blanès, Fabrizio's tutor.[46]

In London, Lucien was also trying to gain literary fame, but the first volume of his memoirs was a commercial failure. Readers had expected some intimate revelations about his brother, but he had kept all the notes about his private dealings with Napoleon in a separate file, called *Secret Memoirs*— and he felt it was too early for him to share those turbulent moments with the public. His time in England was coming to a close. In September 1837,

Charles went to London for three months with his own son Lucien (who one day would become a cardinal). He had not received any money from the hefty dowry Joseph had given him for Zénaïde, since it had been used for the mortgage of Canino, and a dispute arose with his father, but Joseph, as ever, quietly settled the matter.

Lucien and Joseph had been in London for a good five years, and they saw no point in remaining there. Lucien finally returned to Italy—to Senigallia—in the summer of 1838. Alexandrine was ill, but the reunion with her long-gone husband revitalized her. The two made peace, and traveled together to Munich in 1839 to visit Alexandrine's friend King Ludwig I of Bavaria, a collector of antiquities.[47]

This would be their last trip together. In the loving recollection of his wife, on May 30, 1840, and still in good form for his sixty-five years, Lucien had been walking in the grounds of Musignano, which included an ancient forest of secular oaks traversed by a stream. He was particularly fond of this forest, which reminded him of the chestnut forests of Corsica, where, in his youth, along with his *babo* Pasquale Paoli, he had often sung verses from *La Gerusalemme Liberata* by Torquato Tasso—the poet who had inspired him in his writing the epic *Charlemagne,* praised by Byron and Mme de Staël. He had continued this singing habit in his land of exile, to the joy of the whole family, for whom it was the signal of his return to the palace. On that day, they heard him recite a canto from Tasso's epic poem. It was an oddly emotional moment for them all. When he emerged from the forest, he was falling ill.[48]

Exactly a month later, Lucien died in the arms of Alexandrine, in Viterbo. They were on their way to Siena, where they were to spend the summer. Father Maurizio and Constance, their youngest child, who would later become a nun, assisted him in his final moments.

Alexandrine wrote to Ingres to ask him to insert, posthumously, Lucien's portrait in his family sketch of 1815. But the painter refused to retouch his drawing, and the head of the family would only appear as a sculpted bust: a beloved father, but absent.[49] Alexandrine lived for another fifteen years, which she spent defending her husband's legacy—writing an eloquent pamphlet against the minister Thiers, who had misrepresented Lucien in his *History of the Consulate and the Empire*.[50] And she published her own literary works, enjoying friendships and acquaintances with the likes of Balzac, Alfred de Vigny, Lamartine, and Victor Hugo. She died in Senigallia in 1855, aged seventy-seven, surrounded by her children and many grandchildren.[51]

Charles became the most renowned naturalist and ornithologist of his generation and remained politically active in the opposition to the papacy.

Antoine settled down to become a celebrated winemaker, whose Italian "champagne" was immensely popular.

Louis, who had been born in England in 1813, when his parents were exiled there, lived in London from 1850. He had inherited his father's ease with languages and became a respected comparative linguist and philologist, learned in many European dialects, and known especially for his expertise in Basque, for which he compiled a dictionary and into which he translated the Song of Songs. He knew Celtic, worked on English dialects (which earned him a Civil List pension that he much needed toward the end of his life), and helped translate Matthew's Gospel into the Asturian, Calabrian, Corsican, Genoese, Milanese, Roman, Sardinian, and Sicilian dialects.

Pierre, after the 1848 revolution and the abdication of Louis-Philippe, returned to France but was a constant source of embarrassment to his cousin Louis-Napoleon, who became Emperor Napoleon III in 1852. He became known as the "Wild Boar of Corsica."[52] In 1870, he shot dead Victor Noir, a man who had come to his house to bring him the summons to a duel. Pierre was tried and eventually released on the basis of self-defense, but the stigma of a violent man always stayed with him. He married a Parisian woman, by whom he had two children. His son Roland, an explorer and geographer, in turn had a daughter named Marie Bonaparte, who married the prince of Greece. She became the first female psychoanalyst, a famed pupil of Freud, whom she saved from the Nazis by arranging for him and his family to be brought to London, the city where Lucien had sought and found freedom of expression in his later years.

Letizia, the other black sheep of the family, married an English diplomat, Thomas Wyse. She was none too faithful, and they separated scandalously. She ended her life in misery in an Augustinian convent in Paris.

Marie, while still a teenager, had left home against her mother's wishes and married a local count from Canino, Vincenzo Valentini. Like her mother, she wrote poems—in Italian. Her daughter Luciana would marry the wealthy Senator Zeffirino Faina; Luciana was Alexandrine's universal legatee, and it is thanks to her that the most intimate papers of Lucien's life were preserved from destruction.[53]

NOTES

PREFACE
1. Iung I, xii. A full critical edition of Lucien's *Mémoires* is in preparation.

CHAPTER 1
1. This section draws from many combined sources, among them: Abrantès, Barras, Bourrienne, Dwyer, Iung, and *Memoirs of Lucien Bonaparte* (hereafter *Memoirs*). See also some unpublished sections of the *Mémoires* 1814, 184r–232v.
2. *Discours de Lucien Bonaparte*, 1799; *Mémoires* 1814, 208v–209r; Iung I, 323–324; see Bourrienne I, 278–279.
3. Ludwig, 148.
4. Iung I, 24; see Napoleon to his uncle Nicolas Paravicini, Brienne, June 25, 1784 (PML, MA 316). See Bourrienne I, 3 (wrongly stating that the two brothers did not meet at Brienne).
5. *Mémoires* 1814, 19r–v; Iung I, 25.
6. *Mémoires* 1814, 16v–17r; Iung I, 11–12.
7. *Mémoires* 1814, 19r, 21v.
8. *Mémoires* 1814, 26v.
9. Ludwig, 14.
10. *Mémoires* 1814, 25r.
11. *Mémoires* 1814, 111v; Iung I, 139v.
12. Boswell, 119.
13. *Memoirs*, 12.
14. Ibid.
15. *Mémoires* 1814, 40r; *Memoirs*, 12.
16. *Mémoires* 1814, 41r.
17. *Mémoires* 1814, 42v; Iung I, 40.
18. *Mémoires* 1814, 19v; Iung I, 25. Graziani, 24ff. questions both the chronology and the truthfulness of Lucien's statements.
19. *Memoirs*, 13.
20. *Mémoires* 1814, 47v; Iung I, 46.
21. *Mémoires* 1814, 46v.
22. Napoleon to Lucien, Paris, June 1792 (Masson, *Napoléon dans sa jeunesse*, 296).
23. Lucien to Joseph, Ucciani, June 24, 1792 (Masson, *Napoléon dans sa jeunesse*, 297).
24. *Mémoires* 1814, 50v; see *Memoirs*, 14.
25. *Mémoires* 1816, 65r.
26. *Mémoires* 1814, 51v; Iung I, 61; *Memoirs*, 14.

27. The following scene is drawn from Lucien's *Mémoires* 1814, 60r ff.; see Iung I, 65 ff.
28. Masson, *Napoléon dans sa jeunesse,* 324; see Abrantès, 218: "A shrewd and perceptive man, he surmised that so much suppressed fire risked overwhelming and destroying the evidently ardent soul of this young Bonaparte and took him under his wing." The man is Huguet de Sémonville; d'Abrantès is listed as a duchess by some publishers, not all.
29. *Mémoires* 1814, 102r.
30. Iung I, 90; *Memoirs,* 18.
31. *Mémoires* 1814, 106v; Iung I, 94.
32. *Mémoires* 1814, 89r.
33. *Memoirs,* 16; *Mémoires* 1814, 97v.
34. Some Napoleonic historians have it that Napoleon was the one to rescue the fleeing family members in a sensational fashion and that Lucien was the one who had endangered them, causing them to flee their home, by writing to his brothers from Toulon a letter in which he announced the decree he had signed for Paoli's arrest. The letter would have been seized by Paoli's agents. That is all possible. But there is no trace of the letter. Paoli knew full well that the Bonapartes were on the French side in any case; and in planning his revenge against the defectors to his cause, he would have meant his promise of not sparing anyone who stood in the way.
35. *Mémoires* 1814, 119v.
36. Iung I, 107; *Memoirs,* 20.
37. *Mémoires* 1814, 84v.
38. Dumas, *Vie de Napoléon,* chap. "La prise de Toulon."
39. Iung I, 122–3; see *Mémoires* 1816, 65v–66r: Lucien denied having written this letter, claiming that it had been forged by some zealous servant of his brother as first consul, or by an agent of Fouché or Talleyrand.
40. *Mémoires* 1814, 133v; Iung I, 112; *Memoirs,* 26. Italics in the original.
41. *Memoirs,* 23–25; see *Mémoires* 1814, 133v ff.
42. Barras, 340–342.
43. Ibid.
44. Iung I, 109; *Memoirs,* 25.
45. *Memoirs,* 28.
46. Iung I, 118; *Memoirs,* 31.
47. Lucien to Rey père, from the prisons of Aix, July 20, 1795 (Iung I, 512–514).
48. Lucien to Chiappe, from the prisons of Aix, July 20, 1795 (Iung I, 130–131; this letter is preserved in Italian, the language it was probably written originally, in AFP).
49. Barras, 119–120.
50. Fraser, 6.
51. See Moorehead, 235 ff.
52. Moorehead, 184, 240, 282; Fairweather, 211–212.
53. *Mémoires* 1815, 81r; Iung I, 136; II, 212.
54. *Mémoires* 1814, 134r; Iung I, 135.
55. Napoleon to Carnot, summer 1796 (Iung I, 149–150); Atteridge, 33.
56. Lucien to Barras, Strasbourg, September 14, 1796 (PIASA, #284).
57. Napoleon to Carnot, October 25, 1796 (Iung I, 150); see Atteridge, 36.
58. Atteridge, 38.
59. Christine to Napoleon, Ajaccio, August 1, 1797 (Iung I, 151) *Mémoires* 1814, 133v.
60. Napoleon to Joseph, on board of the *Orient,* May 19, 1798 (Iung I, 154; 483).
61. *Mémoires* 1814, 134v; Iung I, 199; *Memoirs,* 110–113; Fouché, 56–58. See Alexandrine's *Appel à la justice,* 57.
62. Iung I, 263; see Dwyer, 452.
63. Napoleon to Josephine, June 15, 1796 (Stuart, 197).

64. Rémusat, 42.
65. Gohier, 200; Dwyer, 473.
66. Bourrienne II, 137.
67. *Mémoires* 1814, 184r ff.; Iung I, 283 ff. See Dumas, *The Companions of Jehu,* 260.
68. Dwyer, 476; Iung I, 293.
69. See Stendhal, *Vie de Napoléon,* 46.

CHAPTER 2
1. Dwyer, 511.
2. *Recueil,* 119 ff.
3. *Recueil,* 129 ff.; Fouché, 92, claimed that there was "no fraud" in the counting.
4. Abrantès, 164.
5. Piétri II, 99.
6. Rémusat, 29.
7. *Memoirs of the Private and Political Life of Lucien Bonaparte, Prince of Canino.* 115. Hereafter *Secret Memoirs.*
8. Fouché, 68.
9. Chateaubriand II, 164.
10. Riberette; Lucien Bonaparte, Lettres à Madame Récamier, 1799–1800: BNF, Nouvelles Acquisitions Françaises, 16597. See Caracciolo, 136–139.
11. Abrantès, 165–166.
12. *Mémoires* 1816, 324r; Iung I, 280.
13. Récamier I, 27 ff.
14. Abrantès, 246.
15. Abrantès, 247.
16. Edelein-Badie, 325.
17. *Mémoires* 1814, 288r-v; Iung I, 381–2 (see Caracciolo, 170–172, Cat. 69); Piétri I, 114–115, also recording the malicious slander by Barras, who in his memoirs wrote that Lucien had poisoned her.
18. Ludwig, 167.
19. Lucien to Joseph, Paris, June 24, 1800 (Iung I, 411; see Bourrienne II, 28–29).
20. Ludwig, 169.
21. *Mémoires* 1814, 281r–282r; Iung I, 385.
22. See *Recueil,* 258 ff.
23. *Recueil,* 276 ff., see *Discours prononcé.*
24. Napoleon to Lucien, Paris, July 16, 1800 (Bordes, 32).
25. Delécluze, 231–232.
26. Abrantès V, 86 (June 1806).
27. Bordes, 30.
28. *Recueil,* 146.
29. Duquesnoy to Lucien, Paris, January 21, 24, 29, 1801 (AF); *Mémoires* 1814, 299r; Iung I, 390.
30. *Mémoires* 1814, 303r; Iung I, 395.
31. Roederer, 22.
32. *Recueil,* 321; see Iung I, 409.
33. *Mémoires* 1814, 282r; Iung I, 385.
34. Iung II, 91n; see unpublished *Mémoires* in AF.
35. Iung I, 421 ff.; see Bourrienne II, 52 ff.; *Secret Memoirs,* 111 ff; Fouché, 111–112; Piétri I, 121 ff.
36. Roederer, 53; see Iung I, 432 (with the misleading typo "8 . . ." instead of "S . . .").
37. Roederer, 49.

38. *Mémoires* 1814, 283r.

39. *Mémoires* 1814, 284r; Iung II, 53.

40. *Mémoires* 1814, 285r.

41. *Mémoires* 1814, 285r; see Masson II, 12, who instead claims that Lucien was in awe of Wicquefort's tract. See *Mémoires* 1815, 2r; Iung II, 20, 203n. See also Simonetta, *Lucien Bonaparte ambassadeur en Espagne,* 70 ff.

42. *Mémoires* 1814, 291r; Iung II, 3. The travel letters to Elisa are also in AF.

43. Lucien to Elisa, Montolieu, November 13, 1800 (1814, 294r; AF).

44. Iung II, 6; see Napoleon to Joseph, Paris, December 2, 1800 (*Mémoires du roi Joseph* I, 191); Piétri II, 23 ff.

45. *Mémoires* 1815, 1r; Iung II, 23.

46. *Mémoires* 1815, 3v; Iung II, 19–20.

47. *Mémoires* 1815, 2r; Iung II, 20. See *Mémoires* 1816, 74r; Iung II, 73n.

48. Hughes, 239 ff.

49. *Mémoires* 1815, 2r; Iung II, 23n.

50. Talleyrand to Lucien, Paris, December 24, 1800 (Iung II, 56; wrongly dated as 23). See Iung II, 456, Talleyrand to Lucien, Paris, December 25,1800.

51. *Mémoires,* AF 13–14; see Iung II, 91n.

52. Roederer, 52.

53. Dumas, *Le Chevalier,* 333, 364, 500.

54. *Mémoires* 1815, 3v–25v; Iung II, 23 ff.

55. Hughes, 240 ff.

56. Fumaroli, 305–321.

57. Elisa to Lucien, Paris, February 16, 1801 (AFP, 8365).

58. Elisa to Lucien, Paris, February 20, 1801 (AFP, 8359).

59. Piétri II, 187.

60. *Mémoires* 1815, 4r; Iung II, 48.

61. *Mémoires* 1815, 4r.

62. *Mémoires* 1815, 3r-v.

63. Iung II, 67–68. See *Mémoires* 1816, 64v; Iung II, 130n.

64. Piétri II, 249 ff.

65. *Mémoires* 1815, 27r; Iung II, 89n.

66. Marquesa to Lucien (Madrid?), early summer 1801 (AF).

67. Elisa to Lucien (Paris?), August 20, 1801 (AFP, 8354).

68. *Mémoires* 1815, 29v.

69. Lucien to Napoleon (Madrid?), April 1801 (Iung II, 154).

70. Roederer, 54–56.

71. Napoleon to Lucien, Paris, March 1801 (as quoted in Piétri II, 353).

72. Iung II, 124; P.-N. Bonaparte, *Souvenirs,* 220.

73. Iung II, 126; P.-N. Bonaparte, *Souvenirs,* 225.

74. *Mémoires* 1815, 42v ff.; Iung II, 128 ff.

75. Jefferson to Livingston, Washington, April 18, 1802 (Peterson, 486).

76. *Mémoires* 1815, 46r ff.; Iung II, 136 ff.

77. *Mémoires* 1815, 56r; Iung II, 158 ff.; P.-N. Bonaparte, *Souvenirs,* 158 ff.

78. Mlle Lenormant, Mme Récamier's niece, see *Mémoires* 1816, 71r-v; Iung II, 178–179.

CHAPTER 3

1. *Mémoires* 1815, 128r.

2. The whole section about Méréville is drawn from the unpublished *Mémoires* in AF. No further references to this text will be made in the notes.

3. *Mémoires* 1815, 106r; Iung II, 243 ff.

4. Stendhal, *Vie de Napoléon,* 160.
5. Chateaubriand I, 577.
6. Alexandrine's autograph manuscript of the *Souvenirs* is preserved in AF; a typewritten transcription is in AFP; parts of this text were published by Fleuriot de Langle.
7. Fontanes to Elisa, October 4, 1802 (Fleuriot, *Alexandrine,* 43).
8. Lucien to Napoleon, Paris, winter 1802–1803 (BIF, ms. 2190, folios 29–30; see Caracciolo, 139–140).
9. See entry by Arikha and Simonetta in Caracciolo, 174–176 (Cat. 71).
10. Simonetta and Colesanti, *Lo Sperone del Sotterraneo,* passim (AFP).
11. *Mémoires* 1814, 188r; Iung II, 379; Piétri I, 186–187.
12. *Mémoires* 1815, 36r.
13. *Mémoires* 1815, 193v–194r; Iung II, 389.
14. *Mémoires* 1815, 196v–197r; Iung II, 394–395 (this chapter is chronologically misplaced by Iung).
15. *Mémoires* 1815, 200r; Iung II, 399.
16. *Mémoires* 1815, 209r; Iung II, 411.
17. The whole dialogue entitled "La Reine d'Etrurie" is in P.-N. Bonaparte, *Souvenirs,* 240 ff., Iung II, 272 ff.
18. Ducrest, 9. See Piétri I, 188; Piétri II, 151–152 and 157; Fleuriot, *Alexandrine,* 47.
19. This episode is drawn from the unpublished *Mémoires* in AF.
20. Ibid.
21. Ibid.
22. *Mémoires* 1815, 37v.
23. This episode is drawn from Simonetta and Colesanti, *Lo Sperone del Sotterraneo* (AFP).
24. Lucien to Napoleon, early November 1803 (Simonetta and Colesanti, *Lo Sperone del Sotterraneo,* AFP).
25. The whole episode in *Mémoires* 1815, 140r ff.; Iung II, 310 ff.
26. *Mémoires* 1815, 154v ff.; Iung II, 332 ff. (rearranged chronologically).
27. *Mémoires* 1815, 172r ff.; Iung II, 358 ff. (rearranged chronologically).

CHAPTER 4

1. *Mémoires* 1815, 133r ff.; see Simonetta and Colesanti, *Lo Sperone del Sotterraneo,* 69–70.
2. *Mémoires* 1815, 136r.
3. *Mémoires* 1815, 121r; see Iung II, 268.
4. *Mémoires* 1815, 136v.
5. Dumas, *Le Chevalier,* 464.
6. Fouché, 168; Iung II, 432; see P.-N. Bonaparte, *Souvenirs,* 152.
7. Rémusat, 266 ff. Translation revised by authors.
8. *Mémoires* 1815, 212v (see also 138v); Iung II, 435 ff.
9. *Mémoires* 1815, 225v ff.; see Simonetta and Colesanti, *Lo Sperone del Sotterraneo,* 72–80.
10. *Mémoires* 1815, 334r.
11. Ibid.; see Iung III, 4.
12. *Mémoires* 1815, 335r; see Fraser, 112 ff.
13. Fraser, 119 ff.
14. Bernadotte to Lucien, Paris, June 1804, in *Mémoires* 1815, 219r–222v and 1816, 86r–89r; see Iung I, 362–63 and II, 445–449.
15. Elisa to Lucien, Paris, June 17, 1804, quoted in Alexandrine, *Appel à la justice,* 104–106.
16. From Lucien's unpublished "Brouillards" (AFP).
17. Letizia to Lucien, Paris, April 7, 1805, Bonaparte, *Lettere di Leticia,* 47–48. Hereafter LLB.

18. *Mémoires* 1815, 265v; Iung III, 9.
19. This whole section is drawn from *Mémoires* 1815, 265r–289v; Iung III, 9–48. Copies and originals of the letters by Talleyrand and Fesch are also in AFP.
20. Lucien to Joseph (Pesaro, summer 1805; AF).
21. Ibid.
22. Lucien to Elisa, Pesaro, August 5, 1805 (AF); see Marmottan, *Lettres inédites,* 171).
23. Elisa to Lucien, Lucca, October 1, 1805 (AF); see Marmottan, *Lettres inédites,* 175).
24. Consalvi to Lucien, Rome, August 10 and 17, 1805 (AF).
25. Joseph to Lucien, Saut sur Seine, September 6, 1805 (AN 400/14 AP, 85).
26. Joseph to Napoleon, Paris, October 1, 1805 (Bonaparte, Mémoires et Correspondance I, 282. Hereafter *Mémoires du Roi Joseph.*)
27. *Mémoires* 1816, 72v–73v (see Iung III, 57: long letter by Artaud describing Canova's atelier in Rome, February 19, 1805).
28. Edelein-Badie; see Caracciolo, 241ff.
29. Pauline to Lucien, Paris, March 6, 1806 (AFP, 8384). Lucien's handwritten reply is written on the back of the same sheet.
30. This comment is drawn from the unpublished *Mémoires* in AF. See Fraser, 136–137.
31. Lucien to Letizia, Tusculum, July 1, 1806 (Edelein-Badie, 342); Letizia to Lucien, Pont, September 7, 1806 (LLB, 54–55 in French; but the original in Italian, AF, contains the censored information about the financial situation).
32. *Mémoires* 1815, 329v.
33. Lucien to Fesch, Rome, October 6, 1806 (PIASA #286; see Atteridge, 175; Tyson Stroud, *Man Who Had Been King,* 196).
34. Lucien to Letizia and to Joseph, Rome, October 7 and 9, 1806 (AF).
35. Letizia to Lucien, Paris, November 2, 1806 (LLB, 55–56; see uncensored original in Italian, AF).
36. Lucien to Elisa, Rome, April 4, 1807 (Marmottan, *Lettres,* 180–181).
37. Letizia to Lucien, Paris, May 9, 1807 (AN, 400/14 AP, 9–10).
38. Letizia to Lucien, Paris, July 11, 1807 (AN, 400/14 AP, 12–14).
39. Lucien to Lethière, Rome, January 9, 1807 (We thank Geneviève Madec-Capy for providing a copy of this document from the private archive of Pierre Ordioni).

CHAPTER 5
1. Joseph to Lucien, Venice, December 4, 1807 (AN, 400/14 AP, 101).
2. Joseph to Napoleon, Modena, December 11, 1807 (*Mémoires du roi Joseph* IV, 77).
3. Napoleon to Letizia (without date or place but from northern Italy, December 1807; Edelein-Badie, 347).
4. On this whole interview, see *Mémoires* 1815, 290r–313r; see Iung III, 82–125; see Fleuriot, *Alexandrine,* 87–99; see Ludwig, 271–284; Piétri I, 223 ff.
5. Napoleon to Joseph, Milan, December 17, 1807 (*Mémoires du roi Joseph* IV, 80; see Iung III, 137–138).
6. Letizia to Lucien, Paris, December 28, 1807 (LLB, 62).
7. Joseph to Lucien, Naples, January 1, 1808 (AN, 400/14 AP, 103–106).
8. Napoleon to Joseph, [Paris], March 11, 1808 (Masson, *Napoléon et sa famille* IV, 221–222).
9. Marmottan, *Lucien Bonaparte á Florence,* 327.
10. Letizia to Lucien, Paris, March 28, 1808 (AF).
11. Masson, *Napoléon et sa famille* IV, 224–227 ; Masson, *Napoléon et sa famille* V, 40–42; see BT, Fonds Masson 457, 93–98.
12. Letizia to Joseph, Paris, June 7, 1808 (BIF, ms. 5670, f. 125).
13. Tassoni to Testi, Florence, June 21, 1808 (Marmottan, *Lucien Bonaparte á Florence* 331).

14. Lucien to Joseph, July 5, 1808 (BIF, ms. 5670, f. 146v).
15. Elisa to Lucien, [Lucca?], June 14 and 25, 1808 (AF); August 30, 1808 (AFP, 8369).
16. Letizia to Lucien, Paris, October 30, 1808 (Iung III, 152–153).
17. Letizia to Lucien, September 23, 1808 (AN, 400/14 AP, 17–18).
18. Lucien to Letizia, Canino, December 4, 1808 (Iung III, 153–154).
19. Abrantès, 4, 205–209.
20. Hughes, 261 ff.
21. Roederer, 127, 134.
22. Elisa to Lucien, Pisa, December 25, 1809 (AF; Marmottan, *Lettres,* 234).
23. Lucien to Joseph, Canino, January 1, 1810 (BIF, ms. 5670, f. 159).
24. Piétri I, 242 (from Campi's *brouillon*).
25. Alexandrine to Napoleon, Canino, February 1810 (Fleuriot, *Alexandrine,* 104–105; see R. Bonaparte, ed., *Lucien Bonaparte et sa famille,* 181–183).
26. Letizia to Alexandrine, Paris, March 10, 1810 (PIASA #266; see Iung III, 155–156).
27. All the letters exchanged between Lolotte and her parents are in AF. The Lolotte Dossier is comprised of thirty-four letters by Lolotte to her parents, three by Alexandrine to Lolotte (plus a fifty-page-long list of advice on good religious and moral behavior), twenty one by Lucien to Lolotte, two by Lucien to Campi, fifteen by Campi to Lucien, two by Lucien to Napoleon, three by Lucien to Letizia, and one by Napoleon to Letizia. See Simonetta, *Séjours,* in Caracciolo, 277.
28. Fleuriot, *Alexandrine,* 109.
29. Napoleon to Letizia, Dunkirk, May 22, 1810 (AF).
30. Piétri I, 254.
31. Fleuriot, *Alexandrine,* 109.
32. Alexandrine to Madame . . . , Fort Ricasoli, September 5, 1810 (AF; AFP).
33. Lucien to Piétri, Fort Ricasoli, September 1, 1810 (Piétri I, 260).
34. Napoleon to the president of the Senate Garnier, Fontainebleau, September 27, 1810 (*Lettres inédites de Napoléon 1er,* 276; see Masson, *Napoléon et sa famille* V, 126–134, with the date September 18).
35. The poem is still unpublished (AF; one copy preceded by a handwritten letter by Lucien to Joseph, Tusculum, February 20, 1817, was still in the hands of a Parisian book dealer, Rodolphe Chamonal, in 2009).
36. Tyson Stroud, *Emperor of Nature,* 18 and plate 1. This is the same engraving that appears on the title page to this chapter.
37. Lucien to Campi, Worcester, December 1811 (AF).
38. BL Add. 34584, 74v–75r (see Butler, 79–80).
39. Chateaubriand as quoted in Fraser, 172.
40. Madame de Staël to Lucien, [London], February 20, 1814 (AF); see Madame de Staël to Lucien, [London], April 23, 1814 (Fleuriot, *Alexandrine,* 139–140).
41. Byron to Butler, London, October 20, 1813 (Butler 89–90); see Lucien to Butler, Worcester, November 9, 1813 (BL Add. 34583, 450).
42. The article from the *Champion,* December 1814 is preserved in BL, Add. 34584, 73.
43. BL Add. 34584, 75v (see Butler 80).
44. Father Maurizio to Alexandrine, Brescia, December 24, 1849 (AF).
45. See Lieven.
46. Letizia to Lucien, Portoferraio, August 18, 1814 (LLB, 82).
47. Fleuriot, *Alexandrine,* 154 (Pichot, 341).
48. Edelein-Badie, 121.
49. Pietromarchi, 258, 264; *Secret Memoirs,* 74.
50. Letizia to Lucien, Portoferraio, March 5, 1815 (LLB, 82; AN, 400/14 AP, 27–28).
51. *Mémoires,* 1815, 252v.

52. *Note confidentielle du Père Maurice sur son entrevue avec Napoléon aux Tuileries en 1815* (*Mémoires* 1816, 203r–209r, 213r–224r; Iung III, 232–242. The *Suplément* in 1816, 210r–212v; Iung III, 365–371. Another copy in AFM). See Pietri I, 290 on Lucien ambassador in Rome.

53. Lucien to Alexandrine, Paris, May 8, 1815 (Eugénie, Princesse de Grèce, 16). For the *cordon,* see Caracciolo, 281 ff.

54. *Mémoires* 1815, 255v (see Iung III, 263).

55. The rest of the chapter is drawn from *Mémoires* 1815, 255v–257v. See Atteridge, 443 ff. and Lucien's *La vérité sur les cent-jours* (text largely reprinted in Iung III, 287–346).

56. Miot, 734.

57. Iung III, 309; Piétri I, 299; Atteridge, 449.

58. Atteridge, 455 ff.

EPILOGUE
1. Atteridge, 460.

2. *Mémoires* 1815, 257v; Iung III, 359; Piétri I, 305.

3. Piétri I, 305.

4. Lucien to Metternich, Turin, July 1815 (Iung III, 362–364; see Piétri I, 306–307).

5. Metternich to Lucien, [Vienna,] August 28, 1815 (Iung III, 365; see Eugénie, Princesse de Grèce, 18, correcting the date on the basis on the original).

6. Piétri I, 309.

7. Piétri II, 362.

8. Elisa to Lucien [undated] (Piétri I, 311).

9. Châtillon; Piétri I, 316; P.-N. Bonaparte, *Souvenirs,* 51 ff.

10. Piétri I, 314 ff.; Fleuriot, *Alexandrine,* 168.

11. See Tyson Stroud, *Man Who Had Been King,* 1 ff.

12. Joseph to Lucien, Claremont (near New York), October 25, 1815 (AN, 400/14 AP, 119).

13. Joseph to Lucien, New York, January 30, 1816 (AN, 400/14 AP, 122–124).

14. Joseph to Julie, Point Breeze, April 17, 1818 (Tyson Stroud, *Man Who Had Been King,* 60).

15. Joseph to Lucien, Philadelphia, March 20, 1819 (Tyson Stroud, *Man Who Had Been King,* 61).

16. Tyson Stroud, *Man Who Had Been King,* 77.

17. Joseph to Lucien, Point Breeze, February 24, 1822 (AN, 400/14 AP, 132–135).

18. Alexandrine to Charles, Croce del Biacco, July 17, 1822 (Fleuriot, *Alexandrine,* 188).

19. Charles to Lucien, Rome, October 4, 1822 (AFP, 8387–8388; see Tyson Stroud, *Emperor of Nature,* 29–31).

20. Charles to Alexandrine, Rome, October 6, 1822 (AFP, 8298). Charles to Lucien, Rome, February 28, 1823 (AFP, 8390). On the back of this letter Lucien sketched the draft of his reply; see Tyson Stroud, *Emperor of Nature,* 31.

21. Tyson Stroud, *Emperor of Nature,* 34 ff.

22. Charles to Alexandrine, Point Breeze, November 1, 1823 (AFP, 8299; see Tyson Stroud, *Emperor of Nature,* 42; Tyson Stroud, *Man Who Had Been King,* 109).

23. Charles to Lucien, Point Breeze, June 16, 1824 (AFP, 8394).

24. Fleuriot, *Alexandrine,* 194 ff.

25. Lucien to Joseph, Rome, August 26, 1826 (Fleuriot, *Alexandrine,* 195–196).

26. Letizia to Lucien, Rome, September 30, 1828 (AF; see Fleuriot, *Alexandrine,* 204–205).

27. Joseph to Letizia, Point Breeze, July 27, 1831 (Pietromarchi, 313).

28. Joseph to Lucien, Philadelphia, March 31, 1832 (AN, 400/14 AP, 138–145).

29. Lucien to Pierre, Canino, November 15, 1832 (P.-N. Bonaparte, *Souvenirs,* 60–62).

30. See dated entries from Mailliard Journals in MP (Yale MS 341, Box 7). See also journal of Lucien traveling to England in 1833 (AF) for Lucien's social engagements.
31. Tyson Stroud, *Man Who Had Been King,* 169 (MP, April 30, 1833).
32. Lucien to Father Maurizio, London, June 7 [1833] (AFM).
33. Iung III, 404–420.
34. Tyson Stroud, *Man Who Had Been King,* 165 (MP, August 24, 1833).
35. August 8, 1833 (AF, English travel journal).
36. *La vérité sur les cent-jours;* see Iung III, 287–346.
37. Tyson Stroud, *Man Who Had Been King,* 174 (MP, May 1, 1835).
38. MP, May 18, 1835.
39. Alexandrine to Lucien, [Canino, early 1836, with a copy of Pius VII to Alexandrine, Rome, June 4, 1808] (AF).
40. Lucien to Pierre, [London, late 1835–early 1836]: P.-N. Bonaparte, *Souvenirs,* 97–98.
41. Stendhal to Thiers, Civitavecchia, May 6, 1836 (Stendhal, *Correspondance,* 209–211). See many letters by Alexandrine to various cardinals pleading for Pierre (AF).
42. Tyson Stroud, *Man Who Had Been King,* 186.
43. Ibid., 185.
44 Eugénie, Princesse de Grèce, 147–149; see Pierre to Joseph, London, July 16 and 17, 1837; Christine to Joseph, London, July 17, 1837 (AF).
45. Stendhal to Bucci, Paris, September 6, 1838 (Stendhal, *Correspondance,* 267; see Stendhal to Marie, Civitavecchia, August 14, 1840 [ibid., 380–381]; Marie to Stendhal [Canino], August 8, 1840 [ibid., 578–579]).
46. Pietromarchi, 317.
47. Fleuriot, *Alexandrine,* 211.
48. *Mémoires* 1814, 54r.
49. Fleuriot, *Alexandrine,* 155; Fleuriot, "Monsieur Ingres."
50. Alexandrine, *Appel à la justice.*
51. About Alexandrine's literary acquaintances and her children and grandchildren, see AF. See Stendhal to Thiers, Civitavecchia, July 1, 1840 (Stendhal, *Correspondance,* 372–373).
52. See P.-N. Bonaparte, *Souvenirs* and Eugénie, Princesse de Grèce.
53. See Authors' preface.

BIBLIOGRAPHY

MANUSCRIPT SOURCES

AF = Archivio Faina, Perugia
AFM = Archivio dei Frati Minori di Lombardia, Milan
AFP = Archivio della Fondazione Primoli, Rome
AN = Archives Nationales, Paris
AP (after AN) = Archives Privées
BIF = Bibliothèque de l'Institut de France, Paris
BL = British Library, London
BNF = Bibliothèque Nationale de France, Paris
BT = Bibliothèque Thiers, Fonds Masson, Paris
Mémoires 1814, 1815, 1816 = Archives Diplomatiques, Ministère des Affaires Étrangères, Paris, MD, France
MN = Museo Napoleonico, Rome
MP = Mailliard Papers, Manuscripts and Archives, Yale University Library, New Haven, CT
PML = Pierpont Morgan Library, Literary & Historical Manuscripts (LHMS), New York
PIASA = *Pages d'histoire—Lettres et manuscrits autographes* (sale of February 13, 2009)

WORKS BY LUCIEN BONAPARTE (CHRONOLOGICALLY)

Discours de Lucien Bonaparte, président du Conseil des Cinq-Cents, aux troupes, au milieu de la cour du palais de Saint-Cloud, le 19 brumaire an 8 ([A Saint-Cloud] [de l'Imprimerie Nationale] [19 brumaire an 8 = 9 novémbre 1799]).

La Tribu indienne, ou Édouard et Stellina. Par le citoyen L. B. Paris, An. VII (1799), 2 vols.

Recueil des Lettres Circulaires, Instructions, Arrêtés et Discours Publics émanés des citoyens Quinette, Laplace, Lucien Bonaparte, Chaptal, Ministres de l'intérieur depuis le 16 Messidor an 7 jusqu'au 1er Vendémiaire an 10. Imprimerie de la République, an X (1802); cf. *Discours prononcé dans le Temple de Mars . . . le 25 messidor an 8, pour la Féte du 14 juillet et de la concorde.* Paris, an VIII (1800).

La vérité sur les cent-jours; suivie de documens historiques sur 1815. Paris 1835.

Mémoires de Lucien Bonaparte, prince de Canino. Écrits par lui-même. Tome Premier. Édition originale. Paris 1836.

Memoirs of Lucien Bonaparte. Written by Himself. Part I. London 1836 (Cited in text as *Memoirs.*)

Mémoires de Lucien Bonaparte, prince de Canino. Écrits par lui-même. Tome Premier. Bruxelles 1836.

Mémoires de Lucien Bonaparte, prince de Canino. Écrits par lui-même. Tome Deuxième. Bruxelles 1845.
Lucien Bonaparte et sa famille [ed. Roland Bonaparte]. Paris 1889.

PRIMARY SOURCES BY LUCIEN AND ALEXANDRINE

Bonaparte, Alexandrine. *Appel à la justice des contemporains de feu Lucien Bonaparte en réfutation des assertions de M. Thiers dans son histoire du Consulat et de l'Empire . . .* Paris 1845.

Bonaparte, Lucien. *Memoirs of the Private and Political Life of Lucien Bonaparte, Prince of Canino.* Translated from the French. London 1818. (Cited in text as *Secret Memoirs.*)

Muséum étrusque de Lucien Bonaparte, prince de Canino, fouilles de 1828 á 1829. Vases peints avec inscriptions. Viterbo 1829.

Bonaparte, Pierre-Napoléon. *Souvenirs, Traditions et Révélations.* Part I, Book 1, Vol. 1. De 1815 à la Révolution de Février. Ixelles-Bruxelles 1876.

[Campi, Andrea, but published without author] *Mémoires secrets sur la vie privée, politique et littéraire de Lucien Bonaparte, prince de Canino.* Paris 1816, 2 vols.

Iung, Theodor, ed. *Lucien Bonaparte et ses Mémoires.* D'après les papiers déposés aux Archives Étrangères et d'autres documents inédits. Paris 1882–83, 3 vols. (Cited in text as Iung.)

WORKS BY OTHERS (QUOTED IN ENGLISH WHEN A TRANSLATION EXISTS)

Abrantès, Duchesse d'. *Mémoires d'une contemporaine,* Paris 1828.
———. *Memoirs of the Duchess d'Abrantès (Madame Junot).* New York 1832.
Albany, Comtesse d'. *Correspondance inédite de la comtesse d'Albany.* Nîmes 1879.
Barras, Vicomte de. *Memoirs of Barras Member of the Directorate,* New York 1895.
Bonaparte, Joseph. *Mémoires et correspondance politique et militaire du roi Joseph; publiés, annotés et mis en ordre,* ed. A. Du Casse, Paris 1856–60, 10 vols. (Cited in text as *Mémoires du roi Joseph.*)
Bonaparte, Letizia. *Lettere di Letizia Buonaparte,* ed. P. Misciattelli. Milano 1936. (Cited in text as LLB.)
Boswell, James. *The Journal to a Tour to Corsica and Memoirs of Pascal Paoli.* London 1768; reprint 1996.
Bourrienne, Louis Antoine Fauvelet de. *Mémoires de M. Bourrienne, Ministre d'État, sur Napoléon, le Directoire, le Consulat, l'Empire et la Restauration.* Paris 1829, 10 vols.
Butler, Samuel, ed. *The life and letters of Dr. Samuel Butler: head-master of Shrewsbury school 1798–1830 and afterwards Bishop of Lichfield.* London 1896.
Chateaubriand, François René de. *Mémoires d'Outre-Tombe.* Paris 1951, 2 vols.
Châtillon, Charles de. *Quinze ans d'exil dans les États Romains, pendant la proscription de Lucien Bonaparte.* Paris 1842.
De Las Cases, Emmanuel. *Mémorial de Sainte Hélène. Journal of the Private Life and Conversations of the Emperor at Saint Helena.* London 1823.
Ducrest, Madame. *Chroniques populaires. Mémoires sur l'impératrice Joséphine.* Paris 1855.
Fouché, Joseph. *Duc d'Otranto. Ministre de la police génerale. Mémoires.* Paris 1993.
Gohier, Louis-Gérôme. *Mémoires de Louis-Jérôme Gohier, Président du Directoire au 18 Brumaire.* Paris 1824.
Lettres inédites de Napoléon 1er. Paris 1898.
Miot. *Memoirs of Count Miot de Melito.* London 1881, 2 vols.
Peterson, M. D., ed. *The Portable Jefferson.* New York 1975.
Récamier, Madame. *Souvenirs et Correspondance de Madame Récamier,* ed. Madame Lenormant. Paris 1859, 2 vols.
Rémusat, Madame de. *Memoirs of Madame Rémusat in Two Volumes.* London 1880.

Riberette Pierre. "Vingt lettres inédites de Lucien Bonaparte à Madame Récamier," *Société Chateaubriand Bulletin,* 1978, pp. 39–57.

Roederer, Pierre-Louis. *Bonaparte me disait.* Paris 1942.

Simonetta, Marcello, and Colesanti, Massimo, eds. *Lo Sperone del Sotterraneo. Trittico di memorie inedite e rare.* Rome 2008.

Stendhal [Henri Beyle]. *Correspondance. Book III 1835–1842,* ed. Victor del Litto and Henri Martineu. Paris 1968.

SECONDARY SOURCES

Atteridge, Hilliard Andrew. *Napoleon's Brothers.* London 1909.

Bordes, Philippe. *Jacques-Louis David: Empire to Exile.* New Haven 2005.

Caracciolo, Maria Teresa, ed. *Lucien Bonaparte (1775–1740) un homme libre.* Exhibition catalogue, Musée Fesch, Ajaccio 2010.

Charles, Napoléon. *Bonaparte et Paoli: aux origines de la question corse.* Ajaccio 2000.

Colesanti, Massimo, ed. *Napoleone, le donne. Protagoniste, alleate, nemiche. Atti del Convegno Internazionale, Roma, 9–10 novembre 2006.* Rome 2009.

Delécluze, Etienne-Jean. *Louis David. Son école et son temps. Souvenirs.* Paris 1855.

Dumas, Alexandre. *Le Chevalier de Sainte-Hermine.* Paris 2005.

———. *The Companions of Jehu,* San Diego 2008.

———. *Vie de Napoléon.* Paris 1881.

Dwyer, Philip. *Napoleon: The Path to Power.* New Haven 2009.

Edelein-Badie, Béatrice. *La collection de tableaux de Lucien Bonaparte.* Paris 1997.

Eugénie, Princesse de Grèce. *Pierre Napoléon Bonaparte.* Paris 1963.

Fairweather, Maria. *Madame de Staël.* New York 2005.

Fleuriot de Langle, Paul. *Alexandrine Lucien-Bonaparte, Princesse de Canino (1778–1855).* Paris 1939.

———. "Le Second Mariage de Lucien Bonaparte," *Revue des Deux Mondes,* June 15, 1936, pp. 784–810.

———. "Monsieur Ingres et la Princesse de Canino," *La Revue de France,* July 1939, pp. 34–43.

Fraser, Flora. *Pauline Bonaparte: Venus of Empire.* New York 2009.

Fumaroli, Marc. *Quand l'Europe parlait français,* Paris 2001.

Graziani, Antoine-Marie. *Lucien Bonaparte, l'aigle versatile,* in Caracciolo, pp. 15–33.

Hughes, Robert. *Goya.* New York 2004.

Hulot, Frédéric. *Les frères de Napoléon.* Paris 2006.

Natoli, M., ed. *Luciano Bonaparte, le sue collezioni d'arte, le sue residenze a Roma, nel Lazio, in Italia (1804–1840).* Rome 1995.

Lawday, David. *Napoleon's Master: A Life of Prince Talleyrand.* (New York: Thomas Dunne Books/St. Martin's Press, 2007).

Lieven, Dominic. *Russia against Napoleon: The True Story of the Campaigns of War and Peace.* (New York: Viking, 2010).

Ludwig, Emil. *Napoleon.* London 1954 (1926).

Marmottan, Paul. "Lucien Bonaparte et Napoléon en 1807"; "Lucien Bonaparte á Florence, 17 avril–5 novembre, 1808," *Revue historique,* Book 79, 1902, pp. 57–62, 324–332.

———. "Lucien Bonaparte et sa sœur Elisa, lettres inédites," *Revue des études napoléoniennes,* March 1931, pp. 166–186, April 1931, pp. 229–239.

———. "Lucien Ministre de l'intérieur et les arts," *Revue des études napoléoniennes,* July-August 1925, pp. 1–40.

Masson, Frédéric. *Napoléon dans sa jeunesse.* Paris 1907.

———. *Napoléon et sa famille.* Paris 1897–1919, 11 vols.

Moorehead, Caroline. *Dancing to the Precipice: The Life of Lucie de la Tour du Pin, Eyewitness to an Era.* New York 2009.

Pichot, Amédée. *Napoléon à l'île d'Elbe. Chronique des évènements de 1814 et 1815.* Paris 1878.

Piétri, François. *Lucien Bonaparte.* Paris 1939. (Cited in text as Piétri I.)

———. *Lucien Bonaparte à Madrid (1801).* Paris 1951. (Cited in text as Piétri II.)

Pietromarchi, Antonello. *Lucien Bonaparte, prince romain.* Version française de Reine Artebisio Carducci. Paris 1985 (Original Italian edition: *Luciano Bonaparte principe romano.* Reggio Emilia, 1980).

Plessix Gray, Francine du. *Madame de Staël: The First Modern Woman.* New York 2008.

Primoli, Giuseppe. "Une nièce de l'Empereur, Charlotte Bonaparte, Princesse Gabrielli, fille de Lucien," *Revue des études napoléoniennes,* March-April 1925, pp. 97–132.

Ramage, Nancy. "Vincenzo Pacetti and Luciano Bonaparte: The Restorer and His Patron," in *History of Restoration of Ancient Stone Sculptures.* Getty Museum 2003, pp. 137–148.

Simonetta, Marcello. *Lucien Bonaparte ambassadeur en Espagne,* in Caracciolo, pp. 70–79; *Une œuvre inconnue: les* Mémoires *de Lucien Bonaparte,* ibid., pp. 122–129; *Séjours en Angleterre (1810–1814) et en France (le Cent-Jours, 1815),* ibid., pp. 277–285.

Stendhal [Henri Beyle]. *Vie de Napoléon.* Paris 2006 (1969).

Stuart, Andrea. *The Rose of Martinique: A Life of Napoleon's Josephine.* New York 2003.

Tyson Stroud, Patricia. *The Emperor of Nature: Charles-Lucien Bonaparte and His World.* University of Pennsylvania Press 2000.

———. *The Man Who Had Been King: The American Exile of Napoleon's Brother Joseph.* University of Pennsylvania Press 2005.

Vallet, Huguette. *Les Voyages en Italie (1804). Journal d'un compagnon d'exil de Lucien Bonaparte.* Rome 1986.

INDEX